To Lynne

Dear Josiah,
May the reading book give you & all in this families w. the Lord.
Love in Christ,
Bill & the girls

A Sinner Saved By Grace

A SINNER SAVED BY GRACE

Ed Nelson
with Emilee Nelson

Copyright © 2020 Mile Hi Publishers LLC

All rights reserved. No part of this book may be used, reproduced, or transmitted in any form or by any means, electronic or mechanical, including photocopying or recording, or by any information storage and retrieval system, without permission in writing from the publisher. For more information, contact:

Mile Hi Publishers, LLC
P.O. Box 429
Castle Rock, CO 80104

Published November 2020
Printed in the United States of America

Cover design by Jonathan Chong
Cover photos courtesy of History Colorado, Denver, Colorado, and the Nelson Family photo library.

ISBN (hardcover) : 978-1-953983-00-8
ISBN (paperback): 978-1-953983-01-5
ISBN (e-book)   : 978-1-953983-03-9
ISBN (audiobook): 978-1-953983-02-2

All Scripture quotations are taken from the King James Version of the Bible.

To future generations:

*May you believe in the power of God,
Depend on the Spirit of God,
Preach of the Son of God,
Stand with the Word of God,
And do all to the glory of God.*

*This is the word of the L*ORD *unto Zerubbabel, saying, Not by might, nor by power, but by my spirit, saith the L*ORD *of hosts.*
Zechariah 4:6

Contents

Foreword		xi
Introduction		xv
Chapter 1	The Accident	1
Chapter 2	My Family	7
Chapter 3	Frozen to the Farm	25
Chapter 4	The Call to Preach	35
Chapter 5	The First Soul I Led To Christ	51
Chapter 6	Ministry Lessons 101	55
Chapter 7	A Polka-dotted Ordination	67
Chapter 8	My First Pastorate	71
Chapter 9	Rocky Mountain Evangelist	77
Chapter 10	Guyla	91
Chapter 11	Preparing for the Mission Field	99
Chapter 12	Six Months to Live	107
Chapter 13	"If You Leave on Monday..."	113
Chapter 14	"Canceled" Revival	119
Chapter 15	God's Miraculous Provision	127
Chapter 16	Hoffman Heights	145
Chapter 17	Hard Lessons	163
Chapter 18	Spelling Matters	175
Chapter 19	Building a Church	183

Chapter 20	Controversy	191
Chapter 21	Church Split	199
Chapter 22	Missions and Growth	205
Chapter 23	A Trip Around the World	211
Chapter 24	"Honey, We've Got a School"	223
Chapter 25	Building a School	231
Chapter 26	Revival	237
Chapter 27	Buses, Radio, & A Little Bit of Crazy	243
Chapter 28	The Shenanigans of the Nelson Kids	255
Chapter 29	The Family Grows Up	269
Chapter 30	Family Matters	287
Chapter 31	Fundamental Opposition	295
Chapter 32	Politics	303
Chapter 33	She Kept Her Word	311
Chapter 34	Showers of Blessing	315
Chapter 35	Behind the Iron Curtain	329
Chapter 36	Tucson	357
Chapter 37	"Retired"	369
Chapter 38	"Gettin' Old Ain't for Sissies"	375

Acknowledgments	393
Notes	395
Photo Credits	405

Foreword

"There was a man sent from God, whose name was John" (John 1:6).

THUS IS GIVEN a brief introduction to a unique Jewish man who would fulfill the ultimate office of the prophet in preparing the way for Messiah. John the Baptist was quite a man and quite a prophet.

I have always loved the prophets, those servants of God who were raised up to cry out, "Thus saith the Lord." From Noah's preaching of righteousness to the apocalyptic Revelation of John, the messages of God's faithful spokesmen have stimulated my mind, stirred my imagination and stoked my heart.

No doubt most of you reading this foreword would hold to a cessationist view of the prophet, as I do. That is, when the Apostle John put down his pen at the end of Revelation 22, the office of the prophet was formally and finally fulfilled as Prophecy, the Word of God, was completed. At the same time there is general agreement among conservative theologians that the gift of the prophet that was provided to the New Testament church is exercised to some degree today in the authoritative forth-telling of the Word, as opposed to its fore-telling.

So even though the mission of the prophet has changed, God is still in the business of raising up spokesmen who will declare His message with pathos and power, men who will have an impact on the generation which hears them. The author of this autobiography is such a messenger of God.

"There was a man sent from God, whose name was Ed." Somehow that doesn't have quite the same ring to it as the gospel writer's introduction of John the Baptist. But the ministry of Ed Nelson shares many parallels with this special messenger of the Lord, and his testimony resonates loudly in every life that he has touched for the glory of God since his conversion to Christ in October of 1944 at a Colorado revival meeting.

I first met Dr. Nelson when I was a student at Bob Jones University in the mid-1970s. With some of his children enrolled at the University, Dr. Nelson was a regular visitor to the campus and was easily distinguished by his stature and his dignified manner. Yes, he was impressive in his persona, but it was not until I heard him speak in chapel that I realized that he was a prophet. As I listened to Dr. Nelson, I recognized even as an undergraduate student that I was hearing something different from mere teaching.

During the years following my university studies, I interacted with Dr. Nelson somewhat from a distance, enjoying fellowship with him at pastors meetings and hearing periodic news of his successful ministry at South Sheridan Baptist Church in Denver, Colorado. In 1990, Dr. Nelson resigned his pastorate and went on the road for the cause of Christ in Russia — and a new relationship was born between us. I remember as a young pastor having Dr. Nelson into our church to share his vision for the persecuted believers of Eastern Europe. My heart was knit to his as I witnessed his vision for the souls of men and his unswerving commitment to Christ and His Word.

Old Testament scholars have written of the three-fold role of the prophet: he points us to God's sovereignty, he preaches God's holiness, and he proclaims God's love. As you will read in this wonderful volume, Dr. Ed Nelson's life and ministry align with each of these characteristics.

You will learn of God's sovereign working in a farm boy's life, allowing him to suffer an "accident" which would factor into his conversion experience. You will see the sovereignty of God in keeping the Nelsons off the foreign field when they were repeatedly approved for missionary service in Japan. You will witness the divine hand restraining him from church-planting in southern California and directing him to the eastern slope of Colorado where many churches would be established and impacted. Yes, Ed Nelson's life speaks of God's sovereignty.

A prophet also proclaims God's holiness. My extended family experience began indirectly with Dr. Nelson in the early 1960s in Colorado when he, along with my future father-in-law and other fundamentalist Baptist pastors, stood against the "Soft Core" within the Conservative Baptist movement, leading to the founding of separatist churches, pastors fellowships, Christian schools, and a mission agency. Biblical separation has been the hallmark of this choice servant of Christ, and his biography preaches the holiness of God both by his life and his lips.

Finally, a prophet proclaims the love of Christ. Dr. Ed Nelson has been a soulwinner throughout his ministry. As a pastor, he has led many to Christ across Colorado and Arizona. As an evangelist, he has seen sinners around the world walk the sawdust trail. Recently, my wife and I were in Russia, and I noticed Dr. Nelson's picture hanging in a local church that we were visiting. We were told that he had been instrumental in many of the members of that congregation coming to Christ and being strengthened in their faith.

Yes, when a prophet speaks, we must both listen and learn. You will be thrilled to read the stories of this dear man's life — but more importantly, you will be strengthened as you behold this man's God. Such is the objective of the prophet.

I cannot close this foreword without speaking of the importance of Dr. Nelson to Baptist World Mission (BWM) and to my own ministry with the organization. He, along with godly leaders such as Dr. Monroe Parker, Dr. Ernest Pickering and Dr. Wayne Van Gelderen, founded

BWM in 1961, birthing it out of a burden for separatist Baptist missions. Under the leadership influence of such men, the mission eventually grew to more than 350 missionaries serving in over 50 countries.

Of the original mission founders, none of them was alive when I was elected Executive Director in 2009 — except Dr. Nelson. When I joined the board in 1999 as a young and inexperienced trustee, Dr. Nelson took me under his wing, taught me much about missions and church planting, and encouraged me by word and example to have vision and to trust God. That is what prophets do — and I am eternally grateful for this BWM patriarch who has been my mentor and my friend.

My prayer is that you will be greatly impacted for Christ as you read this prophet's story.

Bud Steadman

Executive Director
Baptist World Mission

Introduction

After a service, someone approached me and asked, "Pastor Nelson, when are you going to write your autobiography?" This was not the first time I had been asked. People had been asking me for years. But what did I have to write about? I am nobody special.

But as I began thinking about my life, I realized that I actually have a *lot* to write about. In fact, there are 96 years worth of God's working in my life — work such as saving me from death on multiple occasions, opening my eyes to my need for Jesus, calling me to preach the Gospel of Jesus Christ, working the miraculous through the power of the Holy Spirit, and so much more. It really is quite the story of how God took me, a sinner, saved me by His grace, and used me to proclaim the precious message of the Gospel.

So, I finally decided to write my story. I still believe I am nobody special. But God has shown me again and again what He can do with people who are surrendered to His will. He takes them and uses them to bring Himself glory and to bring others to faith in Jesus Christ. That is my goal with this autobiography — that you would not finish and say, "Wow, what an amazing man Ed Nelson was!" But that you would say, "Wow, what an incredible God Ed Nelson served."

So let us begin. We will start nearly 80 years ago on a simple farm in Windsor, Colorado.

Chapter 1

THE ACCIDENT

WHEN I WOKE up on Monday morning, I had no idea that my life would change forever. It was Labor Day, 1941, and it was just like any other day on the farm — lots of work.

I got up around 4:00 A.M., dressed, ate the breakfast Mother had prepared, fed the animals, and headed out to the corrals, straw hat on my head. There was something unusually exciting about this day, however. Dad was always trying out the cutting edge of farming technology, and we had a new machine to try!

Our farm spread across 280 acres of land a few miles east of Fort Collins, Colorado. In addition to farming sugar beets and various grains, we fattened sheep and cattle to provide income during the winters. A huge benefit of the animals was the true organic fertilizer they provided. For years, I had hand-forked the manure into a manure spreader for fertilizing the crops. It took a long time to fill the spreader. Dad was always looking for ways to speed up the process and make our farm more efficient.

Finally, he found a way! Earlier that year, a blacksmith and Dad discovered a fork that they could build to custom-fit our row-crop John Deere tractor. It had taken all summer to build, but it was finally ready.

Dad had started me farming at an early age and I quickly became his right-hand man. I loved the farm and thrived on the hard work. Even though I was only 17 years old, Dad let me be the first to try out this new machine. We went to the corral and I hitched up the horses, Bob and Dolly, to the manure spreader. Then Dad and I carefully attached the new fork to the tractor, and I began loading the spreader with manure.

The machine worked amazingly well. I was astounded at how quickly I filled the spreader. In my excitement, I loaded the spreader so high that I was unable to put the seat down where I normally sat to drive the team of horses. Today, I had to stand on a small platform instead.

The field to which I was headed was about a half mile from the farmyard. I slapped the reins on the backs of the horses and we headed down the trail toward the field. The trail was bumpy, situated between the fields — it was not an actual road. But I was driving our best team of horses, and I had driven that trail so many times, I could have driven it with my eyes closed.

As we bumped along the road, the weight of the large load caused the drive chain to engage the gears. That activated the machine with a tremendous jolt. I was instantly thrown forward and landed between Bob and Dolly on the tongue of the spreader. The horses took off at a full gallop. I was terrified and did not know what to do.

My father and Grandpa Magni had both warned me about runaway horses and had given me advice for what to do if it ever happened to me. I had listened carefully, but never in my wildest dreams thought I would actually *need* those instructions. Now, as I was barreling down the trail in between the horses, I realized how wrong I was.

Somehow, I still had the reins in my hand and was able to clamber up to the driver's stand by grabbing the horses' harnesses and pulling myself up. I could hear the instructions racing through my head:

"If you are ever driving with runaway horses, jump as quickly as you can from the vehicle," Grandpa Magni had said.

*"It takes the horses a **long** time to slow down, and many times, the vehicle wrecks and is destroyed,"* Dad had added.

I muscled all my strength and jumped as far and as hard as I could. It was not far enough. I hit the racing spreader and felt the jolt as I hit the ground in front of the front wheel.

Miraculously, the wheel froze on my body and dragged me. Just as miraculously, the horses stopped instantly. The vehicle which had been careening down the trail just seconds before was now completely still.

I was badly shaken up. I knew that if the wheel had run over me, I would have been killed instantly. I lay there in stunned shock for a moment, not believing that I was alive. Finally, I was able to wiggle my body out from under the wheel. I stood up and saw that my shirt and pants were badly torn. I looked down the trail from which I had come and saw my straw hat lying on the ground.

I limped over to my hat and picked up what was left of it. I was shaking all over, but because I did not know what else to do, I took the reins, climbed back onto the spreader, and continued on to the field.

After spreading the load, I drove back to the corral. Everyone else was out working, so no one was there and no one had seen what had happened. I managed to climb down from the spreader and stumble toward the house. Mother heard some commotion and met me at the door.

"Edward!" she cried. "What happened?"

"I had an accident," I mumbled as she led me to the couch. "I was going out to the field and loaded that spreader too full. The machine engaged and threw me forward which caused the horses to take off. I jumped, but didn't make it past the spreader. It caught me on the front wheel and dragged me until Bob and Dolly stopped."

For the next few days, I lay in bed motionless. Everything hurt. I could not move. I had trouble talking. Mother was by my side all day every day, trying everything she could to help me feel better, but I just got worse. Three days after the accident, Mother and Dad decided to take me to the doctor.

"This boy is sick!" the doctor exclaimed. "Take him to the hospital immediately. He needs more care than I can give."

So we drove to the Weld County Hospital in Greeley where I was admitted right away. Preliminary x-rays and tests showed that I had broken most of my ribs and had punctured my left lung.

"This doesn't look good," the doctor told us. "I want to call in a specialist from Denver to help."

It just so happened that the specialist they called had been my dad's best friend in grade school. I knew him as Dr. Bob. Once Dr. Bob and the local doctor had assessed the situation, they talked to my parents.

"This is not good at all," they said solemnly. "His pleura cavity is filling with fluid. Even though he is in an oxygen tent, his oxygen levels keep declining. His ribs are broken. His left lung is punctured. There isn't much we can do."

"There isn't even a surgery that I can try," Dr. Bob added. "I am so sorry, but Edward likely will not make it through the night."

I knew that I was in bad shape, but I did not know just how serious my condition really was. When my parents and the doctors came back into the room, no one had to tell me what the doctors had said. I could see that my parents had been crying and knew I probably would not live. At just 17 years of age, I was going to die!

"Well, Edward," Dr. Bob began, "I can't put you through any surgeries. They won't fix the problem. I do want to try a new medicine on you. It's called Sulfathiazole. The nurse will be in shortly to give you your first dose. It should help take some pain away and make you more comfortable. I'm sorry, but there just isn't anything else we can do."

Mother and Dad stayed for a few more hours until the hospital forced them to leave. Visitors were only allowed at specific times during the day. No one could stay the night, and no one could visit outside of the visiting hours. They stayed as long as they could, and then headed home to the responsibilities waiting for them on the farm.

Once I was alone, I lay in that hospital bed giving some serious thought to eternity. I was going to die! And that thought *terrified* me! I turned my head to the side, closed my eyes, and prayed.

"Oh God, if there is a God, I would like for you to hear my prayer right now. Please give me health enough so that I can get a Bible and read it to come to know the truth. I'd like to know what the truth is. And if I get a Bible, I will read it."

The next day, I woke up. I had lived through the night! I was not much better, but I was alive. Mother and Dad came back and stayed with me for much of the morning. Nurses kept giving me the medicine and checking my vital signs. This became my daily routine — lying in bed unable to move, family members visiting, and nurses and doctors checking on my progress. For weeks, I lay there fighting for my life.

Every day, my parents would drive the 23 miles to the hospital to visit me and check on my progress. Some days, I showed improvement. Other days, no one expected me to make it through another night. Often, they brought my younger brother, Ken, with them.

"I remember one night in particular," Ken told me years later. "Mother and Dad were so discouraged about your progress. You had taken a step backward again, and we had lost hope that you would ever be well. Mother was so sad and just stared out the window the entire drive home. Then all of a sudden, we saw the Northern Lights* brighten the Colorado night sky! Once Mother saw that, it was like a sign sent from God. She somehow had peace that you would be well again."

Six weeks after being admitted to the hospital, the doctors let me go home by ambulance. I had convinced the doctors that Mother could take better care of me at home — I just wanted to be out of the hospital.

I had told my parents about my prayer that first night in the hospital, and when I got home, one of the first things I asked my parents for was a Bible. I began to read, but I could not understand it.** For me, a farm boy who had not trusted Christ, reading the Bible became frustrating because of my lack of understanding. I now believed there was a God,

---

* The Northern Lights came to Colorado on Sept. 18, 1941, according to *Greeley Daily Tribune*.

** The Bible gives the reason for this in 1 Corinthians 2:14 — "*But the natural man receiveth not the things of the Spirit of God: for they are foolishness unto him: neither can he know them, because they are spiritually discerned.*"

but I did not know anything about Him other than the fact that He had answered my prayer and let me live. Soon after I started reading the Bible, I quit. It just did not make sense to me.

Since I was so weak and still had difficulty moving, we had a hospital bed brought to the house for me to sleep on. Mother set up the bed in the living room and was by my side nursing me back to health for months. She fed me. She bathed me. She read to me. She took care of me like only a mother can do — she was incredible.

I had always been tall and lanky, but this accident made lanky seem large. I had dropped from 180 pounds to 120 pounds. At 6′4″, I was literally skin and bones. For months, I could not get out of bed. I felt like a burden to my parents, Mother especially, but there was nothing I could do about it. I was completely helpless.

Lying on a couch unable to do anything was awful. I felt lazy and good-for-nothing. I had been enrolled in the Colorado State College to study agriculture that fall. The semester began just a few days after the accident happened. Obviously, I was not able to participate in school that year. I was too weak.

I gave almost all my time and energy to exercising and gaining my health back. When the Japanese attacked Pearl Harbor three months after the accident, I was still in that hospital bed in our living room. I had the radio on when they broke in with a special announcement that the Pearl Harbor attack had taken place. I was consumed with the same patriotism that swept across the United States. I wanted to get well quickly so I could be part of the war — I wanted to go fight!

But for six to eight months, I was unable to go outside or do much of anything. Eventually, I got stronger and stronger until I was able to be back on the farm working with the other farm hands, Ken, and my dad.

Facing death was terrifying, and fighting for my life shook my very soul. I should have died, but there is a God in Heaven Who heard the prayer of a Colorado farm boy, and He let me live.

Chapter 2

My Family

I AM A full-blooded Swede, which for my family meant two things: good morals and hard work. All four of my grandparents emigrated from Sweden to the United States in the late 1800s.

My father's dad, John Magni Nelson, was a carpenter in Sweden. As a young man, he became an alcoholic and was prone to fits of anger. However, in a free church in Sweden one night, he heard the Gospel. He knew that he was a sinner and desperately needed help — he needed Jesus. He trusted Christ that night and his life was forever changed. He quit drinking. He regularly attended church. He was no longer angry. He had a tremendous conversion and lived his faith well.

When he ran out of work in Sweden, he decided to come to the United States to find a job. He arrived in Chicago on May 21, 1884. For six years, he labored in Chicago as a carpenter. While in Sweden, he had known a girl named Christina who had also moved to the United States. However, she lived in Denver. They corresponded via letters, and when Magni ran out of work in Chicago, he decided to move to Colorado. Continuing in his trade of carpentry, he began working on several of the now-iconic Denver buildings such as the Oxford Hotel and the old county courthouse. In his spare time, he courted Christina. They were married on September 30, 1890.

In 1886, Colorado began constructing its State Capitol building and hired many carpenters to work on it. When Magni moved to Denver, they hired him, too. While he was working on the Capitol, Magni and Christina were thrilled to welcome their first child into the world, George Nelson. In 1893, when the Capitol was close to completion, my father, Ernest Denver Nelson, was born.

Magni and Christina seemed to really love the city of Denver, so they named Ernest after it. Soon after the Capitol building was finished in 1894, Magni moved his family to a farm near Loveland, Colorado, to begin an entirely different career. It was there that they welcomed two baby girls. One died in infancy; the other, Grace, became the baby of the family and the only Nelson daughter. In 1904, the Nelson family moved to a farm just north of Windsor, Colorado.

The Nelson children grew up in a solid Christian home. Every afternoon, Magni would take a break from farming, gather the family together, and read the Bible and pray. He did this every day. They faithfully attended church and lived out their faith. However, because Magni and Christina grew up in Sweden, they believed that they should not push their children toward any religious decisions. Magni let people know he believed the truth about Jesus, but never once did he ask his children or grandchildren, "Would you like to know how to become a Christian?"

Even though there were no pointed questions about the Gospel, Magni and Christina reared their children well. My father attended a small country school about a mile from the farm with his two siblings and other farm kids in the area. My Swedish grandparents believed that children should work just as they did in the "old country." Therefore, my father learned farm work early in his life. He finished 8th grade and then quit school to begin working full-time on the farm.

His older brother, George, was permitted to complete high school and continue his education with college. He graduated in engineering and immediately got a job in New York at a factory; but eventually, he came home and worked on the farm too. Magni gave the farm to George, the oldest Nelson boy. So my dad, who loved farming, went out and bought his own farm a mile north of the homestead.

* * * * *

My mother's parents, John and Tekla Peterson, came from Sweden to Colorado in the 1880s looking for gold. They lived in the mountain town of Idaho Springs in a modest home while John sought his fortune mining for gold. He staked a claim on a gold mine near Black Hawk. My mother, Anna Marie Peterson, was born in 1895 and was followed by three other siblings: John, Gertrude, and Ellen. The Petersons recognized the importance of education, and all four of the Peterson children graduated from high school in Idaho Springs.

However, during the late 1890s and early 1900s, the Petersons' gold vein petered out. John decided to move his family to Pierce, Colorado, where he became a sharecrop farmer. Rather than owning the land, he rented it from someone who would get a share of the harvest each

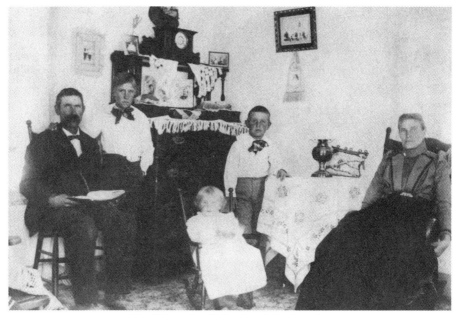

The Nelson family having daily devotions
Left to right: John Magni, George, Grace, Ernest, & Christina Nelson

year. He worked hard to provide for his family, yet they were very poor and had a difficult time making ends meet.

When the Peterson family moved to Pierce, my mother moved away from home to Greeley. For a while, she worked in the Greeley Dry Goods Company as a sales clerk. In the meantime, my father had purchased a dilapidated farm a mile north of the farm his parents owned. In 1918, he began changing that farm from a run-down operation to a successful farm still operating to this day. At a dance one evening in the nearby town of Severance, Ernest and Anna met. They soon fell in love and were married on December 29, 1920. For their honeymoon, they took a first class train to Los Angeles and watched the Rose Bowl on New Year's Day, even though neither of them were big football fans.

At first, Mother had a difficult time adjusting to farm life. Because of her job in Greeley, she never experienced farm life with the rest of her family. Now, she had to live on a farm without the conveniences she had grown accustomed to in the city. My parents lived in a small house without running water and with no indoor bathrooms. Over their first several years of marriage, my father began remodeling our house and making many improvements to the home.

A year or two after they were married, Dad and Mother found out they were expecting a baby! They were overjoyed to welcome their first baby boy into their family. But within an hour of Mother's delivering the child, their world was devastated as their newborn son died. During that time, many women lost babies during childbirth, and sadly, many mothers died in the process too. Thankfully, that was not the case for my mother. While she grieved deeply over the loss of her baby, she and Dad continued working on the farm and making improvements on the house. Mother never spoke of this loss.

Spring of 1923 brought much joy as Mother discovered she was pregnant again! On December 1, 1923, I was born. My parents were thrilled to have their second boy and named me Edward John Nelson after my Uncle John and both grandfathers. I even shared a birthday with Grandpa Magni.

Mother doted on me, and Dad started teaching me farming at a very young age. I followed Dad around the farm wherever he went and watched him as he worked. I learned much from my observations.

When I was two, the Nelson/Peterson family relationship grew stronger. My mother's brother, John, married my dad's sister, Grace. It was a double family marriage now! John and Grace moved to Kansas City, Kansas, shortly after their marriage, and Mother and Dad promised that we would visit them each summer. And we did. From as early as I can remember, each summer included a week or two in Kansas City with Uncle John and Aunt Grace.

In spite of the farming demands, Dad continued making improvements on the house, and by the time my brother, Kenneth (Ken), was born in February of 1928, Dad finally had the updated house complete. I was thrilled to have a brother to play with, even if he was a little over four years younger. He became the best punching bag there was!

In the remodeled house, we had running water and an indoor bathroom. Dad even went ahead of the times and installed his own electricity. No electrical companies were coming to farms in those days, so Dad installed a 32-volt electric plant with a number of 32-volt batteries to store the power. We were the only farm in that immediate area that had electricity. We were even able to find a 32-volt electric refrigerator. What a blessing that was. We no longer had to have the ice-man stop by our farm each week to sell us a supply of ice for the ice box.

These improvements to the house made a huge difference for Mother. She adapted well to farm life and always had the house spick-and-span. She was an incredible lady who took care of her family and farm. She kept a tight house and a strict schedule.

Monday was laundry day. Her goal was to have her laundry out before anyone else in the area. It was on the lines by 5 A.M. — even in

The house where I grew up.

the dead of winter. But the work did not stop there. The clothes were ironed, folded, and put away before Mother would go to bed that night.

Tuesday was mending day. If there were any tears in the socks or any other clothing, she fixed them.

Wednesday, she cleaned the living room area.

Thursday, all the bedrooms were cleaned, as well as the hall.

Friday was bath day. At the end of the work day, Mother set up the bathtub in the kitchen, filled it with hot water, and each of us took our baths in turn using the same water. She made sure our fingernails and toenails were clipped then too.

Saturday was the baking day. We never bought bread or sweets; she made it all, and wow, was she a fabulous cook. Her Swedish Rye Bread was legendary, and we boys always *loved* her Chicken and Noodle Dish.

Dad and Mother were very successful in building a growing farm enterprise. They prospered even during the Great Depression caused by the financial collapse of 1929. I was just six years old and did not understand or know what many children my age were facing during that time. I heard a few stories of people without food, but I did not realize how serious it was until I was older.

On the farm, we always had enough. Sugar was expensive and many families had to give up sugar altogether. However, my family raised sugar beets, so we had plenty of sweets during the Depression.

My parents were very careful about what and how much we ate. Even though we always had enough, they were frugal with their money and their food. We did not waste anything. Whatever was set before us, we ate. We learned to be grateful. They taught me to save as much as I could. In the fall, I helped Mother can food to store in the cellar for the winter months. Mother and Dad were always planning for the future and saving as much as possible, while still providing for our immediate needs.

We had many men who worked for us, and during that time, Dad paid them each $25 per month. They worked hard every day of the month for only $25. They were glad to get it, too, because many others had no work at all. Dad also provided each family with housing, potatoes, meat from some farm animals, and eggs from the chickens. They were well taken care of, but even so, money was tight.

I watched my parents through that time and learned to be frugal. I learned the difference between a need and a want and was taught that just because I wanted something did not mean I should buy it. I saved my money and learned to be wise with what I had.

As the Depression continued, Mother and Dad enrolled me in school. Ken was still too young to attend, so he stayed at home with Mother and watched Dad farm like I had done at his age. School was exciting and opened up a whole new world for me as I learned to read. In my spare time, I loved to read and tried to teach Ken how to read too, even though he was only two. When Dad finished work in the evenings, we often played baseball or catch outside before Mother called us for dinner. It was a great life: chores, school, play, family.

When I was 11 years old, Dad decided it was time for me to get serious about working on the farm. Mother tried to persuade him otherwise. "He's only 11!" she said. "That is much too young to be out with you men."

Nevertheless, Dad prevailed and insisted I learn how to farm. My first job was rolling a field. One of the farm hands plowed the field with a team of horses and a plow. Someone else harrowed the ground with equipment that had a flat piece of steel with teeth on it that sank down

Working on the farm began at an early age

into the ground. The men used horses to drag it across the field to break up any clods. Then, another man leveled the field to ensure the water flowed evenly throughout the entire area.

Finally, came my job. Dad wanted me to roll the field. We attached a big roller to a team of horses, and then I drove up and down the field rolling out any of the remaining clods of dirt before we planted the seeds. It was hard work for my 11-year-old body to handle, but I loved it. I was finally able to help Dad with his work!

Three years before America came out of the Great Depression, Mother and Dad brought us into the living room. "We are having a baby!" they told us excitedly.

A few months later, my youngest brother Donald (Don) was born. I was 12 and Ken was 7. We were thrilled to have another brother.

Two or three days after Don was born, Mother noticed a problem. "Something is wrong with this boy. Look at his eyes," she said as she held Don up for Dad to see.

They took him to our family doctor who diagnosed the issue. "It's a condition called Aniridia," he said. "He doesn't have an iris. His eyes are just pupils. He can see a little, but we will have to watch him as he gets older because this could develop into other eye problems."

All of us watched him grow from a baby to a little boy. We played with him, read to him, walked with him, but most of all, we protected him. Dad spent a lot of time with him. Every day after a long day working on the farm, Dad came inside, washed his hands and face, got on the floor, and played with Don until it was time for supper. Life was not easy, but we certainly had a happy home.

Ken and I were both in school now and very active with extracurricular activities. We were members of the 4-H club and went to county fairs with our various products. One year, I won first place for the best peck of barley and Ken won an award for the best 12 pickling cucumbers. Every year we participated in the Denver Stock Show and brought our best sheep or cattle or whatever we had at the time.

One year, Dad and I drove to the mountains and bought a steer that we thought would have a chance to be the champion steer. The winner of that competition would receive a *lot* of money from a big company in Denver which sponsored the stock show. Unfortunately, there was so much competition that year that we were nowhere close to winning the prize. Every year, though, we received a nice addition to our income by selling pigs, cattle, and sheep at the show.

Along with my fellow classmates, I participated in school dances, plays, lectures, and other activities. When I was in high school, Ken decided he wanted to learn to play the violin. The screeching from his practicing was awful. But he was diligent in his lessons and eventually the screeches turned into beautiful music. I do not have a musical bone in my body, so I turned to other hobbies such as hunting, fishing, and photography.

In the cellar downstairs, Mother let me set up my own dark room where I developed my own films and pictures. I loved it! Each year, when we took our family trip for a few weeks either to the mountains or to visit Uncle John in Kansas City, I brought my camera with me. When I was old enough to drive, I spent the weekends in the mountains fishing and hunting.

There was not much time to be spared from the farm for these hobbies, however. Dad had been reared to value hard work, and he taught us boys to do the same. We worked all day every day except Sunday when we went to church.

As Don continued to grow, his eyesight got worse, and the pressure began building around his eyes. When he was six, Mother and Dad decided to enroll him in the Colorado School for the Deaf and the Blind in Colorado Springs. It was an all-day ordeal when we moved Don into the school. I was preparing for college in a few weeks and Ken was going into 9th grade. Our entire family drove over 130 miles from Fort Collins to Colorado Springs and checked Don into his school.

My Family

The Ernest Nelson Family, July 1939
Left to right: Ken, Mother, Don, Dad, Ed

When we got there, the school staff told Mother, "You will have to leave him here for two months. No visits. Don't come back until the two months are over."

"I promise," a lady said, "I will take care of your son as if he were my own child. We will teach him how to read. We will teach him Braille. Even though he can still see, we are going to help Don know how to take care of himself as if he was blind."

Mother was a wreck, but finally she left her six-year-old son in the hands of the capable school staff. She cried the entire way home. "How are we going to get along without our boy?" she lamented.

Life was very different without Don around, but Mother and Dad honored their word and did not go back to visit until the two months were up. The school did wonders for Don. It opened up an entirely new world for him. He could read! He learned to read with his fingers too — they taught him Braille. When he returned home again, it was amazing to watch what he was now able to do.

* * * * *

Until the early 1900s, Colorado farming was "dry-land" farming. With very little moisture for the crops, dryland farmers selected crops such as wheat that were drought-resistant or drought-evasive. They also supplemented their income in the winter months by fattening livestock, mainly sheep and cattle, to ship to the market each spring. In the early 1900s, farmers in northern Colorado sought to change the type of farming from dryland to irrigated in order to produce better and more diverse crops.

Several companies were formed to solve the problem. Their solution was to bring water from the Rocky Mountains to the farms on the Eastern Plains through canals that would cross from one farm to another. Many of the companies had farmers as stock holders, so the canals proved to be a great solution.

One of these companies, the Larimer-Weld Ditch Company, had built one of these canals through the middle of Dad's farm. However, they had failed to survey the ditch properly so that the water would flow through the farm. Therefore, they had to move the ditch farther north on the farm. That meant that there were two large canals in Dad's farm — one now unused, and the other about 400 feet north that delivered water for the farmers east of us. The empty, useless canal (20 feet wide) stretched across the entire width of our farm. The huge ditch made it almost impossible to cultivate the land. The ditch had been there so long that the cottonwood trees that had been planted along the banks were now large trees.

At that time, farming and excavating were still done by horse power. Dad wanted to regain that part of his farm, so he used a small, horse-drawn excavating implement called a slip. He cut down the trees growing on the banks with a hand saw and an ax. Often, he blew the roots out with dynamite. As a little boy, I watched him as he worked tirelessly to fill in the ditch. It took several years before the canal was completely filled in and we could farm it as part of the fields.

After that, there was more work to be done on the farm. The new canal flowed through our farm, but the seepage from it caused much of Dad's land to be alkaline — unable to produce a crop of anything. He realized he had to drain water underground away from the farm so it could be good for farming again. And again, he had to do this by hand.

He had a spade with which he dug small ditches from each field to end in a low place that had natural drainage. That low area was natural to our farm and the farms below it. Water would flow down from our farm through the other farms and eventually empty into another one of those lateral canals carrying the water from the mountains for irrigation. Dad dug the ditches from the higher areas of the field to drain the water down to flow through the natural drainage. He would lay porous tile in the ditches and cover them with dirt. The drainage worked! The alkaline soils became productive once again. This also took years to accomplish, but he finally had turned a worthless farming area into one of the outstanding farms in Colorado: The Cactus Hill Ranch.

My father's success as a farmer is evidenced by the fact that he was honored in 1959 as the "Soil Conservation Farmer of the Year" and in 1977 as the "Rotary Club Master Farmer of the Year." He deserved those honors, for he had taken a run-down farm and turned it into a most successful operation.

* * * * *

Both of my parents were moral individuals. Both Sweden and the United States were much more moral societies than they are today. Both sets of grandparents came from Sweden with definite moral values to instill in their families. Those values were the basis for the way I was brought up.

Dad and Mother never drank alcohol or any intoxicating drinks. I never heard my father use a curse word of any kind — and I believe he never did. We were disciplined if we used any foul language at all. They taught us boys that we should take care of our bodies, and that meant

Cactus Hill Ranch, 1958

never smoking or using tobacco of any kind. Values like these were drilled into us constantly by parents who lived what they taught.

Despite our solid morals and the habit of regular church attendance, my family did not attend a church that really believed and taught the Bible. Dad tried to have us in Sunday School and the main service every Sunday morning, even though Mother would only occasionally attend with us. The church was a liberal church, however, that did not preach anything about sin or hell. When I had my farming accident in high school, the pastor visited me in the hospital. He told me I was such a good young man that everything would be just fine with God. That year, when teaching my Sunday School class, he used Dick Tracy comics for his Sunday School lesson.

Even though we did not get truth from the church, my 8th grade Sunday School teacher was a lady who was a born-again believer who truly taught us the Word of God. I remember at Christmas that year, she gave each student a plaque that read:

Did I say anything today I would not want to be saying when Jesus comes?
Did I do anything today I would not want to be doing when Jesus comes?
Did I go anyplace today I would not want to be found when Jesus comes?

I treasured that plaque, and Mother hung it over my bed where I could see it every day. I did not understand it, but even at an early age, God was planting seeds in my heart. I do think my father had accepted Christ as a child in his home; but as a busy adult man, he neglected God's Word. We never used or read the Bible in our home. Yet in spite of all this, Mother and Dad taught us to be moral people. Several lessons that my parents instilled in me as a little boy have stayed with me to this day.

When I was four or five years old, my mother stopped me right by the telephone that hung on the wall in the hall of our house.

"Edward," she said, "do you realize neither your mother nor your father use any form of tobacco?"

"Yes, Mother, I do," I answered.

"And do you realize that none of your grandparents and aunts and uncles and cousins smoke or have smoked?" she continued.

"Yes," I said.

"Will you promise me right here, right now, that you will never smoke or use tobacco in any form?" she asked.

"Yes, Mother," I said solemnly. "I promise."

Fifteen years later, I was out in the field working for Dad. It was summertime, and I was irrigating the crops. We had a field north of our house, and I drove the farm pickup to that field. My job for the day was to guide the irrigation water through the field. One of our big Colorado summer hail storms was approaching. I could see the line of rain and hail marching its way closer and closer to me. I had been taught by my father and grandfather never to stay in a field with a shovel when one of those storms came. Lightning might be attracted to the metal on the shovel and strike me and the shovel. I definitely did not want *that* to happen, so when I saw the storm approaching, I headed back to the pickup dragging the metal part of the shovel on the ground behind me.

The skies opened up about the time I arrived at the pickup. I tossed the shovel into the bed and hopped into the front seat of the truck. It was a violent storm with sheets of rain pouring from the sky and hail pounding the metal roof and sides of the truck. Lightning flashed above and around me, and the thunder was deafening.

As I sat there anxiously waiting out the storm, I noticed a pack of cigarettes that one of the hired farm hands had left on the seat. I had heard that cigarettes were good to calm nerves, so I decided to try one. I took one out of the pack and pushed in the cigarette lighter. I brought that lighter right up to the cigarette. Then a vision came to me: I saw myself as a little boy, promising my mother in the hall of our house that I would never use tobacco. Instead of lighting the cigarette, I opened the window and threw the cigarette and the rest of the pack outside to be soaked by the rain and thus made useless. I wanted to honor my word, and I did not go back on my pledge to my mother.

As I continued sitting in the truck waiting for the storm to pass, I saw a bolt of lightning hit the ground on a neighboring farm not far from where I was. Finally the storm passed and I, being a curious teenager, drove over to where I had seen the lightning hit the ground. There on a ditch bank lay the body of a man I knew well. He was the officer of the company who checked to see that each farmer received his proper share of irrigation water each day. Some tumble weeds had blown into the ditch and were causing a back up that could wash out the ditch bank. He was trying to clean out the debris in the middle of the storm, and the lightning struck the pitchfork he was using. He was killed instantly.

I sat there pondering the situation and was deeply impressed with the fact that none of us knows when we are going to meet the dreadful enemy of death. I certainly was not ready to die, and I doubt that this man expected he would die that day. I had not yet trusted Christ, but that day, I began to wonder what would happen if I died — and most certainly I would die! At the end of my life, whenever that would be, I would face God. That thought terrified me, so I tried to dismiss it, but I kept thinking back to two short years prior when I had almost died in the farming accident. Medically and logically speaking, I should have died right then and there. Death had become very real to me in the past two years, and I realized that I could die at any time. God was beginning to do a work in my life that would eventually bring me to the point of salvation.

I never forgot my promise to my mother. I never forgot that man and how quickly he was taken out of this life. And I never forgot the reality that all of us will die, whether we are ready for it or not.

* * * * *

Growing up on a farm was always an adventure and always a lot of work. Dad was a firm believer in hard work. Mother was a firm believer in education. Thus, I became an educated farm boy. I attended Windsor High School, graduating on May 16, 1941. I was active in 4H, class discussions, fair competitions, occasional public speaking, and school musicals and plays (even though I could not sing very well). I enjoyed my high school days. In my senior year of high school, I was the Senior Class President — quite the honor!

In addition to being Senior Class President, I had the reputation of being the boy who did not drink. Several of my classmates would tease me frequently about not drinking alcohol, but I did not budge. I would not drink. This was probably instilled in me as a boy by my parents, who also did not drink.

One day each school year, the seniors would plan a "senior sneak day" unbeknownst to the teachers. The whole senior class would just skip school for that day. I believe it was April of 1941 when I participated in Sneak Day. Several of my classmates and I took cars up from Loveland to a park in Thompson Canyon. We hiked for a while up and down hills and over some big boulders. There were about six guys ahead of me, and just as I reached the top of one of the hills, four of the guys grabbed me and pinned me to the ground. I had no clue what was happening. The two other boys opened my mouth, grabbed a bottle of liquor, and started pouring it into my mouth. I could not do anything to stop them, but I refused to drink alcohol!

I took a huge breath right before they started pouring the liquor in my mouth. When they had finished pouring, I spewed the alcohol all over them. They were furious! However, I graduated from high school still being the "guy who did not drink."

Even though I was very active in both my school and my community, I also continued to work hard on the farm. Work was important to Dad. Farming was his

Senior Class President, 1941

life and it had become my life too. I learned so much from him and was his right-hand man for as far back as I can remember. Because I wanted to be the best farmer I possibly could be, I enrolled in the Colorado State College in Fort Collins to study agriculture. I even got a scholarship for $100 to help continue my education. After the accident with the runaway horses, however, attending college was out of the question. I was in the hospital fighting for my life, and then I was at home trying to regain my strength little by little. My plans, my world, had turned upside down. I still wanted to be a farmer like Dad. I still wanted to go to college. But that would all change on December 7, 1941.

Chapter 3

FROZEN TO THE FARM

SEVENTEEN WEEKS AFTER my accident with the team of runaway horses, I was still in bed at home working on my recovery. Just before Mother brought me lunch, I was listening to a radio program. Suddenly, an announcer interrupted the program with a special announcement that changed the course of U.S. history:

> *From the NBC Newsroom in New York. President Roosevelt said in a statement today that the Japanese have attacked Pearl Harbor, Hawaii, from the air. I'll repeat that. President Roosevelt says that the Japanese have attacked Pearl Harbor in Hawaii, from the air. We will interrupt all programs to give you latest news bulletins. Stay tuned to this station. . . . Ladies and Gentlemen, a special announcement. . . . The regular county defense program is functioning in an orderly manner and citizens are urged to remain calm and avoid all unnecessary confusion because of hysteria. Citizen volunteers are asked to go quietly to their nearest police or fire station and offer their services if they wish to help. There is no immediate cause for alarm and coolness will accomplish more than anything else.**

The next day, President Roosevelt addressed the nation via radio and declared war on Japan. I vividly remember his words!

---

* WeAreHistoryTeachers, 'The Pearl Harbor Attack Emergency Radio Broadcast Announcement (December 07, 1941),' YouTube video, 04:02, 14 June, 2018.

Yesterday, December 7, 1941 — a date which will live in infamy — the United States of America was suddenly and deliberately attacked by naval and air forces of the Empire of Japan. No matter how long it may take us to overcome this premeditated invasion, the American people in their righteous might will win through to absolute victory.*

In that moment, there was a patriotism that spontaneously came to our country. In fact, it was a patriotism that has not been matched since. Even the great patriotism following the attack by Al-Qaeda on September 11, 2001, did not match the patriotic response following the Pearl Harbor attack in Hawaii.

My response was no different than that of almost every other American. I wanted to volunteer to serve my country. I was old enough to serve since I had just turned 18 the week prior, but I was still lying in a hospital bed recovering from my accident. As I regained my strength and abilities during the next six months, that passion to serve my country never dwindled.

Finally, the day came when I thought I was strong enough to enlist. The first step was passing a physical examination. I failed. I waited a few days and then tried again. I failed again. No matter how hard I tried, I just could not pass that physical test. My heart had been damaged in the aftermath of the farming accident, and it just would not beat slowly enough for me to pass the test for any of the armed forces. The draft of men into various military forces was in place at that time. However, because of my physical condition, the draft board gave me a 4-F rating. In the vernacular of that day, it was called "frozen to the farm."

I was devastated. I wanted to be in the military like the rest of the young men my age. I wanted to fight to defend America and the liberty we enjoyed. But there was nothing I could do to pass that test, so reluctantly, I continued working on the farm.

---

* "The United States Declares War On Japan," HISTORY.

Three years later, I was still farming. World War II raged on, and the government continued to draft men into armed services. But due to my 4-F rating, I had not been called. It was October of 1944 now, and we were harvesting our main cash crop, sugar beets. My job every day was to operate the Model B John Deere tractor that had the beet puller equipment mounted on it. This equipment lifted the beets up by the roots from the ground so that a crew of toppers could cut the tops off the beets and put them in piles. Another crew would then fork the beets onto a truck bed and haul the beets to a factory where they would be processed into sugar.

One Monday morning, I was driving the tractor in one of the beet fields close to where our mailbox was, about a quarter-mile from the house. The mailman, Mr. E. M. Spoon, was a Christian. On this particular morning, he left his car at our mailbox and headed to the field where I was driving the tractor. He worked his way through the barbed-wire fence and came to greet me. I stopped the tractor, climbed down, and asked, "How are you, Mr. Spoon?"

"I'm doing well, thank you, Ed," he replied. "I just wanted to stop by to see if you would come to a revival meeting at my church tonight. It's at the First Baptist Church over in Fort Collins. We are having special meetings this week with the evangelist Dr. Bob Jones, Sr. I sure would love it if you would join me tonight."

Frankly, that was the last thing I wanted to do at that moment. My parents had warned me not to attend revival meetings. They said meetings like that were "holy roller" types of events, and we certainly did not want to be known as "holy rollers." I *wanted* to tell Mr. Spoon that I would not be coming, but he was a kind man whom I respected for his faithfulness and testimony for the Lord.

"All right. I will come with you tonight," I told him.

"Wonderful!" he exclaimed. "I will see you tonight at 7 o'clock then. Looking forward to it."

I hopped back on the tractor and finished the work for that day. After dinner, I honored my word to Mr. Spoon and went to the service. What a shock that was!

I heard real preaching from the Word of God. Dr. Bob Jones, Sr., said that all people are sinners. I had certainly never heard that before. When I was sick in the hospital, my pastor had reassured me that everything would be fine with God because I was such a good young man. Now here is this strange evangelist telling me that I am a sinner? And he did not even know me! I was furious.

As I drove the 11 miles home, I was so upset over the message I had heard that I determined I would never go back to hear that kind of preaching again. I was a good person! There was no way that Dr. Jones could know my thoughts and see inside my heart. I was motivated by money and wanted to get rich as quickly as possible.

The next day, as I was driving the tractor in the field, I started thinking about the message some more. It still made me mad. *I wonder what he will preach about tonight that could make me mad again?* I thought. *Surely he can't make me **that** angry two nights in a row.* I changed my mind and decided to attend the Tuesday night service too.

That night, Dr. Jones preached the Gospel and showed us the verse: *"For all have sinned, and come short of the glory of God" (Romans 3:23).* Then he said that because of our sin, we actually *deserve* to die. I don't remember his exact words, but he preached something like this:

> Romans 6:23 says, *"For the wages of sin is death; but the gift of God is eternal life through Jesus Christ our Lord."* Each of us deserves to die. This isn't just death here on this earth. This is eternal death in a place called Hell. Ladies and Gentleman, this is a real, terrible place of fire and weeping and wailing and gnashing of teeth. It's not a place where anyone wants to go, but many of you are on the pathway to Hell!
>
> But I have good news too. Jesus came and took the punishment for your sin on Himself so that one day when you do die, if you believe in Him, you will spend eternity with Him in Heaven.

Wow, did that preaching make me mad again — even more so than the night before! Again, I vowed I would never go back. But God was convicting me of sin. That night, I realized that the lustful thoughts I had thought about for years were not so good. I had problems inside, but nobody knew about them. Surely, God would see that I really was a good man.

While working in the field the next day, I changed my mind again and attended the third night with the same, angry response.

On the fourth night, something changed.

On that Thursday evening of the revival meeting, I gave in to what the Holy Spirit had been convicting me of for a long time. I realized it had not been Dr. Jones I was angry at this whole week. Rather, it was God, and I had been against Him my entire life. I knew deep down that what Dr. Jones was preaching from the Bible was true. I *was* a sinner, and I really *did* deserve to die. The times I had already faced death in my 20 years of life all pointed to one thing: God wanted my attention.

I realized how He had graciously spared my life. He answered my prayer while I was alone in that hospital room just waiting to die — He let me live! And that Thursday evening, I acknowledged in my heart that I truly *was* a sinner, but that Jesus had come and paid the punishment for my sin. I prayed to God and accepted that truth. I believed that night what I still believe to this day. Jesus is my Savior!

My life changed drastically, and I have been a different man ever since. I immediately quit reading some bad magazines. I vowed I would not listen to or tell illicit jokes. My whole mindset on life changed.

I immediately began attending Sunday School and the services at First Baptist Church of Fort Collins. Daily Bible reading became an integral part of my life. I really began to grow in my relationship with God. As I read my Bible, I came across passages like Philippians 1:6 — *"Being confident of this very thing, that he which hath begun a good work in you will perform it until the day of Jesus Christ,"* — and 2 Peter 3:18 — *"But grow in grace, and in the knowledge of our Lord and Saviour Jesus*

Christ." I realized that these verses were speaking of the change that was happening within me.

This happened in October of 1944. Within one month of my salvation, I received the letter I had been waiting three years for: I was being drafted into the United States military. I was thrilled! I could finally serve my country in the fight for freedom. I was to report to Fort Logan in Denver where I would undergo the physical examination before I was officially accepted.

Considering my past experiences with the physical exams, I immediately called my doctor and asked what I should do.

"Do no work for three days and rest a lot," he replied. "Maybe your heart will beat slowly enough after the days of rest and you will pass the exam."

I followed his instructions and arrived at Fort Logan on the date assigned. I went through each examination, anxious that I would fail again. But when I reached the end of the exams, everything seemed to be fine.

I only needed to pass one final interview. A sergeant pointed me to a door. When I entered, I found a Navy Captain sitting behind a desk. He motioned for me to be seated at the front of the desk. I did not know he was a doctor — in fact, he was a psychiatrist.

"What do you do for a good time?" he began with the first question.

"I go to church," I replied quickly. It was now one month since I had been saved.

He exploded, jumped out of his chair, and leaned over the desk.

"You go to *church* for a good time?!" he shouted.

"Yes," I responded calmly. "I enjoy going to church."

His questions came with rapid fire. "Do you hear voices talking to you?"

"No."

"Do you date girls?"

"Yes."

"What do you do on a date?"

"We go to church and then might go out for some refreshments afterwards."

"That's not what I mean," he exploded. "Here's the question: Do you commit adultery?"

"Absolutely not!" I replied.

He looked very angry. He pointed me to another door and said, "Go in there and talk to the Lieutenant."

I stepped into the next room where an Army First Lieutenant had me be seated. He walked into the Captain's office, closed the door, and they talked briefly. When the Lieutenant returned to his office, he interacted with me in a manner exactly opposite to that of the Captain. This man seemed cool and collected in his demeanor.

"The Captain tells me you are a religious fanatic," he began.

It was my turn to be upset. "I am not a fanatic!" I answered quickly. "But, I do enjoy going to church."

"Do you read your Bible?" he asked.

"Yes, I do. Every day."

"How much time do you take to read your Bible?" he continued.

"It varies," I responded. "Some days it's 20 minutes. Some days it's less."

"Why the difference in time? Are you better some days than others?"

"No," I replied. "It's just a matter of time. Some days I have a little more time than I do other days."

The Lieutenant stood and said, "Well, I have the same problem with time. Thanks. You are dismissed."

He opened the door and I left the office. Shortly after that meeting, all of us draftees were called into a large room to receive our orders. One after another, the sergeant read the names from the list and asked each individual to come forward to receive his orders. One by one, others went up until I was the last man standing.

"What's your name?" the sergeant asked.

"Nelson. Edward John Nelson," I answered.

He searched his records and finally said, "Nelson, there is nothing here for you. Go home. The draft board will give you a report in about a week."

I returned to the farm and waited anxiously for a whole week. Finally, the letter came in the mail. The report read:

"A paranoid schizophrenic — unfit for military service."

I was shocked and, quite honestly, offended. Believe me, I was such a weak, new Christian that had I thought my answers in the interviews would have kept me from entering the military, I would have given very different answers.

My mother, who was none too happy with me for becoming a Christian, said, "I'm not surprised. You've been getting a little crazy being around those Baptists!"

I called my doctor and asked him about the report. I just did not understand why the draft board would say such a thing. He, too, was shocked.

"Ed," he said. "I know you quite well. I do not agree with the diagnosis. You are not paranoid, and you are definitely *not* schizophrenic."

If it were to happen to me today, I would not be offended as I was then. In fact, I would gladly accept the term "religious fanatic." It actually meant that I had become a fan of Jesus Christ. This was persecution of someone who trusted Jesus Christ and loved the Bible as God's holy inspired Word. It was 1944, and there was persecution of Bible believers then. Such animosity against Christians has continued for three-quarters of a century, and today, it is a very real threat always looming in the future. However, for 1944, it was shocking for me and many others to experience that kind of persecution.

As a result of the psychiatric evaluation report, the draft board continued my 4-F rating. I continued working on the farm and faithfully attending the services at First Baptist Church. During the next year,

I enrolled in a correspondence course from Moody Bible Institute in Chicago. It was very good for me to learn some basic, Gospel instruction that helped me grow in the Lord. I also re-enrolled in the Colorado State College agriculture classes and was able to complete the year of schooling that had been disrupted by my accident on the farm.

When the war ended in September of 1945, I was still plugging away at the farm. I never did have the opportunity to serve in the U.S. Military. But for the life-changing salvation and spiritual growth experiences during the war, I am forever grateful that I remained "frozen on the farm."

Chapter 4

THE CALL TO PREACH

One year after my salvation, another dramatic, life changing event took place. Pastor MacIntosh from First Baptist Church of Fort Collins invited Dr. Bob Jones, Jr., to hold revival meetings at our church. Nearly all the young men who were military age from the church had either enlisted or had been drafted at the beginning of the war — except me due to my health issues. This meant that I was the only young man left in the church. World War II had just ended, but my peers were not yet home. Pastor asked me to lead the singing for the revival meetings — clearly he had no one else, because I have no musical talent. I have trouble finding the right pitch. But I agreed and did my best. At least I could wave my arms and gesture as I had seen others do.

Every night after the service, Dr. Bob, Jr., would say something like this to me: "Ed, you need to come to Bob Jones College and get some training." He could see very clearly that I needed training if I hoped to do *anything* public for the Lord.

The last Sunday of that meeting was life-changing for me. After the morning service, a godly lady, Mrs. Williamson, walked up to the platform where I was still standing.

"Ed," she called.

"Yes, ma'am," I said as I stepped toward her. I will never forget what she said.

She pointed her finger at me and said, "Ed, you have been called to preach."

I am ashamed of my response. I had a very strong voice at the time, and when she told me that, I slapped my hands on my knees and gave her a big horse laugh that echoed throughout the building. Many of the people still visiting together turned their heads to see the commotion: me bent over with my hands still on my knees laughing at what this dear lady had just said.

My rude reply did not seem to faze Mrs. Williamson at all. She kept looking right at me and said, "Ed, will you pray about this?"

What was I to say? "Yes, ma'am," I responded. "I will pray about it." Preaching was the last thing I wanted to do, so I was convinced praying about it would do nothing to change my mind.

That afternoon, Dr. Jones invited me to visit him at his hotel before the evening service. He asked what I planned to do for my life's work. I told him that I planned to be a farmer, and then maybe someday, I could enter politics and run for a public office. I had high aspirations of being elected to Congress.

He just looked at me and said, "I think it is commendable that you would like to try to serve others in public office. But there is one thing you must remember. Even if you do *some* good in public office, you are only putting props under something that is eventually going to fall. You would be far wiser to surrender your life to the Lord's will. Then, you will be laboring in something that will last forever."

I left that room with a heavy heart and with thoughts racing through my mind. First, I had agreed to Mrs. Williamson's request to pray about becoming a preacher. Now, Dr. Jones was telling me to invest my life in that which is eternal rather than temporal. My heart was deeply burdened about what I should do.

That night, as Dr. Jones closed the service with an invitation to pray, I stepped off the platform, knelt at the altar, and prayed briefly for God's will to be done in my life.

The Call to Preach

The next morning, I was back on the tractor in sugar beet harvest, just as I had been the year before when Mr. Spoon had invited me to the revival meetings. As I drove that tractor around the field, I was deeply burdened by the Lord. Finally, I stopped the tractor, climbed down, knelt behind it, and prayed.

"God, I yield my life to Your will. Whatever You desire me to do, I will do it. I will be a preacher of Your Word if that is Your will for me."

I boarded the tractor again and continued on with my work. When I got close to the farmyard, I stopped the tractor and went into the farmyard to tell my father what I had just decided.

"Dad," I called to him, "I have surrendered my life to the Lord to do His will. I think He is calling me to preach. Can you believe it? I'm going to be a preacher. You should probably look for another man to take my place here," I suggested. "I am going to see if I can go to college for the beginning of the second semester this school year and that's just a few months away."

"You'll starve to death!" he stated emphatically. All he knew was that the church I had attended with my family before my salvation paid the pastor a very small salary.

"I will trust the Lord to take care of me," I replied.

Then Dad told me something I had never known. "I expected that one day you would tell me this — that you would give your life for the ministry. My father, your grandfather, often prayed that his oldest grandson would become a preacher."

My Grandpa Magni had passed away five years earlier but had never said a word to me about his prayers for my life. I realized that my defiance to the Lord's will had taken place against the prayers of my grandfather. And his prayers had won the battle. That confirmed in my mind that I had made the right decision. God had called me to preach.*

---

* Early on, there were times when I wondered if I should really continue on in the work of the Lord. Every time I doubted my calling, God gave me assurance that I was serving in the will of God. For over 70 years now, I have never doubted that I was called of God into the ministry.

Dad soon hired a man to take my place on both my farm and his. At the age of 19, I had purchased a 260 acre farm several miles north of Dad's farm. It was a *good* piece of land. I did not live on my farm, but rented it out to a family who worked on it with me and for me. Like my dad's farm hands, they received a place to stay, wages, and meat and produce to help supply their family needs.

I had purchased the farm for $26,000. At the time, I only had $7,000 in my savings, so I planned to get the rest in a loan from the bank. When I told Dad my plan, he said, "Let's not get the bank involved in this. I will loan you the $19,000 you need and you can just pay me back. That way we will own it in its entirety."

Now that I had accepted God's call into the ministry, I knew that I must give up the farm. Instead of selling my farm, I just handed it over to Dad. He had paid for most of it anyway. My farm was now officially part of the Cactus Hill Ranch.

It was October of 1945 when I was called to preach. The spring semester for colleges did not begin until mid-January, but I was out of work now and did not know what to do. I mentally stepped back and evaluated my life.

I'm now 21 years old, going on 22. I've always wanted to see a farm bureau organization started here in my area. I wonder if I could maybe get something started in the few months I have left before school.

I decided to give it a try. I went to two well-known farmers and told them I wanted to start a farm bureau in Weld County. "Well," they responded, "we think it's a good idea, and we'll back you if you want to go ahead and try."

With their word as my support, I went out into the community knocking on doors. "We're going to have a meeting about organizing farmers," I said. "Would you like to come and hear what it's about? We are meeting several nights this week."

Community by community, I knocked on doors and invited people to come and learn about the farm bureau. Then in the evening meetings, I answered questions, signed people up, and collected membership fees. Almost everyone wanted to be a part of it.

At the time, there was a small farm bureau several hundred miles away in the San Luis Valley, and that was the largest one in the state. As I continued going to surrounding communities, farmers from all over Colorado heard about me and came to the meetings.

The group I had started was growing rapidly. One of the last meetings I held was just southwest of Greeley in a farming community. Right before the meeting started, some men came up to see me. "We're from the San Luis Valley," they said. "We heard about this, so we've come up to talk to you. We want to see a statewide farm bureau. You've done such a phenomenal job here, but we understand you are going away to school soon. Why don't you stay home and we'll organize a state farm bureau together. You will be the Executive Director. What do you think?"

I was thrilled. This is what I had always dreamed of. And to think, I would have this opportunity before I was 22! But, I had been called to preach and knew that the ministry was where I belonged. "Thank you for your offer, but I can't," I told them. "I have been called to preach, and that is what I'm going to do. I wish you well."

They did not understand completely, but they did not argue with my decision either. They ended up starting the Colorado Farm Bureau and called a man to be the Executive Director who later became the Secretary of Agriculture in Washington. Did I regret my decision later? Absolutely not. I knew without a shadow of a doubt that God wanted me in the ministry, and so it was not difficult for me to say no, even though farming and politics were the two things I had dreamed about my entire life.

* * * * *

WHILE I was working on starting the farm bureau, I was also applying to Bible colleges for the spring semester of the 1945–46 school year. I had made spiritual decisions under the ministries of Dr.

Bob Jones, Sr., and Dr. Bob Jones, Jr., who were both executives of Bob Jones College in Cleveland, Tennessee. I considered that as one of my options, but a problem arose that needs a little back story to explain.

My mother's brother, John Peterson (Uncle John) lived in Kansas City and had become a very successful businessman owning several dime stores. In those days, we called the variety stores Dime Stores — we could actually buy things in the stores for a nickel or a dime! Uncle John had started working at one of these stores, quickly became a manager, and eventually owned several of them.

Uncle John and my family were quite close, and as a teenager, I would travel each summer by train to Kansas City for a month to visit him and his family. Like Mother, he was a good, moral person, and as part of his good works, he and his family faithfully attended a Lutheran church. During my first few summers, I would attend the services with them. We would come home immediately after the morning service, quickly eat lunch, and then we would begin counting money from his many stores. Every Sunday I was with them, I remember Uncle John pouring out the money on the dining room table, and then all of the family and I would get to work. One dollar bills would be in one pile, dimes in another, nickels in another, and so on. We would gather the coins and roll them into the proper containers to take the money to the bank the next day. It was actually quite fun!

When I was 15, something changed. Uncle John and his family had gotten saved. And what a story that was when I heard it.

One day, the Lutheran pastor had said, "John, you're attending here regularly. How would you like to teach a Sunday School class?"

He said, "Well, I'd love to."

"Great! We'll have you take the Junior High boys' class," he replied.

They scheduled the Sunday on which he would start and then John went home. "Grace," he called to his wife, "I'm going to be a Sunday School teacher. I ought to teach the Bible, I guess. But we don't have one in our house."

John and Grace Peterson

"Well, you sell them in your stores," she responded. "Why don't you go pick one up?"

He drove to one of his stores, got a Bible, and began reading in the Gospel of John. He came to John chapter three and read, *"Except a man be born again, he cannot see the kingdom of God" (John 3:3).* He had never heard that before in his church.

I don't think I've been born again, he thought to himself. He studied and thought some more and finished reading the book of John. One day, he said, "I'm going to accept the Lord." He got on his knees in his living room and told the Lord that he accepted Him as his Savior. Immediately, his life changed. Within a few weeks, Aunt Grace and my cousins also accepted Christ as their Savior.

Shortly after his salvation, the Sunday came on which Uncle John was to begin teaching the junior high boys. The first lesson he taught them was, "You Must Be Born Again."

After the church service, the pastor came in. "What did you teach in Sunday School this morning?" he asked.

"I taught the new birth — that you need to be born again," Uncle John replied.

"You can no longer be a teacher," the pastor said firmly. "We don't allow that to be taught here."

Uncle John, Aunt Grace, and my cousins started looking for a new church and found Central Bible Hall in downtown Kansas City, Kansas. It was pastored by Dr. Walter Wilson who was a solid Bible preacher. He taught the new birth and the whole counsel of God from the Bible. Uncle John and his family really began to grow spiritually.

From that point on, Uncle John was always trying to tell me that I was a sinner and needed Jesus. I still remember sitting in a service between Uncle John and Aunt Grace. I was rather bored with the message; the pastor was preaching about the blood of Christ. I had no idea why you would ever want to talk about blood in public — that was gross and weird to me. I could easily fall asleep anywhere, so I started dozing.

As I started nodding off, Aunt Grace poked me in the ribs. I leaned the other way, but Uncle John poked me too! They poked me all the way through the entire message, so I heard my first message on the necessity of the blood to pay the penalty for sin. I did not understand it at the time, but I did not forget the message either.

Sunday afternoons were very different that year. Instead of counting money like we had done in prior years, Uncle John spent the afternoon reading his Bible. The entire trip, whenever I would go with him to visit his stores, he would witness to me. He would witness to his employees. Everywhere he went, he diligently told people about their need for Christ as Savior.

When I accepted the Lord as Savior in 1944, I immediately wrote Uncle John. He was thrilled! As a diligent Bible student and man of spiritual stature, he had my highest respect.

When I wrote to tell him about surrendering my life to preach, he wrote back something to the effect of:

I am thankful you were saved through the ministry of Dr. Bob Jones, Sr., and that you have been called to preach under the ministry of Dr. Bob Jones, Jr. They are good preachers. However, I advise you not to enroll in their school, Bob Jones College. I believe Wheaton College in Wheaton, Illinois, is a much better school. I want you to enroll there.

I took his advice and wrote to Wheaton College saying I would be interested in enrolling there beginning in January of 1946. I did not hear back. Members in my church also recommended Houghton College and Taylor College, so I sent a similar inquiry letter to both schools. Again, I did not hear back.

Time was passing. I needed to get enrolled if I was to start in January. Finally, out of desperation, I wrote Bob Jones College. Within a week, I had a reply. The envelope even had an airmail stamp — the first airmail letter I had ever received. Regular first class mail cost three cents. Airmail cost six cents. You knew if you ever received an airmail letter, it was very important. I ripped the letter open and read a note from Dr. Bob Jones, Sr. He said the college was interested in having me apply and had enclosed the application for me. Soon thereafter, I was enrolled at Bob Jones College.

On my way to Bob Jones College in Cleveland, Tennessee, I had to take the train from Colorado through Chicago with a long layover there. Out of respect for my uncle and his advice, I decided I would use my layover time to visit Wheaton College. I was able to speak with the Registrar, Dr. Enoch Dyrness. He explained that they had not answered my letter because the school was full and had no room for any other students that semester.

"Why don't you finish your trip to Cleveland and attend Bob Jones College for this semester," he suggested. "Come fall, we will have room and you can transfer here in September. I will make a reservation for you now for the next school year."

The following night, I arrived at Bob Jones College. I was greeted by school staff members at the train depot and was given a first class reception.

Bob Jones College, 1947
Cleveland, Tennessee

I loved my classes that semester. The course that really caught my attention was "The Preacher Boys Class." (The actual title was "The Preacher and His Problems.") Twice each week, I was privileged to be under the direction and tutelage of Dr. Monroe Parker for this class. Every class period would open with the hymn, *Souls for Jesus*:

> *Souls for Jesus is our battle cry;*
> *Souls for Jesus — we'll fight until we die.*
> *We never will give in,*
> *While souls are lost in sin!*
> *Souls for Jesus is our battle cry!*
>   — Gillis Partin

Hearing and singing that song with hundreds of other men made chills go up and down my spine. We all sang it with such gusto!

The class was much more than a thrilling song, though. Dr. Parker was a constant challenge to each of us to become men of God who would serve Him wherever He sent us. I was a new believer, having been saved just over a year; but I felt right at home. I immersed myself in the spiritual atmosphere into which the Lord had placed me. I loved it!

I was so pleased with what I was experiencing at Bob Jones College that within a month after arriving, I wrote a letter to Dr. Dyrness of Wheaton, telling him I was canceling my reservation for the fall term at Wheaton College. I would stay at Bob Jones College and finish my schooling there.

A major challenge arose during my first month at school — one I was not prepared for. Mother was opposed to my going to Bob Jones College. During the first month of school, every day, I received a letter from her with a signed blank check in it. She requested that I gain some sanity and leave the school. I was to use the check to buy the ticket to come back home. These letters came daily. Every day, I tore up the check and threw it away. That did not deter Mother. She had a similar letter with a signed blank check in it arriving the next day. This continued for three weeks!

I wrote her several times saying I was very satisfied with where I was and that I believed Bob Jones College was the school where I needed to be. She finally heeded my letters and the checks stopped coming.

I thoroughly enjoyed that first semester of school. The highlight of each day was the Chapel program. Administration, faculty members, and visiting preachers gave sermons that were a tremendous blessing. I particularly enjoyed the messages by Dr. Bob Jones, Sr., Dr. Bob Jones, Jr., and Dr. Monroe Parker.

I loved the fact that every class period opened with prayer. All around the campus, there were posters with different sayings by Dr. Jones, Sr. These principles were burned into my heart and mind. Throughout my entire ministry, I have referred back to many of these sayings, such as,

> "Do right — even if the stars fall."
> "The greatest ability is dependability."
> "The way to keep from having trouble is to have trouble."

That first semester at Bob Jones College was truly life-changing for me. I was encouraged to read and study my Bible in ways I had never done before. I grew in my faith dramatically. I also made many decisions for the Lord during that time.

I remember one day during my first semester, Dr. John R. Rice unexpectedly stopped by the college. I did not know who he was. He was an evangelist and the editor of *The Sword of the Lord*, a Christian newspaper sent to thousands of subscribers. As Preacher Boys, we were required to subscribe to the newspaper, but I had yet to receive my first issue.

During the lunch hour, Dr. Jones, Sr., announced that Dr. Rice had come and that he would preach at a special additional chapel that afternoon. He spoke from Luke 11 about putting bread before the family. He emphasized the fact that we students should become soul-winners. In that service, I dedicated my life to become a soul-winner.

When the meeting was over, I ran to my room and knelt to pray. I remember telling the Lord that I did not know whether or not I would be able to preach, but I asked the Lord to make me a soul-winner — a fisher of men.

That very week, I decided I should go off campus on Saturday and find somewhere I could talk to souls about Christ. I longed to get busy at the job to which I had just dedicated my life.

On Friday, I went to the school's business office and asked if I could get 2,500 Gospel tracts. The one the school used at the time was a small pamphlet entitled, *"THIS IS IMPORTANT!"* The tract presented four truths that are the basis of many other tracts.

1. The fact is, we are all sinners (Romans 3:23)
2. The wages of sin is death (Romans 6:23)
3. Christ paid the price for us by His death on the cross (Romans 5:8)
4. Each person must receive Christ as his personal Savior (Romans 10:13, John 1:12)

That evening, I went to my room and carefully folded all 2,500 tracts. I planned to go from the campus in Cleveland to Chattanooga — about 30 miles away. In those days, students who did not have a car would hitchhike their way to wherever they needed to go. I did not have a car, so on Saturday morning, I caught rides on the highway and eventually ended up in Chattanooga.

I started down a street in the business district and handed out some tracts. At the center of town, I came to Terminal Station which was one of two railroad stations in the town. All trains traveling south would pass through this station, so it was quite busy. There were lots of people there, so I began passing out tracts.

I handed one to a man dressed in a black suit, a white shirt, and a black bow tie. He was carrying a black instrument case. I turned around, and there was another man dressed in the same attire also holding a black instrument case. Two other men dressed alike came up to me with their instrument cases in hand and asked me for tracts. Two more appeared. There were now six musicians standing together reading these tracts.

I have six men of a group together. Maybe this can be my congregation and I can preach my first sermon, I thought.

Terminal Station — Chattanooga, Tennessee
Photo by Will H. Stokes Family / ChattanoogaHistory.com

I climbed onto one of the benches nearby, stood up, and asked the men to look up. "I have a message from the Bible for you," I told them.

Amazingly, they turned and faced me. I had done zero preparation for this, but while sitting in class one day, I had thought that Romans 6:23 would make a good sermon.

"Romans 6:23 says, *'For the wages of sin is death; but the gift of God is eternal life through Jesus Christ our Lord.'*" And that is how I started the first sermon I ever preached.

I did not preach very long, probably less than 10 minutes. During those minutes, other men from the music group joined us until we had about 20 altogether — each one was carrying an instrument case. I closed the message and did what I had seen other preachers do: I had them bow their heads and gave them an invitation to step forward and take my hand. To any who did so, I would show him how to be saved.

There was no response, so I closed in prayer.

A man stepped forward then and introduced himself. His name was Sigmund Romberg and he was the leader of this band. They had just finished a concert in Chattanooga and were heading to the Metropolitan Opera House in New York City for their next concert.

Just over five years later, I read in a newspaper that Sigmund Romberg had died. I do not know if he ever heard any other sermons or if he ever accepted Christ, but I do know that he had a chance to believe the Gospel. He had heard a young preacher boy in Chattanooga, Tennessee, tell him that every person is a sinner and the only way for anyone to go to Heaven is to trust Jesus Christ Who died to pay the penalty for sin.

After my message was over and the band had moved on, I continued passing out tracts throughout town the rest of the day. I met a lady later that afternoon. "Do you believe in Hell?" she asked.

"I do," I replied.

"Prove it to me from your Bible," she demanded.

That was not a question I was prepared to answer. I had heard preaching on the reality of Hell, but I had never studied the Bible to know where to find verses to prove it actually did exist. I had been saved for just over a year at this point, so there were many things I did not know and had not yet studied for myself.

As soon as I returned to campus that evening, I took my recently-purchased *Strong's Concordance* and found verses on Hell. I added them to my daily memory verse pack, and from that day on, I have had Scriptural proof on the teachings of a very real place called Hell.

I learned a valuable lesson that day. Soul-winning was a lot of work, but it is key to growing in grace and helps believers know more truth from Scripture. Many times, people are fearful of witnessing to others because they think they might get asked questions to which they do not know answers or because people might laugh at them. That may be the case (and likely will be), but that first day of my soul-winning effort showed me a truth I did not know how to prove. I studied the answer and continued to grow substantially in my faith and spiritual understanding. Witnessing for Christ and reaching others with the Gospel message is a key for anyone to grow in the Lord as he ought.

Though I had worked all day to reach someone with the Gospel, I had not led anyone to Christ. It was discouraging, but I determined I would continue trying. The next week, I picked up more tracts and headed back to Chattanooga. This time, I went to a residential area of town and began knocking on doors.

Door by door, I covered hundreds of homes and spoke to several people. However, the day ended and again, I had not seen any souls trust Christ. I was very discouraged. I determined I would not go back to Chattanooga, for it seemed there was no one there who was interested in hearing the message. As discouraged as I was, I still told God I would not quit.

So the next weekend, I decided to try Knoxville, Tennessee.

Chapter 5

THE FIRST SOUL I LED TO CHRIST

My reception in Knoxville did not start out much differently from my reception in Chattanooga. I went through the downtown section of Knoxville passing out tracts with no good conversations. I tried a residential area and started knocking on doors. For about two hours, I walked door to door throughout the community, but no one seemed to be interested at all.

I was terribly discouraged and ready to quit. I was so discouraged that I was probably asking those who opened their doors, "I imagine you don't want to be saved, do you?"

After a few more houses, I began talking with a man who said, "I'm not interested. But I do know someone who is."

"Really?" I anxiously and eagerly replied. "Who is he? Where is he?"

"He is my father-in-law, and he lives in Cleveland."

Cleveland? That was exactly the town I lived in and had been hitchhiking *out* of each Saturday. For some reason, it had never occurred to me that I should witness in my own city. I thought I had to go away some distance in order to reach souls; like a missionary to another country.

"My father-in-law just had a stroke and has been begging to see a Baptist preacher," the man told me.

I did not tell him that I was only a freshman student at a Bible college. "I am the man," I said. "I will go see him."

He gave me the man's address and I hurried away to the bus depot. A bus was just about to leave for Cleveland, so I bought a ticket and headed back. I figured this was an urgent matter and hitchhiking would take too long — Knoxville was over 80 miles from Cleveland.

The bus arrived in Cleveland and I went outside to find a taxi. I had grown up on a farm where there were no taxis, so I had never called for one nor ridden in one. But I had seen some other fellows stand at the curb and yell, "Taxi! Taxi!" until a taxi came and picked them up. So I did just that and pretty soon, a taxi pulled up in front of me. After I was seated, I gave the driver the address from the man in Knoxville.

He took one look at it and said, "How did it happen that you called on *me* to take you to this address?"

"Well," I responded, "I called for a taxi and you were the first to come."

"That's interesting," he replied. "I think I am the only taxi driver in this town who knows where this address is."

I silently thanked God for leading me to this particular taxi driver. I was quite excited now — I was going to see a man who might want to get saved! We had driven a short ways out of town when the asphalt pavement became a dirt road. The driver turned right onto a much smaller road and then turned left into what seemed to be a field. He drove a short distance, then stopped.

"There's the house," he said as he pointed. It was no more than a run-down shack that looked like it was falling apart at the seams.

I paid the fare, stepped out, and went up to the shack. As I knocked on the front door, it began to open itself. I quickly pulled it back, then tried knocking again, this time, holding the door shut as I knocked.

I thought I heard someone inside, so I pushed the door open to listen. I heard a weak voice coming from a room down the hall. I stepped in and walked to the dimly lit room. There, on a single bed, I saw a stricken man calling for help.

The man chewed tobacco, and as I walked in, I could see he was chewing some right then. But since he had been afflicted by the stroke, he could not spit. Someone had made a little trough out of paper and put it to his mouth. The tobacco juice would ooze from his mouth onto the trough which then carried the juice down to a coffee can on the floor. The stench in the room was almost unbearable. But this was the man whom I was supposed to see.

I knelt down beside his bed and said, "I was in Knoxville today and met your son-in-law. He told me you were calling for a Baptist preacher. Is that correct?"

"Yes," he answered feebly. "I am very sick, and I want to get saved."

"Well, I'm a student at a Bible college and came here to show you how to be saved," I responded. "May I do that? May I show you how to become a child of God?"

"Oh, yes!" he said, as eagerly as he could.

I gave him the Gospel showing him first Romans 3:23 — *"For all have sinned, and come short of the glory of God."* He was a sinner! Then I went to Romans 6:23 which reveals clearly that *"the wages of sin is* [eternal] *death."* Next, I read to him John 1:12 which states that *"as many as received him, to them gave he power to become the sons of God, even to them that believe on his name."* I asked him if he wanted to receive Christ Jesus as his Savior right then.

"Yes!" he exclaimed.

"You can repeat this prayer after me. This prayer doesn't save you — it's just a tool to help you talk to God. My words can't save you. This prayer must come from your heart as *you* believe what you are saying and confess this to God."

"I will mean it from my heart," he promised.

"Okay," I said. "Dear God, I know I am a sinner. I know I should pay for my sins with spiritual death. And I know that You love me and gave Your Son to pay my penalty by dying in my place."

He was repeating after me as I continued to pray. "Right now, I accept Jesus Christ as my Savior. I trust Him. In Jesus' name, Amen."

As I looked up from finishing this prayer, I saw the man's paralyzed lips endeavor to smile. His whole countenance had changed! He gripped my hand as tightly as he could. My heart started pounding within my chest. The hand of the first person I had ever led to Christ was squeezing my hand as strongly as his stroke-smitten body would allow. I have never forgotten it!

I walked out of that little house into the dark of a February night and found my way down a little trail that led to the road. I discovered that this house was not too far from campus, so I walked all the way back to campus. The journey seemed but a moment, for I realized that there is no greater joy in life than that of leading someone to Christ. Not only was this precious soul saved and changed, but my life goals were transformed. I wanted to win more souls for Christ!

I arrived back at the campus just as the 10:00 P.M. Saturday night prayer meeting in my dormitory began. As I came into the room, the leader asked for testimonies.

"Just this evening," I spoke up, "I had the privilege of leading my first soul to Christ." A loud "Amen" rang through the hall — it seemed like all the boys joined in.

A few days later, I learned that the man had died. I rejoiced (and still rejoice) that I will one day see him in Heaven where there is no more sickness, no more pain, no more strokes — he trusted Christ, and God had used me to reach him. I will never forget that day.

That experience changed the course of my life. From that day on throughout my college years, I spent nearly every weekend away from campus doing various activities trying to reach souls. I would always pray before beginning to study for my classes. After this man accepted Christ, I added something to my prayer: "Lord, use my studies and my classes to make me an effective soul-winner."

Chapter 6

MINISTRY LESSONS 101

I HAD ALREADY completed a year of college before God called me to preach. After I had sufficiently recovered from my accident, I had enrolled at the Colorado State College to study agriculture. College was nothing new for me, but Bob Jones College was *very* different from the state school I had attended.

The amount of required events and rules was somewhat shocking initially. Every morning at 6:00 A.M., the bells rang throughout the dormitories. Breakfast was served promptly at 7:00 A.M., with the first classes starting at 7:30. Every day except Friday, we were required to attend chapel at 11:00 A.M. Lunch was served in two different shifts to accommodate the growing number of students. Then afternoon classes commenced and went on until 6:00 P.M. when we attended dinner which was required every evening.

The most unusual thing was that we were assigned tables for meals. Each table had a host and hostess. The host and hostess might be a faculty or staff member couple, or perhaps two students. Occasionally, one student and one staff member would act as host and hostess. Every few weeks, the table assignments changed so that everyone met different students and staff members.

It was a great way for me to meet new people! As I began making friends that first semester, I noticed something else unusual. There were many World War II veterans who were about the same age as I was (older than the average student), but they had a spiritual maturity that rebuked me! In getting to know them, I discovered that many of these men had been saved during their time in the U.S. military. I learned that most of them had been influenced by The Navigators, an organization led by Dr. Dawson Trotman based in southern California.

The Navigators program emphasized one-on-one discipleship with the goal of creating many "spiritual generations of believers." One of the methods The Navigators used was Scripture memorization. These discipled men, now fellow students, had memorized the 108 verses in The Navigators' *Basic Scripture Memory* program. Almost all of them could quote all the verses perfectly.

Because I wanted to catch up with these men and continue to mature in my faith, I wrote The Navigators and enrolled in that basic memorization program. Along with my studies that first semester, I also memorized the 108 verses which proved to be a tremendous blessing to me. I have quoted those verses often in my preaching ever since that first year.

Also during that first semester, I read a book by E. M. Bounds called *Power Through Prayer*. In it, he states, "Every preacher who does not make prayer a mighty factor in his own life and ministry is weak as a factor in God's work and is powerless to project God's cause in the world." Repeatedly, Bounds emphasizes that someone can be the most eloquent, knowledgeable, personable, likable preacher in the world, but unless he prays, and prays earnestly and sincerely, pleading alone with God, his ministry will be dead and the words of life he is preaching about will actually be the words of death.

Wow, did that ever get my attention! Along with my decision to preach and to be a soul-winner, I determined that I wanted to be a man of prayer — sincere prayer, asking God to work the impossible and miraculous. And He did! I learned first hand what Zechariah 4:6 says,

> "This is the word of the Lord unto Zerubbabel, saying, Not by might, nor by power, but by my spirit, saith the Lord of hosts."

It says "not by might" — letting the personality come in and doing things by my own personality. It says "nor by power" — that is, power of a denomination or something like that. It is only by the Spirit of God that my ministry can have an impact. It has nothing to do with me.

At that time, the charismatic movement had arisen. Many Christians did not want to emphasize the power of the Holy Spirit in their ministries because they were afraid of being called charismatics. I was apprehensive, too, but after reading *Power Through Prayer*, I understood the *need* for Spirit-filled prayers and ministries. I determined that I would believe the Scriptures and not worry about movements. I needed the Spirit of God to make a difference in my life — and He did.

* * * * *

After I had determined to be a soul winner and had led my first soul to Christ, I endeavored to leave campus each Friday after my last afternoon class and preach all weekend, returning Sunday night. I traveled all over Tennessee and the surrounding areas preaching the Gospel. This was not only something I had decided to do on my own, but something Dr. Bob Jones, Sr., had encouraged us Preacher Boys to do.

"The way to learn to preach is to preach," he would say.

Part of the way the school helped us accomplish good preaching was by requiring us to take Speech and English classes our freshman year. Dr. Bob Jones, Sr., explained that he wanted the school to prepare young people to serve in local churches. To do that effectively required that they be able to speak and write correctly.

My speech class proved to be most valuable in shaping the direction of my ministry and the rest of my life. At the beginning of the semester, every student was required to stand before the class and give a five minute speech about his or her background prior to enrolling in Bob Jones College. I remember standing before the class and speaking about my farming background. That was all I knew.

One man in the class was older than the rest of us. He had done evangelistic work and pastoral ministry for 12 years, but had never received any college training. At the time, he was pastor of South Dalton Baptist Church in Dalton, Georgia, about 45 minutes from the school. In his background speech, he informed us that he had worked at soul winning, and for the last 12 years, he had averaged leading 500 people to the Lord every year.

Wow, were we ever shocked and in awe of this man! What a successful ministry he had! I decided to get better acquainted with him and as a result, he took an interest in me. He invited me to work with him that summer. He was preparing to launch into full-time evangelism once the semester finished in May. In April, he resigned as pastor of the church in Dalton, and together, we started planning for the summer travels. He informed me that I would need a car, so as soon as the semester closed, I carpooled my way back to Colorado to get my car. I was under the impression that we were leaving right away for my new job, so I only stayed one night with my parents. They were sorely disappointed, but I explained I needed to get back to Georgia as quickly as possible. The next day, I was on the road to Dalton.

My mother knew that I had difficulty driving long distances. I tended to get sleepy and needed to stop for naps. She was worried that I would not make the 1,400 mile drive by myself, so they asked my brother, Ken, to go with me and gave him the money to take the plane home.

Until that point, I had never shared Christ with my family. After I decided to be a soul winner that semester, I was determined that I was going to witness to everyone, but especially my family. Even though I only stayed one day, I shared Christ with both of my brothers and my parents. They did not trust Christ, but on the trip down to Dalton, I had the privilege of seeing Ken profess Christ as Lord. I was thrilled!

As we were driving, Ken said he would like to go to a Christian college also, but he did not want to go to Bob Jones College. I had heard talk of a Christian school, John Brown University, that was in Siloam

Springs, Arkansas. I discovered that it was not too far out of the way for our trip to Georgia, so we decided to stop and visit. Ken was impressed with the school and enrolled for the fall semester. He graduated from that school four years later with a degree in engineering.

When Ken and I arrived in Dalton a few days later, I was shocked to learn that the evangelist had decided to take a three week vacation and would be gone for two more weeks. I could have easily stayed at home longer and spent some time with my parents, but now that I was in Dalton, I could not change it. Ken traveled home while I figured out what to do with my time. Though I was somewhat discouraged, I believed it was God's will for me to be there. I rented a hotel room and walked the streets of Dalton each day passing out tracts and witnessing to anyone I found.

On Sunday, I attended South Dalton Baptist Church where I met the Jake Shields family. They realized my plight and offered to have me stay in their home, saving me hotel and meal expenses. The deacons offered for me to use the church office since the pastor had resigned.

It was the perfect situation for me and I was grateful for their kindness. Every morning when Jake left for work, I left for the church and spent my time in devotions, studying, and prayer. I continued to witness and pass out tracts, but during those two weeks, God revealed a lot to me.

The former pastor — the man for whom I was waiting to return to Dalton from his vacation — had moved his library from the church. He left one book, a book on missions, by Robert Savage, a missionary to Latin American countries. In his book, *Lord, Send Me,* Savage encourages every Christian young person to consider yielding his or her life to the Lord to be used in missions.

When I walked into the study on that first day and saw the book, I immediately dismissed it. Missions was the *last* thing I wanted to be involved in. During my first semester at school, missionaries often spoke in chapel. I remember one missionary who told us that he felt that he needed to accept the customs of the Mongolian people in order to reach them with the Gospel. One of those customs was drinking tea made from cow dung! Another missionary, this one from the high mountains in Mexico, informed us that a common delicacy among the Indians with whom he worked was fried ants. I was so disgusted by these examples of what was required of missionaries that I determined I would never be a missionary.

But that book was the only one left in the pastor's office, and I had nothing better to do. So, I picked it up and read the first chapter. It was well written and began to make me consider going to the mission field. But missions was the last thing I wanted to think about, so I laid the book aside and began studying and working on other things, trying to distract myself from the conviction of the Holy Spirit.

The next day when I returned to the study, I saw the book, still lying on the desk. I read the second chapter and experienced the same conviction but responded again by just putting the book aside and busying myself with other work.

This happened for several days until I read the entire book and became so convicted that I finally knelt down and prayed, yielding my life to missions if that was the will of God. That decision voiced in prayer did as much to shape my future ministry as any decision I ever made. I realized the importance of missions and the Christian's responsibility to be involved in worldwide missions. From that day on, I was dedicated to promoting and advancing Biblical missions to spread the Gospel around the world.

I learned something else during my two-week wait in Dalton — the former pastor was also running a home construction business. I think that his business and the time it required away from the church created some dissension among the congregation and helped cause the pastor to tender his resignation. I tucked the information away in the back of my head and continued my studies and witnessing in Dalton.

At the end of two weeks, the former pastor returned from his vacation and informed me that we would start right away in revival-evangelistic meetings. The first meeting was at a church in a suburb of Cleveland, Tennessee — the town in which I attended school.

The first Sunday of the meeting, in both the morning and evening services, I was not asked to do anything. He led the singing, the prayers, and preached; he conducted the entire service without having me participate in any way. After each service, we went out to a fancy steak house and had a big, expensive meal. I was not used to eating like that. I had grown up on a farm and had been taught to be very frugal — definitely *not* the way this man was living.

The entire week went by and nothing changed. He did everything for the services, and we would eat fancy meals afterwards. Worst of all, no souls were saved. I was shocked.

The following week, we were in a different church, but again, I had no part in anything. I was just another person in the congregation. Again, no souls were saved, and no one made decisions for Christ.

The third week, I confronted the man. "I am confused," I began. "You told me that we would be working together in this ministry, and so far, I haven't done anything. You lead the singing. You pray. You preach. You do everything. This isn't what I signed up for. Is there something you can have me do?"

"Actually, there is," he replied. "Let me take you for a quick drive and show you what you can do."

We drove to Chattanooga where he showed me a large semi-trailer. It had been used commercially for hauling produce around the country. He had hired carpenters to convert this trailer into living quarters for him and his wife while they traveled in evangelism. His plan was to buy a large diesel truck to pull it from meeting to meeting.

"You can help these carpenters build this trailer for me," he told me. "Just ask them what to do and help however you can."

My parents had raised me to work hard, no matter the task, so I rolled up my sleeves and went to work as best I could. I had no construction background though, so I was almost worthless to the carpenters. I was miserable. This was not how I had envisioned spending my summer. I lasted three days at the task.

On the fourth day, I resigned as his helper, telling him, "I thought this summer would be preparing me for the ministry, not carpentry work."

"You are acting in the flesh!" he fumed. "Your carnality crushes me."

"I am sorry," I said, "but I have made up my mind. I want to train for the ministry. I believe it is best if we part ways."

Before I left, he asked me to lend him some money. "The money I have is saved up for my next year of college," I told him.

"I just need $300 right away," he said.

"In order for me to lend you the money, I'll need something as collateral," I said.

"Well, I have a sound system for my car," he replied after thinking a minute. "It has two large Navy speakers that are on a platform fastened on the top of the car. It has an amplifier that works off the car battery with a turntable to play recordings. You can have that as your collateral."

The system was worth more than $300, so I lent him the money, and he gave me the equipment to use until he could pay me back. I never did receive any payment, so I kept the sound system. I was still determined to do the work of the ministry, and that sound system ended up being a tremendous help to my work.

I bought some records of the quartet that sang on Dr. Charles Fuller's *Old Fashioned Revival Hour*, a gospel radio program heard every Sunday all over America and around the world. I began to hold street services and other services in Dalton and other north Georgia towns. There were many days that I conducted five services in five different places.

I would set up and preach a street meeting in the morning. At noon, I would preach to the employees of a textile factory. I visited several different factories and asked if I could have a service each week on a

Using Navy speakers mounted to my car to preach the Gospel. Dalton, Georgia 1946

certain day and preach during their hour-long lunch break. In no time at all, I was booked for each day of the week. I spent the noon lunch hour at a different factory each day. I preached the Gospel and gave an invitation for souls to accept Christ at each service.

Praise the Lord, a number of workers professed to receive Christ as their Savior. If anyone raised a hand showing a desire to know more, I would get his or her name and address and then visit them that week explaining the Bible's plan of salvation.

In the afternoons, I had one or two more street meetings. Then every evening except Wednesday, I would go to a neighborhood, knock on doors, and ask each family if I could have a Gospel meeting in their yard. Usually, within the first four or five houses, one family said, "Yes, we would be glad to have a service in our yard."

I set up my car speaker, played some of the *Old Fashioned Revival Hour* quartets, and announced on my loud speaker that we were having a Gospel service at such-and-such an address. Most people recognized the music from the radio program. On nice summer evenings, we would have between 15 and 30 people attend. I preached a short message and gave an invitation to step out and receive Christ, and we had several people saved in those yard services. For those who were interested or had trusted Christ, I recommended that they attend South Dalton Baptist Church, the church I had joined.

Not long after I began preaching at the bedspread factories, a thought popped into my head as I was driving from one town to another: *I should preach at the jail in this town.* As quickly as it entered, I dismissed it. *That's foolishness. Why would I go out of my way to preach in the jail here?*

I continued driving down the road. It was summer, and my windows were open to the breeze, what little there was in the South. No sooner had I dismissed the jail from my mind, than a bee flew through my car window and stung me. Instantly, I knew why. God had used the sting of a tiny bee to convict my thoughts. It was not "just a thought that popped into my head." It was the leading of the Holy Spirit. And I was so foolish that God had to use a *bee* to cause me to listen to Him.

I immediately turned the car around and drove to the jail. When I got there, I found a man who had been praying for someone to come and present the Gospel to him. He trusted Christ as his Savior that day, and I learned a valuable lesson on listening to the voice of the Holy Spirit. From that day on, I included jail services in my daily preaching schedule. I was a busy man, but I loved it!

As Preacher Boys, we were required to give a weekly report to Dr. Parker detailing our summer ministry opportunities including the places, times, and results from any services we had preached. One week, I remember reporting over 30 different services where I preached the Gospel.

With all of the busyness during my summer and God's blessing of fruit from my services, I made a mistake. I thought it was a good idea to give people the opportunity to support my ministry. Preaching on the streets and in the factories and neighborhoods did not bring in any income. I was living on my savings, so I decided that I needed some income.

A friend who was a cabinet maker made me a little tract box that I could put out at each meeting. At the bottom of the shelves holding the tracts was a box with a lid fastened with a small padlock. There was a slot in the lid so that individuals could drop money into the box if they so desired.

I purchased some tracts written by Dr. Jesse Hendley, a pastor-evangelist from Atlanta. I put the box out with the tracts and invited people to come get some tracts at the services. Along with that invitation, I said, "If you would like to support this ministry, there is a box at the bottom of the tract box where you can place whatever offering you desire."

What a response I had to that! Every service brought in some money. There were a few times I found over $100 after a service. I began making money. And with that income, I backslid. I began to realize I had cooled off in my desire to reach souls. I was more interested in the amount of money in the offering box than in the souls to whom I was preaching.

One day, a discerning deacon from South Dalton Baptist Church invited me to go with him to a three-day soul winning conference in Toccoa Falls, Georgia. Dr. Hyman Appleman was the principal speaker. In one of the services, God convicted me about my interest in making money rather than having a zeal for lost souls. When he gave the invitation to respond to the message, I went forward and knelt down at the altar. With a repentant heart, I made the matter right with the Lord.

The remainder of the summer, I daily surrendered every phase of my life and ministry to the Lord. He would provide. I was not going to allow personal financial gain to affect any decisions I would need to make in my work as a servant of the Lord.

* * * * *

I LEARNED much during that summer. It was good for me to be forced out on my own in serving God. By His grace, I stayed busy in the work of Christ and gained much wisdom for His service. I learned how to win souls and discovered how to give an effective invitation after a message. I also realized the absolute need to serve the Lord *not* for money, but for a spiritual blessing in the lives of others. Probably the greatest lesson I observed was that just because a man is a preacher does not necessarily mean he is a godly man who is filled with God's Spirit and acting in His power.

Something else happened that changed me during that summer. I received word from home that the pressure had gotten worse in my brother Don's eyes. The doctor had used surgery to try and help alleviate the pain. The surgery was successful, but it was not a complete success.

My 11-year-old brother Don was now completely blind.

Chapter 7

A Polka-dotted Ordination

In August, the South Dalton Baptist Church finally called a new pastor, Dr. LeRoy Perry. He was a humble, godly man who was a great blessing to me and the church. He immediately became interested in the ministry I was doing in the area with the neighborhood services, street meetings, and lunch-hour factory services. After a few weeks, he pulled me aside.

"Ed, I've noticed the work you have been doing in our town. You are a busy man," he began. "I know you love what you are doing, but I have a proposition for you. I know of a church, a little country church in North Georgia, that is looking for a pastor. It's Bethel Baptist Church located on a highway between Adairsville and Rome. If you are willing, I would like to recommend they consider calling you as their pastor. You could visit and preach there a few Sundays so you and the people can get to know each other. We can see how the Lord leads. What do you think?"

I did not know what to think. I had preached much over the summer, but I knew nothing about being a pastor. I was also just six weeks away from starting my second semester at Bob Jones College. I expressed my concerns to Pastor Perry who replied, "I will help you as best I can. It's a good church and the people will assist you too."

"Well, thank you," I said. "I'll give it a try and see what the Lord does."

One month later, Bethel Baptist Church called me to be their pastor. I immediately called Pastor Perry who said, "That is great news! The only step left for you is to be ordained. We can do that here at South Dalton Baptist Church. I will make the arrangements."

I had been a believer less than two years when the ordination took place. Even after a month of candidating at the church, I knew *very* little about being a pastor and did not have any idea what an ordination meant. The pastor and three deacons of the church met with me for about 15 minutes and voted to recommend to the church that I be ordained. The people voted and the ordination was scheduled for two weeks later on Sunday, September 15, 1946.

At that very time, I was reading through the book of Acts for my devotions. I noted the fact that baptism always followed after a person believed on the Lord Jesus Christ. The example that was really impressed on me was from Acts 8:36-37. This is the account where Philip teaches an Ethiopian eunuch from the book of Isaiah while the eunuch was on his way home from Jerusalem. This Ethiopian man was very receptive and accepted the Lord in the chariot that day. As the chariot approached a pool of water beside the road, the eunuch asked, *"See, here is water; what doth hinder me to be baptized?" (v.36)*. Philip responded in verse 37 by saying, *"If thou believest with all thine heart, thou mayest."* The eunuch's answer was, *"I believe that Jesus Christ is the Son of God."*

Based on the eunuch's answer, Philip stopped the chariot, took the man down into the water, and baptized him. The passage clearly shows that for baptism to be scriptural, it must be administered after a person has been saved.

After I had accepted the Lord, the pastor of First Baptist Church in Fort Collins had told me I should get baptized. I had responded with, "I have already been baptized." When I was 12, I had been put under the water at a Disciples of Christ church. I had been baptized, but not scripturally. The pastor of the Disciples of Christ church had told me I should be baptized, but never once did he tell me that I needed to believe on Jesus Christ as my Savior before I could be baptized. I was just put under the water. For the pastor of First Baptist Church in Fort Collins, my answer of "I have been baptized" was satisfactory enough. I received no further questioning and thought nothing about it.

As I was reading the passage in Acts about the eunuch's being baptized after his salvation, I realized that I had *not* been baptized according to the instructions in the Bible. I was about to be ordained as a pastor, and I had not been scripturally baptized! Sunday, September 15 came, and as soon as I arrived at the church, I went straight to Pastor Perry.

"Pastor," I said, "Do you think it is right for the church to ordain a man into the ministry who has never been scripturally baptized?"

"What?" he exclaimed. "You haven't been baptized? How did you become a member of this church without being baptized?"

"Well, you accepted me into the membership on the basis of a letter from my church in Fort Collins. But I have been reading my Bible in the book of Acts over these past two weeks and realized that I have never been baptized according to the Bible. I want to be baptized before the ordination takes place."

Pastor Perry immediately had the baptistery filled with water. Following the morning service, I was scripturally baptized *after* I had received Christ as my Savior, and the South Dalton Baptist Church congregation was witness to this act of obedience. As soon as I was baptized, I changed into dry clothes and sat in front of the ordination committee.

I had recently bought a new suit just for the occasion. I had very little money, so I had found a suit on special — $15 instead of $30. I was known to buy things at the cheapest place possible too. So the suit I bought was made of thin wool. It looked nice though, and I thought it would do for the ordination.

Pastor Perry and a few others took me into the pastor's study and asked me a few questions. Then we went to the auditorium where they presented me before the congregation. I knelt behind a chair with my back toward the congregation. As I got on my knees, I thought I heard some snickering, but did not pay much attention. Once Pastor Perry and the others had prayed over me and officially ordained me, I was ushered to the front door for a receiving line. Mrs. Shields was one of the first in line and offered her sincere congratulations. Then, she said in a soft voice so only I would hear, "Don't bend down or make any big movements. As soon as you are through here, come *immediately* back to the house. We need to fix your pants."

"What's wrong with them?" I asked, confused. "This is a new suit."

"Put your hand on the seat of your pants."

I did and was horrified to discover my pants were gaping open clear from Dan to Beer-Sheba. Then I remembered — I was wearing my red polka-dotted underwear. No wonder I had heard snickers. I was ordained on September 15, 1946 — with wet hair and polka-dotted underwear.

Chapter 8

MY FIRST PASTORATE

THE NEXT DAY, I began my second semester at Bob Jones College. A *lot* had changed over the summer. I had experienced many lessons that I knew would stick with me through my entire life. I was eager to get back into the classroom and soak up all the instruction I could retain. I was now a second-semester freshman, but I also had a great responsibility: I was the pastor of a church.

Every Friday, after my classes were finished for the day, I left the school as early as possible and drove the hundred miles to Bethel Baptist Church. A family in the congregation provided lodging and meals for me every weekend. I always scheduled visitation in the area on Friday night and all day Saturday for any who would join me in inviting people to the church. The labor paid off and the Lord blessed our efforts. The church began to grow. I had the privilege of leading several to the Lord and scripturally baptizing them. It was a wonderful, busy time for me in which I learned more key lessons.

My third Sunday at the church, I preached a message on Exodus 17:8–16 where Israel had a battle with Amalek. Moses had Joshua choose men who would follow him and fight with the Amalekites. Moses then went to the mountain and held up his hands before the Lord in prayer. While Moses held up his hands, Joshua and the Israelites prevailed in the battle. But Moses was unable to hold up his hands all the time. Whenever he rested his hands, the Amalekites prevailed. Aaron and Hur were with Moses and saw the problem. They had Moses sit on a rock, and when his arms became too weak for him to hold them up, Aaron and Hur held up Moses' hands for him until the sun went down and the Israelites defeated the Amalekites.

In my message, I asked the people to hold my hands up before the Lord in prayer to God. When the service ended, I went out onto the little porch at the front door so I could greet the people as they left the building. This morning, one of the elderly ladies came out, spit tobacco juice over the railing of the porch,* and then shook my hand while saying, "Young feller! I believe preachers should use the *New* Bible for us today, not the *Old* Bible. That was for Israel!"

I had no clue what she was talking about, so I just said, "Thank you, ma'am," and continued greeting other people.

I went back to the room where I stayed the weekends and pondered what she had said. Finally, it dawned on me that she was talking about the two testaments of the Bible — the Old and New Testaments. She was saying that for our day and age, we should only preach from the New Testament. I did not know why I had not thought of that before. It made a lot of sense to me as a still-young Christian, so I decided that day that I was going to preach only from the New Testament in the future.

Then, one day in a class at school, the professor stated that the Bible was one book made up of two testaments. "These two testaments are bound together in a wonderful way," he taught. "The New Testament is in the Old Testament concealed. The Old Testament is in the New Testament revealed."

I realized my mistake — deciding to preach from only the New Testament was foolish. I had been missing *much* of the significance of the Bible. I began preaching from the Old Testament again and a whole new world opened up before me. Yes! The Bible *is* one book with *one* pri-

---

* In those days in the South, there were many women who chewed tobacco. In this church, some women actually brought coffee cans into the church with them so they would have a way to spit during the service. Believe me, the church building stank *terribly!*

mary message: the redemption of man from sin through the shed blood of Jesus Christ, God's Passover Lamb.

In addition to being a student and a pastor that year, I put into action the decision I had made at the beginning of the summer: I was going to promote missions and would prepare to be a missionary if that was the direction God led me.

Bob Jones College had a Mission Prayer Band that met every night after dinner in the Dining Common. From the messages I had heard the semester before about missionaries drinking cow dung tea and eating fried ants, I had wanted no part in missions or Mission Prayer Band. I did not care to eat fried ants, even if they were covered in mustard or ketchup! I had been completely disinterested (and quite frankly, disgusted) with missions up to that point. But God had changed my heart over the summer and I had surrendered to serve as a missionary if that was God's will for my life.

Therefore, the first thing I did when I returned to school that fall was attend Mission Prayer Band. I joined with a Latin-American student who was the son of a Baptist pastor in Mexico. We labored together to enlist more students to attend the prayer meetings. When I joined Mission Prayer Band that semester, 25-40 students met every weekday evening except Wednesday since we attended a local church service that night.

The Lord had so deeply impressed upon me the need for missions, and for *every* Christian to be involved in missions, that I made it my goal to get as many students as possible to attend Mission Prayer Band.

Many times, while walking down the sidewalk at school, I overheard students saying, "Quick! That's Ed Nelson. He's going to try and get you to join Mission Prayer Band." And I did! I believed that every Christian should be involved in missions and what better way to learn than to pray for the missionaries themselves?

Every Friday afternoon, I left the campus as early as I could to make the 100-mile drive to Bethel Baptist Church. I was learning a lot about preaching, being a pastor, and working with people in the months since I had taken the little country church. I was growing in my faith too.

One day, I was visiting with a deacon who was the definite leader in the church. He had a daughter who was a senior in high school and wanted to attend a Christian college after she graduated. I encouraged her to consider enrolling in Bob Jones College, but her father wondered if their family could afford the tuition. He owned a saw mill and cut wood to sell to lumber yards. It was a small business and finances were tight. Finally, he made the decision that she should enroll in Bob Jones College. That same week, his equipment broke down. The repairs were extremely expensive, requiring him to rebuild parts of the mill. There was no way he was able to provide financially for his daughter to go to Bob Jones College or any other private college.

I heard about the problems and was discouraged. Bob Jones College had meant so much to me and had truly changed my life. I wanted this girl to experience the same kind of growth that I was getting through the school. Therefore, as a kid-preacher, I challenged this deacon to step out in faith and watch God provide. He did and kept his daughter enrolled. Miraculously, God provided. His business grew, and he was well able to have his daughter attend Bob Jones College. The whole family grew in their faith and I saw firsthand how God provided for His children.

I continued my studies, my pastorate, and my involvement with missions throughout the entire school year. I went home to Colorado for Christmas and enjoyed spending a few weeks with my family. In the spring semester of 1947, I did some serious thinking. I became very burdened for the people of my home state. They needed the Gospel too. My *family* needed the Gospel. Finally, I made the tough decision to resign from the pastorate of Bethel Baptist Church in North Georgia. When the semester ended in May, I preached my last sermon at the church and headed back home. I had learned *much* during my time of preaching in the South. God had stretched me and grown me in ways I never would have grown otherwise. But God had new work for me to do, and it happened to be in my beloved Rocky Mountains.

Chapter 9

Rocky Mountain Evangelist

The semester had ended, goodbyes were said, and I was finally back home in the beautiful state of Colorado. It was the very end of May 1947, and Mother and Dad were thrilled to have me back, even though they still did not like that I was a preacher. I spent a few days with my brothers — much had changed in a year and a half!

Ken had grown and was doing quite well in his studies. He still helped Dad much on the farm. Don had changed too. He was blind. That was hard for me to get used to. We had always helped him with his studies and chores around the house, but he had still been able to see. Now his sight was totally gone. He faced the days with cheerfulness and showed me how he could read with his fingers using the Braille he had learned at the Colorado School for the Deaf and the Blind. It was amazing to watch how quickly he could read with his fingers.

Although it was good to be home, I became restless after just a few days. I wanted to work in the ministry and reach the people of Colorado with the Gospel. I had already been witnessing to my family, and both Ken and Don had professed a belief in Christ as their personal Savior. Mother, however, was still as hard as ever, and I knew I needed to continue the witness to her. But there was also a different work to which I felt God was calling me. I just had no idea where to start.

I had heard of the Spurgeon Memorial Foundation in Englewood, just a few miles south of Denver. It was an organization that helped in sponsoring evangelism. Dr. Carl Harwood was the leader of the organization and was a strong, Bible-believing pastor in the area. I had heard of him while at school and wrote to him asking for suggestions of places where I could try hosting a revival-evangelistic meeting.

"Thanks for your letter, Ed," was the reply a few days later. "There is one town where I would love to see an evangelistic effort being made: Dillon. It's high up in the Rockies, so they are still likely to get snow storms in June. If you come, I will take you there, and you can host a two-week revival service. But I don't want to go until the end of June."

I wrote back that I would love to try preaching in Dillon and we set a date to meet on Friday, June 27. I still had a few weeks before that time came though, and did not know how I was going to fill my time.

The first day of June, a young man from Beth Eden Baptist Church called me. I forget his name, but I remember that he was studying at Rockmont College. Over the summer, he was endeavoring to start a church in the mountain town of Idaho Springs. Idaho Springs was the town my mother had grown up in, so I was quite familiar with the area. We did not visit often but I had been there many times. Once a thriving community, it was now just a small mining town as much of the gold from the Gold Rush days was gone.

"I'd like to have you come help me get started up here, Ed," he told me. "I've already spoken with one couple up there who would like to start a church. Would you come hold a revival meeting?"

"I would love to!" I said. So I rented a tent that could seat up to one hundred people and eagerly prayed for revival and souls to be saved.

On Sunday, June 8, we started the first meeting in Idaho Springs with just me, the young man, and the couple from town, Mr. and Mrs. Shrieve Whitlow. The Whitlows were a godly couple in their mid-seventies and had been earnestly praying that someone would start a church. Even though we were few in number that first night, we did not lose heart.

Idaho Springs, Colorado — 1938
photo courtesy of The Denver Public Library, Western History Collection

The next day, the young man and I spent our time encouraging townspeople to come to the service that night. Someone warned me that some residents of Idaho Springs were planning to tear down the tent at night, so I slept in it. I had an army cot that I set up, and an extra tent stake right beside me just in case someone ever did come. Fortunately, I never needed to use the tent stake as a weapon and the meetings proceeded without any disturbance.

For two weeks we passed out fliers during the day, and then I preached a sermon in the tent every night. The attendance rose and fell, but we saw some nights where a crowd of 25 or more participated in the service. Some were saved and desired to obey Scripture by being baptized.

The meetings were to close on Sunday night, June 22. That afternoon before that last service, we scheduled a baptismal service at an outdoor pool on the edge of town.

If you have ever been to Colorado in June, you know that afternoon thunderstorms develop almost every day. In the mountains, the lightning and thunder can be quite terrifying and dangerous due to the closer proximity to the clouds. In addition, being in the mountains with lots of rain means there is a high likelihood of a flash flood as the rain waters rush throughout the canyons.

That June Sunday afternoon was like so many others. As we prepared for the baptismal service, dark clouds began gathering in the west and we could see that they were heading straight for us. It looked like it was going to be a doozy of a storm with a torrential downpour.

I looked at the sky and then looked at the people who had gathered for the service. "Let's pray," I told them.

"Lord," I said, "You know we are trying to honor You with this service. Souls have been saved and they want to obey Your Word and follow their salvation with baptism. But You know we need the rain too. We just can't have it come here. Would you send it right over that mountain to the south of us? They need the rain too. Thank You, Lord."

As we opened our eyes, we looked at the storm and immediately the cloud moved over the top of the mountain and dumped its much-needed moisture on the other side. God answered our prayers! The sun came out again and we had a wonderful baptismal service free of rain.

The young preacher continued his work in Idaho Springs with the faithful couple and the new converts. He started the First Baptist Church of Idaho Springs that has continued for over 70 years.

After the meetings concluded in Idaho Springs, I went home and spent a few days on the farm with my family. On Friday, June 27, I eagerly met Dr. Harwood in Englewood at the appointed time. We drove up to the mountains, him leading the way and me following in my own car. We passed Idaho Springs, wound around US 6 over Loveland Pass, and finally entered the town of Dillon. It was a little town of just under 200 residents and was situated at the confluence of three rivers — the Blue River, the Snake River, and the Ten Mile River. It was surrounded by mountains on every side. The scenery was truly breathtaking, but the town itself was filthy and very wicked.

As I got out and looked around, I counted eight saloons and only one food store. The town also included a grade school, a town hall, a Conoco gas station, a few miscellaneous shops, and an empty, boarded up Methodist church building.

"They shut it down," Dr. Harwood said as he motioned to the church building. "I know the lady who has the keys. I'll get them from her so we can look inside. You can use this building for your revival meetings."

He obtained keys to the Methodist church building, unlocked the door, and gave me the keys. I walked inside and immediately shivered. It was just as cold inside as it was outside, and the temperature was dropping by the minute. *Maybe we aren't done with winter yet*, I thought. I saw a little kerosene heater, so I walked over and lit it.

"You can stay here," Dr. Harwood said. "I see you brought your army cot — that's wonderful! The Conoco down the street has a room where you can wash up. Let's pray, and then I need to be on my way home again."

We prayed together for God's blessing on the meetings and then he left. "I will continue to pray for you," he said as he walked out the door. "This is a wicked town. I consider Dillon to be the most wicked town east of California and Nevada." And with that, he was gone. I was alone in Dillon.

I brought in a few dishes that I had and fixed a peanut butter and jelly sandwich for dinner. I did not sleep much, but I was grateful for a roof over my head and a dry place to sleep.

The next morning, I walked to the Conoco, washed up as best I could, and got to work. All day Saturday, I took the boards off the windows of the church, cleaned the building, and prepared for the first service which was to be the next morning. I had printed some fliers to pass out advertising the revival meetings. Every house and business in the town received a personal, hand-delivered invitation for the services. I met a 70-year-old woman and her handicapped daughter who lived together just a few miles north of the town and up near the top of the mountain.

Dillon, Colorado — early 1950s
photo courtesy of History Colorado, Denver, Colorado

The Methodist Church Building in Dillon — early 1950s
photo courtesy of The Denver Public Library, Western History Collection

"We're so glad you have come!" they told me excitedly. "We are believers, but as you can see, there is no church here in town. Sometimes we drive to Frisco just to attend the Bible church there. It's not terribly far, but driving can be difficult for us coming down the mountain."

"Will you come to the service here in Dillon tomorrow?" I asked.

"Oh yes!" the mother answered. "We will be there."

That evening, I finished setting up my quarters in a small section of the church. I had the army cot set up against the wall. On a small chair a few feet away, I laid out the supplies for my meals — peanut butter and jelly sandwiches. I found a small pot in which I attempted to heat water on the kerosene heater for a cup of tea. It was not much, but I was happy. I was going to be able to preach the Gospel to a town that really needed it. I put my head on the pillow after the long day's work and prayed that God would bring the people who needed to hear the truth.

The next morning, I washed up at the Conoco gas station again, ate breakfast, and reviewed the Scripture passage for my message. Fifteen minutes before the service was to begin, the elderly lady and her daughter arrived at the church. I eagerly waited for other townspeople to come, but no one else did. So I walked to the pulpit and began the service.

After the service, the ladies informed me about the condition of the town. "During the school year, the police have picked up grade-school children walking down the street roaring drunk. It's awful."

"I have heard a few stories from other people around here," I replied. "And Dr. Harwood told me that it's a very wicked town. I just had no idea how wicked it was until I got here. We desperately need revival!"

The ladies agreed and over the next two weeks, they faithfully attended the services each night. Many nights, a group of believers from the Frisco Bible Church came and helped build a crowd. I was especially grateful for those evenings because they brought a pianist with them who was able to accompany our singing — the rest of the nights, I struggled through leading the singing. I was just not musical at all. But I gave it my best shot.

On the Fourth of July, I woke up to snow. It was summer, and it was snowing! But it was an unusually cold summer for the mountains that year. We carried on with our revival meetings despite the weather and the holiday.

A few residents from Dillon attended sporadically. One night, a man who was a cook at a tourist lodge on the edge of town came to the service. Throughout the entire message that night, I had his undivided attention. When I gave an invitation to come forward at the end of the service, he immediately stepped out and came down the aisle. He grasped my hand and said, "I want to be saved."

"Be seated a moment, and then I will personally show you how to be saved," I responded.

I closed the meeting, dismissed the crowd, and then sat down with this man. I took my Bible and showed him Romans 3:23 which tells us that "*all have sinned, and come short of the glory of God.*" He agreed with me that he was a sinner. Then I showed him Romans 6:23 which says, "*For the wages of sin is death,*" and I stopped. "Because of your sin," I told him, "you deserve to die. Because of sin, you **will** die, and it isn't just a physical death. This is talking about spiritual death and separation from God for eternity."

"But the verse doesn't stop there," I continued. "It finishes with, '*but the gift of God is eternal life through Jesus Christ our Lord.*'"

"I want to believe in Jesus," he said. "I want the gift of God."

"Then pray," I said. "Romans 10:13 says, '*For whosoever shall call upon the name of the Lord shall be saved.*' Confess your sin to God and ask Him to save you. He promises He will."

Right then and there, the man prayed and trusted Christ as his only hope for eternity with God. He was gloriously saved. He attended every service for the rest of my time there.

Shortly after his salvation, the man discovered that I was sleeping on an army cot in the church building. He rented a room for me in a motel nearby. Then he asked what I was doing for my meals. I told him I just had peanut butter and jelly sandwiches.

"I will send meals over to your room each day," he said. "I direct the preparation of all the meals at the lodge. Some of the steaks we get aren't big enough to sell, so they just get put aside."

From that night on, he prepared T-bone steaks for me each night and had someone from the lodge bring over the food for me.

The Monday before my two weeks was up, the cook came to me and said, "I have given the lodge my two-weeks' notice. I resigned from my position and am moving back to Arkansas. Since I accepted the Lord, I have become completely disillusioned with the moral conduct of this town. Arkansas is my home state, and I'm moving back there. I want to be baptized and join the Baptist church there. I really want to do right and live a life that will glorify God."

"I am proud of you," I replied. "I believe God will use your testimony for His glory. Thanks for all that you have done for me. You have been a blessing to me."

I closed the meetings on my third Sunday in Dillon, July 13. The cook from the lodge was the only person who had accepted Christ during the weeks of meetings. On the Monday after the meeting ended, I boarded up the doors and windows of the Methodist church building and returned the keys to the lady who had given them to us. I loaded my car with my few belongings, checked out of the motel, and drove to the city-limit sign on the east side of Dillon.

In my Bible reading, I had come across the passage which says,

> "And whosoever shall not receive you, nor hear you, when ye depart thence, shake off the dust under your feet for a testimony against them. Verily I say unto you, It shall be more tolerable for Sodom and Gomorrha in the day of judgment, than for that city" (Mark 6:11).

I stood beside the Dillon city-limit sign, stomped my feet, pointed my finger toward the town, and said, "God, I want you to curse that town because they did not hear Your Word." Then I got back in my car and returned to my dad's farm in Fort Collins.

A few years later, an article came out in the Denver Post with the headline: "Dillon, Colorado Faces Extinction If Denver Builds Dam." The Denver Water Board had realized the city of Denver was growing too rapidly to sustain the population with their current source of water. As a result, they planned to channel the Blue River and create the Dillon Reservoir and Dam. In order to build the new water source, the town of Dillon as I knew it had to be relocated. A few buildings including the school were moved, but the rest of the buildings were bulldozed. It is said that the town was so contaminated and filthy that the construction crews had to bulldoze six feet past the lowest foundation just to clear the contaminates before they could begin building.

I am not certain whether the Denver Water Board had planned to bulldoze Dillon before I had my revival meetings there in 1947. I do know that nothing was ever printed in the papers about it until years after I was there. I believe God answered the prayer and faith of a naive, 23-year-old college student and destroyed the town of Dillon for their unbelief in the Gospel of Jesus Christ.

* * * * *

After the experience in Dillon, I continued the summer travels by driving further west to Vernal, Utah, about 30 minutes west of the Utah/Colorado border along US Highway 40. Someone had challenged me to try and start a church in a predominately Mormon town, so I accepted the challenge and away I went. This time, I brought with me a couple of young men including a musician to help lead the music for the revival services.

As I had done in other towns, I rented a tent, set it up, and started passing out fliers for revival meetings. I did not get much of a crowd with the usual methods, so I decided to try the radio.

I walked over to the radio station and asked the manager if I could buy some time on the station and preach. "Sure," he said. "I have a short slot available right now. You just cannot say anything against the Mormon church." And so I began preaching on the radio in addition to the tent services.

Still, no crowd gathered to hear the Gospel. After a few days of both radio and tent services, I approached the radio station manager. "Sir," I began, "I know that you're Mormon. You have allowed me to speak the Gospel here, and it's worked out so far. But now, I've decided I would like to announce the topic for my message on Thursday night. I would like to preach on *What Is Wrong With The Mormon Church*. Could I announce that?"

"Oh," he said, "yes, just announce it, but that's all." So I made the announcement and proceeded with the revival service efforts like usual.

Thursday night came and the tent was packed. As I pulled up to the tent that night, I saw the sides were rolled up and there were people gathered outside. There was not a seat left inside the tent!

I had prepared a message, but I did not know very much about Mormonism. I just preached on what I saw was not Scriptural about the Mormon Church. Mormons put more faith in the Book of Mormon than they do in the Bible. It is a religion based on works — you work your way to Heaven — and that is completely opposite of what Scripture teaches: "*Not by works of righteousness which we have done, but according to his mercy he saved us*" *(Titus 3:5a)*. After sharing this and giving the Gospel, I closed the message with an invitation. Three girls came forward and accepted Christ. I was thrilled.

Then, as I began to close up the service completely, a man stood up. "You preached on what's wrong with the Mormon church," he said. "And you said you want to be fair. If you're fair, you'll let us get up and speak and tell you what's wrong with what *you're* doing."

I said, "No, I won't do that." The people were angry. The crowd got up and began moving toward the platform. I tried to calm them down and encourage them to leave, but they would have none of that.

The musician who was with me had also been a Golden Glove boxer. When he saw the people continuing to come closer, he doubled up his fists and was about to launch into the crowd with fists flying. The moment I saw that, I ran over, grabbed him, and said, "Don't you hit. Don't you dare strike anybody!"

I saw another Christian fellow close by. "Go turn the lights off," I told him. "We'll make it dark so they have to leave." The young fellow found the lights and switched them off. We just stayed put and did not move. Eventually, the crowd dispersed and we were able to breathe calmly again. Fortunately, we had avoided an all-out riot.

The next day, one of the girls who had accepted Christ was walking down the street in downtown Vernal. A car stopped near her, and she saw it was her brother. Instead of cheerfully greeting her, he jumped out of his car, hit her, and knocked her out cold. She, along with the other two girls who had received Christ, were no longer welcome in their own homes. A Christian lady who had been attending the services heard of this and opened her home for the three girls.

A few days later, I was walking around the town and suddenly, a Mormon Bishop appeared in front of me. He looked me straight in the eye and began speaking in a deep, dark voice. "We're right," he said. "You know we're right."

Try as I might, I could not get my eyes off of him. They were locked into his eyes, and I began to feel a hand closing around my throat, even though his hands were both at his sides. *There's demonic power here*, I realized. *I better get out of here!*

The hand on my throat was getting tighter each second. "Lord Jesus," I managed to gasp out, "I plead the blood of Jesus for deliverance!"

Immediately, the pressure around my throat was gone and my eyes unlocked from the Bishop. I turned around and quickly returned to where we were staying.

When I walked into the hotel, the other men who were helping with the meetings were gathered together. They took one look at me and exclaimed, "What happened? You're as pale as a ghost!" Briefly, I explained what happened, and then we praised God together for His deliverance.

* * * * *

OVER THE remaining months of the summer, I traveled all throughout the Rocky Mountains preaching the Gospel of Jesus Christ. I visited the Frisco Bible Church, which had supported my revival services in Dillon. I traveled to some lesser known towns in the heart of the Rockies.

I stayed with my parents in between meetings. To my regret, I was hardly home that summer and did not spend as much time with my family as I should have. But God grew me that year. He grew my faith, my ministry, and my endurance. He gave me tangible expressions of His power. And He enabled me to stand for the truth of the Gospel despite opposition from family, friends, religious leaders, and even fellow laborers. These were lessons that I would keep with me for the rest of my life.

While I preached faithfully throughout the Rockies that summer, someone else was faithfully serving the Lord thousands of miles away. Someone I had yet to meet.

Chapter 10

GUYLA

Frances Guyla Pearson was the epitome of brilliance and beauty, though she would never have said so herself. As the third of seven children and the first girl in the family, she spent a lot of time with her mother, Nanette Pearson. "Mother was an amazing woman," she would say years later. "She taught me everything she knew."

It was her mother that taught her how to make the 1-2-3-4 Cake base: 1 cup of butter, 2 cups of sugar, 3 cups of flour, and 4 eggs. "I don't remember what all she put into her cakes," she recalled. "But every single cake she ever baked started with that base."

Shortly after starting classes at the town school in West Point, Mississippi, Frances realized she had been given the nickname "Fannie" and ran home crying. "Don't worry," her mother said kindly. "We will just call you Guyla instead." And so from that day on, she was known as Guyla.

Guyla was named after several relatives with the Guy or Guyla name. Her great-grandfather, John Guy Lofton, fought for the Confederates during the Civil War and was killed in the battle of Seven Pines in Virginia in 1862. His wife, Elizabeth, had borne their last child alone, and named her Margaret Guyla Lofton, the lady who would become Guyla's grandmother. From then on, Guy or Guyla became a family name. Margaret named her son Guy, and her daughter, Nanette. Nanette then named her first daughter Frances Guyla Pearson.

Guyla's mother diligently taught her children to read properly. After working tirelessly all day every day, she would light a candle, pull up a chair, and help Guyla with her homework. It was Nanette, as well as the school teacher, who taught Guyla to read phonetically, giving each letter its own sound. As a result, Guyla excelled at almost everything she did in school, though she never thought she was any smarter than anyone else.

Dave and Dolly (Margaret Guyla) Guyla's grandparents

The teacher did her best to keep all her students busy, but as the sole teacher for five grade levels, sometimes the students had to wait their turn for the next subject.

One day, Guyla had finished her writing assignment ahead of everyone else her age. She was very bored and began glancing around the classroom looking for something to occupy her thoughts.

"Guyla!" the teacher called sharply. Instantly, her head snapped to attention. "Come to the front please."

Quickly, Guyla made her way to stand in front of her teacher. "Stand in that corner with your back to the class for five minutes. You should know better than to slack from your lessons."

Mrs. Pearson had taught all her children to obey immediately when told to do something and to do it without excuses or questions. This day in the classroom was no exception in Guyla's mind. Obediently, she faced the corner for the required time. She was mortified and never once appeared to be bored in class again.

In high school, she competed in track and field as well as many 4-H competitions. Her mother trained her to be a lady and encouraged her to take courses in cooking, needlework, and decorating.

She learned much in school, but had already been taught much at home. From as young as she could remember, she was helping her brothers and her mother with the chores, the dishes, and anything else that needed to be done. With seven children, five of whom were boys, there was always a *lot* of laundry! Guyla prided herself on being able to starch and iron one of her dad's or brothers' shirts in under five minutes — with irons that required being heated and reheated on the stove.

Guyla's father Noble, or "Daddy" as she called him, worked hard to provide for his family, but money was tight. During the Great Depression, Noble earned $25-$30 a month — less than the needed amount for his family to make ends meet. Although they never went hungry, each one of the Pearson children learned to work hard to earn their own spending money.

In addition to her studies and chores, Guyla also worked at various jobs outside the home to earn extra money. One such job was selling shoes at a store in town. She had another job taking care of a widow's children so that the widow could go to work herself. Wherever Guyla could find some extra work, she was there diligently and faithfully. In her spare time, she took the opportunity to advance her skills even further by learning shorthand and typing.

Though times were rough for the Pearsons, there was a simple joy that Guyla learned from her mother that helped her in almost every situation of life. Noble dearly loved his children and tangibly showed it; but to his wife, he was very unkind. Many nights, after the children had gone to bed, Guyla could hear her father yelling at her mother. At breakfast the next morning, her father would be very curt and short-tempered, especially toward Nanette. As soon as Noble left for work, the tension left the room, and Nanette began to sing. Through all the chores, all the dishes, all the laundry, wherever she went, she would sing

The Pearson Family, 1945
Back row: Eugene, David, Sammy, Noble, Nanette
Front row: Paul, Clyde (Buddy), Sue, Guyla

or hum. Guyla noticed and often joined her mother's voice as they carried on sweet tunes of forgiveness and hymns of praise.

The Pearson family attended a small Methodist church in town, and by God's grace, it was a church that fervently believed and preached the Gospel of Jesus Christ. At a young age, Guyla professed salvation through Jesus Christ alone, but over the next decade, she had many doubts. Grandma Margaret prayed earnestly for her daughter and the rest of the family, but Guyla was the only grandchild who accepted Christ at the time.

Plagued with doubt as to her eternal state, Guyla eagerly accepted a friend's invitation to a two-week revival meeting at the local Baptist church. The speakers were two student preachers from Bob Jones College. It was at one of those revival services that Guyla finally had peace that her soul was secure in the hands of God.

In 1942, West Point High School graduated a brilliant class. Some students went on to be veterinarians, others became doctors, but the valedictorian of that graduating class was Miss Frances Guyla Pearson. She finished high school with a 99.3% average, according to the *West Point Daily Times*. However, family members are convinced that

Guyla actually had a perfect score, but the principal believed that no one is perfect and refused to give her a 100%.

Following graduation, Guyla was torn about what she should do. Her family advised her to stay home and work to earn her living. But she had her heart set on further education. Her daddy always said that anybody who wants to go to college can go. If any of his children wanted to go to college, he would support that decision, even though he was unable to help financially. Guyla had not forgotten the two preachers from Bob Jones College, and when she had asked her pastor about the Jones family and the school, he replied that he had nothing against them.

Because Guyla had worked at various jobs during her high school years, she had been able to save $300. This, she discovered, was enough to pay for one semester at Bob Jones College. Three of her brothers, David, Paul, and Buddy, were away fighting in World War II. Her mother had two children under the age of five, Sue and Sammy. Her family did not want her to leave, and she felt as though her mother needed the help with the chores and her younger siblings. Besides this, she only had enough money to stay in school for one semester. She loved learning, and she dearly wanted to go to college. Her parents assured her that they would make it without her at home if college was really what she wanted to do. Her daddy even encouraged her to go. Yet still, she felt plagued by the choice before her.

As she wrestled within her spirit, she heard of a Bible Conference that Bob Jones College was hosting. Some family friends told her that they would be driving through Tennessee and could take her to the school.

She decided to attend the conference, and while there, she enrolled for the fall semester.

In September of 1942, Frances Guyla Pearson officially became a student at Bob Jones College. She was the first of her family to attend college.

Guyla quickly realized that she could take her classes and work as secretary to one of the staff members to help pay for school. Her brother,

David, also sent her monthly checks to help with her expenses. Between her job and her brother, Guyla had enough money to make the payments for another semester.

One day, Dr. Bob Jones, Sr., announced that he needed an additional secretary immediately. His load was so great that his existing secretary, Marjorie Parker, could not keep up. He needed someone who could type quickly and who knew shorthand. Guyla was the only girl applying who could do both, so she got the job. She loved it.

For the next five years as she worked to pay her way through college, she continued to work for Dr. Jones, Sr., by writing letters, answering phone calls, proofreading letters for others, and any other task he asked her to do. The hard work ethic instilled in her from childhood was paying off. She graduated in 1947 with honors — and completely debt free.

* * * * *

THE SUMMER of 1947, Bob Jones College underwent some major changes. Because the student body had grown so rapidly after the war, the Joneses realized that the college needed a new facility. They purchased land in Greenville, South Carolina, and began constructing the buildings for a new campus in September of 1946.

By the following summer, the school began the move from Cleveland to Greenville. All summer long, Guyla moved file after file and organized the new office in Greenville. The location was not the only change, however. According to the school's historical documents, in 1947, six academic schools were added, Bob Jones College became Bob Jones University, and the Board of Trustees elected Dr. Bob Jones, Jr., president of the University. Who did he choose as his personal secretary? None other than Guyla Pearson.

That year, Guyla worked hard, but she became increasingly burdened that she wanted to marry a preacher. Pray as she might, the Lord did not bring anyone along her path whom she found to be suitable. She wrestled with God and asked advice of both Dr. Bob, Sr., and Dr. Bob,

Guyla Pearson, 1946
Bob Jones College — Cleveland, Tennessee

Jr. They simply encouraged her to pray that the Lord's will would be done.

Lord, if I'm not supposed to marry a preacher, she prayed, *please take this desire away from me. I want to serve You and do what is Your will for my life. I surrender this desire to You.*

Sometime during the spring semester of 1948, Guyla was assigned as a staff hostess at a dinner table. Across from her was a Preacher Boy who had been assigned as the host. His name was Ed Nelson.

Chapter 11

PREPARING FOR THE MISSION FIELD

When I returned to school in the fall of 1947, many things were different. Over the summer the school had moved from Cleveland, Tennessee, to Greenville, South Carolina. The campus was brand new, but honestly, it was not much to look at. There was red clay everywhere — quite the mess during the frequent rain showers. The school had also achieved a new status over the summer: I now attended Bob Jones *University*.

Thus far, my time at Bob Jones University had been a time of learning and growing in my walk with the Lord. That fall, I was asked to be a prayer group leader. Each evening, three or four rooms near mine would meet in my room for a required time of prayer. As the prayer group leader, I was tasked with leading discussions and times of prayer each evening.

That fall, the Dean of Students, Dr. Edwards, came to me and said there was a student who was coming to the school who had some problems. They were not sure what was wrong with him, but they wondered if I would be willing to have him live in my room and be in my prayer group.

Bob Jones University, 1949
(The 1948 campus did not have much grass.)

"Yes, that would be fine," I told Dr. Edwards. The student had some major problems, and I tried to help the best I could, but it was difficult.

Shortly into the semester, the school had a day of prayer. We were given the day off from classes, had a few chapel services that spoke on the topic of prayer, and then were encouraged to spend time in personal prayer.

After one of the services, I returned to my room and after a while, my troubled roommate came in. "I just don't know what's wrong with me," he said. "I don't understand what's going on, and I need help. Would you pray with me?"

"I would be glad to," I replied. We knelt down by my bunk bed and began to pray. When I had finished praying, I asked him to pray. He started to pray, and all of a sudden he started jumping around and yelling unintelligibly.

I immediately looked up and saw that his eyes were wildly rolling around, and he was foaming at the mouth. I grabbed him, pinned him to the floor, and held him as still as I could. I began praying over him: "Lord, I plead the blood of Jesus Christ."

Then I said, "In the name of Jesus Christ of Nazareth, demon, I command you to come out of him!"

He wilted on the spot and passed out. After a few minutes, he came to and was an entirely different person. He looked at me and quietly asked, "What happened?"

"I don't know," I said. "One minute you were praying and the next you were wildly thrashing around and screaming unintelligibly. Do you remember anything?"

"Well," he said, "there was a voice talking to me and it's not talking to me anymore. Something came out of me."

His life changed dramatically. He was no longer the weird, quiet kid in the room. He was fervent about seeing souls saved. Every weekend after that, when I would go on extension to nearby towns to witness, he came with me.

One day, we ended up at a carnival and started passing out tracts. After a while, I did not see him around, so I went looking for him. I found him at a bar, passing out tracts and preaching the Gospel to all those around him.

A few weeks later, Dr. Parker, Assistant to the President and Director of Religious Activities, called me into his office and asked, "Whatever happened to that young man we put in the room with you?"

I told him about the day when we knelt in prayer and all of a sudden, he went foaming at the mouth, blabbering, and ended up passing out. He had awakened a different person.

"You must have seen a demon cast out!" he exclaimed. "That's wonderful. See if you can cast some more out around here."

I had not been very frightened before and had not thought much about demonic power. But after Dr. Parker said that, I realized that what he said was likely true. God had enabled me to see a demon cast out through the power of the Holy Spirit and the Name of Jesus Christ.

* * * * *

I was now a junior in college and had become very involved in the campus activities. I was vice-president of the Ministerial Association, chaplain of the Sidney Lanier Society, vice-president of the Baptist Boys Sunday School class, and a member of the *Vintage* yearbook staff. In addition to all that, I was elected Student Body Chaplain. This meant that every Wednesday, I preached for the student body chapel. I also worked closely with the Student Life leadership to help them disciple the students, although that did get me in a bit of trouble.

From my living in the dorms and interacting with fellow classmates, it appeared to me that there were some students who were not living godly lifestyles. I wanted to point out the problematic areas and help them grow as others had helped me.

So during the weekly student chapel services, I spoke from Bible passages that dealt with godly living. There were some students who told me they had made decisions to be more godly. However, there were other students who spoke to Dr. Edwards, the Dean of Students, about this. He called me into his office one day.

"Ed," he began, "we have gotten complaints from some students about your student body chapel messages."

"Oh?" I questioned. "No one has talked to me about my messages other than a few students saying that they experienced conviction and got things right with God."

"Well, that is wonderful," said Dr. Edwards. "Praise the Lord for that." He was a kind man who really loved the students and cared deeply for the student body and our godliness.

"However," he continued, "the school administration has chapel four days a week, and we know best what should be preached in chapel. The purpose of having a Student Body Chaplain is just to encourage the students with more of a devotional-type message. Why don't you change your messages and let us do the harder preaching that provokes the students to conviction?"

I was sorely disappointed, but agreed. "I had no idea," I said. "I will change my messages. I am sorry to cause you trouble."

Though I changed my preaching for the student body chapels, I did *not* back off on my exuberance in promoting Mission Prayer Band and helping my fellow students grow in their relationship with the Lord. Our little missions group had really begun to grow.

* * * * *

I LOVED being in school. I developed some tremendous, life-long friendships with some fellow Preacher Boys. I thrived under the leadership and encouragement of Dr. Monroe Parker. Both Dr. Bob, Sr., and Dr. Bob, Jr., preached often admonishing us to "Do right — even if the stars fall."

Though I had made many friends, I had not met anyone who was a suitable help meet for me. I occasionally took girls out for ice cream or a soda, but never met someone who fit — until, one day, I received my new seating assignment for dinner. I was asked to be host of a table with a staff lady as hostess. Her name was Guyla Pearson, secretary to Dr. Bob Jones, Jr.

She was quite the lady and hostess for our table. I learned a lot from her quiet, graceful ways, even though my mother had taught me much about proper etiquette at dinner tables. Guyla was an outstanding conversationalist and had a wealth of knowledge. And she was very organized. She *had* to be in order to be Dr. Bob's secretary!

I decided I would try to get to know her and ask her out for a date. I knew when the school offices closed for the evening, so I figured she would be leaving around the same time. I waited for her at the corner of the administration building.

She dashed out the door on her way to the dining hall, and I quickly approached her. "Miss Pearson," I called, "I'm going to be on campus this weekend — first time I've been on campus on the weekend all semester. I wondered if we could have a date."

Later, she told me that she thought, *Well I wonder why he's asking me for a date. But he is so much more mature than all these other fellas around here. And he's a preacher too.*

Much to my surprise, she agreed! It was not long before both of us knew that we belonged together.

We dated the rest of the spring semester. On our dates, we went to the student dating parlor where we memorized Scripture together, including the entire book of Ephesians. We also spent much time in prayer together, praying that God would use us for His glory until He took us Home.

I returned home to Colorado for the summer while Guyla stayed at school to continue working. I wrote her a letter every day filling her in on the happenings in the Rockies and on the farm. Despite the long distance, our relationship grew deeper.

We discussed many things through the letters, but the primary topic was missions. When World War II had ended and General Douglas MacArthur oversaw the rebuilding of Japan, he had sent back word to America saying that he needed thousands of Protestant missionaries to come and give the Gospel to the Japanese people.

All over the country, people had responded to his call. I had been one of them, and as I continued writing letters to Guyla, I discovered that she had volunteered as well.

Fall came, and Guyla and I were reunited. We began taking Japanese classes together and prepared to go to the mission field upon my graduation in June. One big step in that preparation was marriage. Right before Christmas of 1948, I asked Guyla to spend the rest of her life with me. She readily said, "Yes!"

We applied to mission boards and were appointed by The Evangelical Alliance Mission. Now that we were "officially" missionaries, we could begin deputation and raise support. The unusual thing we experienced was that we did not have to do much work at all. People and churches found out we were going to Japan and wrote me saying, "We'll support you." We never had to go on deputation, and by the time graduation came, we had our full support. We had a vehicle and all the equipment that we needed. Everything was provided.

But then I became extremely ill. I struggled through my last semester. No matter what I tried, I could not get well. I was tired all the time. I ate at the table for people with special dietary needs. Something was not right. Guyla and I were planning on getting married on June 2 and then going back to Colorado for a few weeks before heading to Japan. We decided that once we were in Colorado, I would see a doctor to try and determine what the problem was.

Chapter 12

SIX MONTHS TO LIVE

T HURSDAY, JUNE 2, 1949 was a big day for me. In fact, it was so monumental that the newspaper back home in Windsor even wrote an article just about me.

Big Day for Ed Nelson

Wins Diploma and Bride Today

(Special from the Bob Jones University News Bureau)
GREENVILLE, S. C., June 2— At the Bob Jones University Convocation in the Rodeheaver Auditorium this morning, Edward John Nelson, son of Mr. and Mrs. Ernest D. Nelson of Route 4, Fort Collins, received the Bachelor of Arts degree from the School of Religion with a major in Bible.

The Convocation was held at 9 o'clock today. Degrees were conferred upon 267 graduating seniors by Dr. Bob Jones, Jr., president of Bob Jones University.

—⊠—

Mr. and Mrs. Nelson and Donald left their home north of Windsor late last week to be present for their son's graduation today, and for his marriage which takes place this afternoon at 4:30 in the university chapel. The bride is a West Point, Miss., girl who has been employed in the university offices since her graduation.

Another son, Kenneth Nelson, who is attending John Brown University in Arkansas, joined his parents there for the trip to South Carolina.

Following a honeymoon in the South, the newlyweds plan to spend a portion of the summer at the Ernest Nelson home. In the fall, they are to be placed in charge of a mission field in Japan.

Unfortunately, as glowing as the article was, they got a few things wrong. I actually graduated on June 1, 1949, and was married the next afternoon.

Mother, Dad, Don, Ken, and many friends attended our wedding in the War Memorial Chapel on campus. Uncle John and Aunt Grace were there too. Like most weddings, it was a family affair for the Nelsons.

Unfortunately, only Guyla's mother was able to attend. Guyla was very disappointed, but she also understood that her family had to work.

Dr. Bob Jones, Jr., was the officiant and had become a very dear friend to both of us. He challenged us to continue serving God with our lives, especially as we prepared for the mission field in Japan.

Marrying Guyla was the second-best decision I made in my entire life, the first being salvation. She was an absolutely stunning bride.

Mother and Dad still thought the preaching business was foolishness, but they loved me. And they loved Guyla dearly, especially Mother. Guyla was joyfully and thoroughly welcomed into the Nelson family that day. After a brief reception in one of the parlors on campus, Guyla and I left for our honeymoon.

While I was a student, I had preached in many places, one of them being at Hotel Lake Louise* (also known as Camp Toccoa) in Toccoa, Georgia. Dr. LeTourneau had built it as a Bible Conference grounds, and I had been invited back several times to speak. On the last time I had spoken, I was told, "For your honeymoon, we'll just furnish your room. You can come and stay in our quarters and eat your meals here."

I thought it was a great deal since neither Guyla nor I had much money. I took them up on their offer and away we went to Hotel Lake Louise for our honeymoon. At 10:00 the next morning, the day after we were married, we heard a knock at the door.

"Brother Nelson," a man said when I answered, "we need a preacher this morning. The man who was supposed to preach is not here and the service was to start a half an hour ago. Could you preach?"

I could not say no to that, so I agreed to preach that morning. That evening, there was another knock on the door. It was the camp director asking me to preach again for the evening service. I agreed again. It happened the next morning. And the next evening. Finally, I told Guyla, "We'd better get out of here. This is no place for a honeymoon!"

We came up with an excuse as to why we could not stay any longer and then headed off to Gatlinburg, Tennessee. There, we were able to have a relaxing honeymoon and explored the Smoky Mountains together.

---

* Now the Georgia Baptist Conference Center

Our Wedding Day, June 2, 1949

In Gatlinburg, Tennessee on our honeymoon

Before we headed to Colorado for the summer, we traveled to a few churches to hold revival meetings. The first meeting I held was with a group of churches on the border of North Carolina and Virginia who wanted to have joint revival meetings. All of them were Baptist, so I accepted the invitation to preach. I learned a lot in a hurry. In that area, some of the "Baptist" churches were not really Baptist. These were *very* charismatic.

They put up the tent and every evening, 45 minutes before the service, I went to the back side of the tent, got on my knees, and prayed. When I heard they were about to start the service, I got up and walked down the aisle onto the platform. On the third night, I was still on my knees praying when I heard a group of ladies starting the service by singing, "I'll live for Him 'til my fingernails turn blue. How about you?"

All the churches involved in the revival loved that music. I did not. I preached that night at the conference, but the music really bothered me. Not only that, but the churches believed in speaking in tongues, another item about which I strongly disagreed with them.

The next day, I called the manager of the campaign. I did not realize they had party-line phones where others could listen in. I said, "We can't have any more of that music like we did last night. That was terrible." We talked some more, and then I hung up. Unbeknownst to me, several elderly ladies were listening to every word.

That night, those ladies went to the manager and demanded he fire me and get me out of there. It was a mess. After the service, I asked the manager, "Do you think I should leave?"

"I wish you would," he replied. "It sure would solve a lot of problems."

I said, "I really think we are not agreeing here, and I think it would be best if I didn't stay."

"Could we give you $300 to leave?" he asked. Three hundred dollars was a *lot* of money for us. A semester of school at Bob Jones University was $300.

"You can give me $300 and I'll leave," I replied. And I did.

With the extra $300, Guyla and I began traveling to the next church, but my health took a sudden turn for the worse. We decided we had better get to Colorado to see a doctor. I was really sick. I was not sure what was wrong, but I knew I could only preach 20 minutes before I had major problems. In Fort Collins, my doctor took some tests and gave me the diagnosis.

"You have nephritis," he said. "It's commonly called Bright's Disease. It's a disease of the nephrons of the kidneys, and it's **always** fatal. You have about six months to live."

"You're an evangelist," he continued. "But you can't continue in evangelism. Your body won't take it. I recommend that you find a small church here somewhere in Colorado where you can preach and satisfy that desire in your life. Preach only one service each week."

Guyla and I were shocked. We had known I was very sick, but we never expected something like this. We consulted a few other doctors who all said the same thing: six months left to live.

After further testing, we discovered that my Bright's Disease was actually caused from the medicine I had been given in the hospital when I had the accident with the runaway team of horses. They had given me an over-dosage of Sulfathiazole. Since it was a new drug, only the second of the Sulfa drugs, they did not know how to use it properly. I was given four tablets every four hours. The proper dosage was later determined to be four tablets in twenty-four hours. Many soldiers were given the same drug during the war and died as a result. And here I was, married just six weeks, ready to go to Japan as a missionary in a few months, and I was told I only had six months left to live. Our whole world changed.

After much prayer, we told the mission board my diagnosis. They immediately canceled our appointment and assigned field and said we could no longer be missionaries.

I had a very limited amount of time left, so I told Guyla, "If I'm going to die, I'd like to do something for the Lord." She readily agreed. I tried to take the doctor's advice to preach only once a week, but no church would have me come. Who was going to have a young fellow come when he is about to die and he cannot preach more than once a week? I could not get a church, and we were desperate. I said to Guyla, "Let's go to Casper and start a new church."

So Guyla and I drove up to Casper, Wyoming, and looked over the town. We found what we thought would be a good place for a church and met a few believers in the town. We set a date for revival meetings, talked to a tent company there about setting up a tent, got permission from the mayor, and then went back home. "We will be back the first week of October," we told our new friends there.

I went through July and August without any meetings and without doing much of anything. Guyla and I prayed daily that God would open up a church in which we could minister. One day, I told Guyla, "I believe God will show us what to do this week." That very week, we had a surprise invitation from Flora, Indiana.

Chapter 13

"IF YOU LEAVE ON MONDAY..."

WHEN I RECEIVED the phone call from the pastor at Grace Brethren Church in Flora, Indiana, I was thrilled. God was providing for Guyla and me. We prayed about it and called the pastor back the next day. "We will come," I told him.

We scheduled the meeting for the last two weeks of September. This would allow us to be in Flora and then immediately travel to Casper.

The day came when we arrived in Flora. We were excited about being in revival work again. I was still very sick, but God gave me the strength to make it through the travels and the services. All I wanted to do was to bring people to Jesus with the life I had left.

We had not gone many nights into the meeting when I began to realize that this church really needed revival. There seemed to be a deadness among the church members. The pastor and I met daily for prayer, asking God to do a work in Flora.

Early in the second week, we faced a big problem. I had noticed that the young people all sat together on the back rows of the church and whispered amongst themselves throughout the entire service. This occurred every night for the first week. It bothered me, but I had done nothing about the problem so far.

On Tuesday night of the second week, I could not tolerate it any longer. Three girls in particular were whispering to each other, laughing softly, and writing notes back and forth. Those around them were trying to pay attention, but were having a very difficult time due to the distraction. I decided I should say something.

I stopped preaching and swept my eyes back and forth across the auditorium while avoiding looking directly at the girls. "I have noticed some disturbance among the teenagers during these services," I started. "Tonight, there are some of them not listening and trying to disturb the service. I'm not saying this just because I am preaching tonight. I have reason to believe you do this to other preachers too. It's not right. You are showing disrespect for God's Word and the Gospel message. You probably even do this with your pastor. Please stop the disturbance and pay attention so you can hear the message and not prevent others from hearing God's Word too." I continued preaching.

Almost immediately, the three girls began their disturbance again.

I stopped quickly, raised my voice, and said, "The disturbance is caused by three girls on the back row. We must have it stop! It's ruining the service and keeping blessing from the church. It must stop and it must stop NOW!"

I started to continue with my message and they immediately picked up with their notes, laughter, and talking. I stopped yet again. This time, my voice was strong and definite. I pointed directly at the girls and said, "I am speaking to you three girls on the back row. Because you will not behave, I'm telling you now, get up and get OUT!"

The three girls stood and stomped out of the building. One of the girls turned at the door and cursed me, taking God's name in vain. Once they were out, I continued the message.

After the service, the pastor came up to me. "You'll probably have to leave and not continue with the rest of the meetings," he said. "These girls have been a constant problem. A previous pastor was actually forced to resign because he had rebuked them."

"Wow," I replied. "Well, I think it would be a mistake to discontinue the meetings. We need to see this matter through to victory."

"I agree," the pastor said. "Let's continue the meetings which close on Sunday night."

"By the way," I asked, "who are those girls?"

"Two of them are daughters of two of our deacons," he replied. "The other is the daughter of an evangelist who is rarely home."

I asked for each of their addresses and the next day, Guyla and I visited each girl at her home.

The first house we drove to was a farm house where one of the deacons lived with his family. We intentionally arrived about the time the school bus brought the girl home. When she stepped off the bus, I walked up to her and said, "I'm sorry I had to call you down last night. May my wife and I come into the house and talk with you and your mother?"

She asked her mother, who graciously agreed and invited us in. We had a pleasant visit. I explained the Gospel to the daughter. We showed her that she needed to be born again. She listened carefully and at the end said, "I would like to accept Christ as my Savior." We knelt in prayer, and she was born again. Her mother was overjoyed.

After we finished at the first house, we drove on to the second girl's house. This girl was also the daughter of a deacon, and they lived in a farm house too. Our knock on the door was answered by the mother. I told her I was sorry for what had happened the night before. She invited us in, and we spoke to both mother and daughter. I apologized to the girl and explained the Gospel to her as I had to the first girl. She also responded to God's Word and accepted the Lord Jesus Christ as her Savior.

The visit to the third home brought a very different reception. We were not invited in. The apology was received with contempt, and the girl manifested her rebellion even at the door. "I want nothing to do with you," she yelled with a curse. Guyla and I were sad to have received such a heartless, godless response. As we drove away, we prayed that this girl, too, might one day trust Christ as her Savior.

That night, there was an entirely different atmosphere in the church building. The two girls who had been saved that afternoon stepped forward at the invitation and publicly confessed Jesus Christ as their Savior. The entire congregation was filled with joy. It also produced a tremendous revival in the lives of the teenagers. They all began sitting much closer to the front and paying better attention to the sermons.

Friday night, the chairman of the deacons approached me before the service. He was a godly man with an excellent testimony in the town. "I'm concerned that we are closing the meeting too soon," he told me. "I think we shouldn't end the meeting on Sunday night as we had originally planned. Why don't we consider extending the meeting one more week?"

"I can't do that," I replied. "I have already rented a tent in Casper, Wyoming, for a two week meeting beginning the next Sunday."

The man looked me square in the eye and said, "Brother Ed, if you leave Flora on Monday morning, you will be out of the will of God. I believe God wants you to stay at least another week here. If you do, I believe real revival will break out in this church!"

"It is not your responsibility to determine what the will of God is for me," I answered pointedly. "Determining His will for me is up to me."

"Put it down, Preacher. If you leave Flora, Indiana, on Monday, you will be out of the will of God."

We had the meeting Friday night, and then Guyla and I returned to the Fedderoff home, the family with whom we were staying. About midnight, Guyla suddenly became violently ill. I woke up, and she was writhing in agonizing pain on the bed. I awakened the family, and we decided to take Guyla to the hospital immediately — a decision that definitely saved her life.

Her appendix had ruptured, and she needed immediate surgery. After surgery, she developed a bad infection. The doctor prescribed a heavy dose of penicillin to fight the infection. When she woke up the next morning, she had a severe rash over her entire body. She was incredibly allergic to penicillin, and since it was a newer drug, we had not known that before.

"Well," the doctor said, "we can't let her out of the hospital for quite some time. She is very sick. I hope she will make it, but there are some serious issues that we are watching closely."

"And Mrs. Nelson," he added as he looked at Guyla, "you are expecting a baby."

We were both dumbfounded. Here we were, far away from home; I was living in my last six months; Guyla was in the hospital, fighting for her life; and now, we were told we were going to be parents. I was scared!

"We are watching both Guyla and the baby very closely," the doctor said. "But because of the appendix rupture and the other complications Guyla has experienced within the last 24 hours, she may lose the baby. If the baby does survive, it may have some serious disabilities."

I prayed then like I had never prayed before. I prayed that God would spare my wife, that God would spare my baby, that God would spare my life. He is the God of the miraculous — He could do it if that was His will.

"We will stay through the weekend and see how she is on Monday," I told the doctor.

Sunday morning before the service, the chairman of the deacons came to me and asked, "Are you leaving tomorrow?"

"No," I said.

"Why not?" he asked. He knew why, but he wanted me to tell him anyway.

"Well, my wife is in the hospital," I replied.

"I heard that. I'm sorry," he said. "But I told you that you shouldn't leave. If you're staying the week, could I get the deacons and pastor together right after the service this morning and ask them if we could have the church vote to extend the meeting one more week?"

"I'll be here," I said, "so we might as well do it." I called the people in Casper and informed them I would have to cancel the revival meeting until Guyla was better.

That night, the church voted to keep the revival meeting going another week. Up to this point, the only people who had responded to the Gospel were those two girls. That Sunday night, 21 people came forward — some to get saved, some to get things right with God. Monday night and every night the rest of the week, people came forward to get saved and get things right in their lives. It was amazing!

By the end of the week, Guyla was still in the hospital unable to be discharged anytime soon. The baby was doing fine so far, but the doctor wanted to keep a close eye on both of them. Guyla was still incredibly weak and unable to get out of bed; she was really sick.

"Could you stay another week?" the pastor and deacons asked me. So I preached the fourth week. Many times, I apologized to the chairman of the deacons for not heeding his advice.

The fifth week, Guyla was *still* in the hospital, so the church voted to keep me preaching yet another week. The sixth Sunday in Flora, we finally closed the meeting. Over 100 people had professed Christ as their Savior, and the church had gone from a desolate church to one on fire for God.

Finally, Guyla was able to leave the hospital. The doctor seemed to think that she was still weak, but much improved, and our unborn baby was also doing well. I closed the service on Sunday night and then we drove to Chicago Monday morning. I did not think it was wise for Guyla to ride that long distance home to Colorado in a car, so I got her a Pullman car on a train and sent her home. I called Mother and Dad and asked them to pick her up from the train station at La Salle, Colorado. "Guyla and I have decided that I am going to stay here until I know what I'm to do next. I don't know where I am to go," I told them. "Can Guyla live with you until I can get home too?"

While Guyla went home, I contacted The Evangelical Alliance Mission which had appointed us, and asked if I could stay in their prophet's chamber. They were headquartered in Chicago and agreed to put me up until I was able to figure out what God would have me do next.

Chapter 14

"Canceled" Revival

During the same week I came to Chicago, Dr. John R. Rice was conducting one of his Revival Conferences at the Chicago Gospel Tabernacle. It began Thursday morning, so I decided to attend. There were many other evangelists and preachers there, several from Bob Jones University. One of the speakers was Dr. Bob Jones, Sr.

He recognized me during one of his sessions and after the service, he came up to speak to me. "Ed! Good to see you!" he said. "What are you doing here?"

I started to explain about the meeting in Flora, but he interrupted with, "Can I take you out for lunch?"

"Well, yes," I replied. We drove to a restaurant nearby and sat down to eat.

"You were starting to tell me about some meeting you just had," he said. "Tell me about it."

"I was in Flora, Indiana and had a revival meeting," I said. "It lasted five weeks, six Sundays." I continued explaining a little about the revival we had seen over the weeks.

"Did they treat you right?" he asked.

"Why yes," I responded. "They had me for meals."

"No, no, no," he said. "Did they *treat* you right?"

"They were very nice," I said. "We stayed with a fine—"

"I mean," he interrupted, "did they give you a good offering?"

"Yes," I replied.

"How much was it?" he demanded.

I almost said, "That's none of your business," but I refrained. "They gave me about $500," I told him.

"Five-hundred dollars?!" he exclaimed. "That's a lot of money! *I don't even get that much, ever.* You're an evangelist; I can see that now. The fact that they gave you that size of offering indicates they were blessed by the services."

Dr. Bob was preaching the next session that afternoon, so we finished lunch and headed back to the Tabernacle. When he got up to preach, he began with, "There's a young man out there I want you to meet. Ed Nelson, stand up."

I stood and he continued, "Nelson just graduated from my college and had his first meeting in Flora, Indiana. I have found Indiana to be one of the most difficult states in which to see a successful revival meeting. But Ed had over 100 people saved, *and* they gave him a great offering. It lasted five weeks, and he had outstanding results. He is an evangelist, and I recommend you get acquainted with this young man."

After the service, I was bombarded with preachers asking me to hold meetings for them. I scheduled quite a few meetings, but nothing for right away. Guyla was in Colorado with my parents, and I still had no direction for the immediate future.

That night, Dr. Hyman Appleman spoke. He was a Jew who had accepted the Lord Jesus Christ as his Messiah. He was a very forceful speaker and brought a message on Isaiah 66:8, *"For as soon as Zion travailed, she brought forth her children."* He explained that if we had no travail — no painful or laborious effort of soul for the lost — we would not have God's power for soul-winning work.

When he gave the invitation that night, *many* came forward to kneel at the altar asking God to give them the burden and effort to reach souls

Ed with Dr. and Mrs. Bob Jones, Sr.

for Christ. I was one of them. As I began praying, I felt an arm come around my shoulders. It was John R. Rice, and he was praying for me, "Oh, Lord, this young man here, I believe God is going to bless him. Use him."

After the service, I went up to him and thanked him for praying for me. The Revival Conference ended on Friday. On Saturday, I drove back to Flora to talk with the pastor there.

"I just don't know what to do," I told him. "I don't have any meetings for a while. My wife is in Colorado. *Somehow*, I have to provide for her."

"You can stay here with us until you know what you are to do," he said kindly.

Sunday afternoon, I talked with him again. "I just don't know what to do next. I've got to find out what God wants me to do. Would you be willing to fast and pray with me tomorrow?" I asked.

"Sure," he replied. "Let's start at 5:00 A.M. in my office."

Monday morning at 5:00 A.M., we knelt in the pastor's study, read some Scripture, and began praying, asking God for direction and provision. Two or three hours later, the pastor's wife knocked on the door.

"Brother Nelson," she said, "you are wanted on the telephone."

I answered the phone and heard, "Ed, this is John."

"John who?" I asked.

"John R. Rice. You were just in our meeting here in Chicago. I tried to reach you last night but couldn't find where you had gone, and I never got your address. I knew you had your wife in Colorado, so I got in touch with Dr. Bob and he told me your address out there. Finally, I talked to your parents and found out where you are.

"The pastor of First Baptist Church in Altamont, Kansas, phoned me yesterday afternoon asking for help. They were to have an evangelist for revival meetings, but he became ill and can't come. They asked me to find an evangelist for them. Can you go?"

"When do they want to start?" I asked.

"As soon as you can get there," he replied.

"I'll be there tomorrow night," I said.

"Very good!" he replied. "You'd better take a train. I don't think you can drive there that quickly and I don't want you to be late."

"Dr. Rice," I said, "I've got to have my car. I'll be there tomorrow night."

I immediately told the pastor, "The fast is over. Our prayers have been answered! I'm going to Kansas."

Within a few minutes, my bags were packed, and I was on the road to Altamont. The pastor's wife was kind enough to fix me a quick breakfast before I left.

I arrived in Altamont Tuesday afternoon around 4:30 P.M. and drove up to the church. It was definitely *not* what I expected for a church hosting revival meetings in a few hours. Everything was locked up tight with nobody in sight.

I saw a house nearby and decided to ask them where I could find the pastor. As I walked up to the door, I noticed lots of farm equipment and parts lying all over the yard. *I wonder why all that is lying around here*, I thought. I knocked and a lady opened the door.

"Excuse me, could you tell me where I could find the pastor's house?"

"This is the pastor's house," she replied. "I'm the pastor's wife."

"Oh," I said. "There was no one at the church and I was asked to come and preach."

"Are you Ed Nelson?" she asked.

"Yes."

"Oh, I'm sorry," she said. "We've had word out that we have canceled the meeting. We contacted Dr. Rice and the police in the various states you would travel through to see if they could stop you and let you know, but obviously no one did."

"How do you feel about canceling the meeting?" I asked.

"We are heartsick — my husband especially. We believe this church needs a revival meeting. He will be home for dinner soon. The church can't afford to have him on salary, so he does farm work during the week. Why don't you at least join us for dinner so you can meet him and talk with him?" she asked.

During the meal, the pastor told me what had happened. "Sunday night, after I announced that Dr. Rice had found you to speak for us, the chairman of the deacons stood and said, 'I don't think we need a meeting. It costs money, and that is something we don't have right now. I move that we cancel the meeting.' Another deacon seconded the motion, and so the majority of the church voted to cancel the revival meeting."

"Oh, I see," I replied. I did not know what else to say, but I could see the pastor was deeply concerned. "Do you feel the church needs revival?" I asked.

"Oh, yes!" he replied fervently. "I have been counting on the meeting to see God do a work among these people." His voice was strong with emotion.

"Would you be willing to spend a whole night in prayer seeking God's leadership and praying for revival in the church?" I asked the couple.

"Of course! We *need* revival!" they said.

"Is there anyone else in your church, maybe another family, who would be willing to pray with us?"

He looked at his wife and then said, "Yes, I believe there is a farmer and his wife who would pray with us. Let's go see if they will join us."

The three of us drove out to the farm. When we told the couple what we planned that evening, they replied, "Oh, this church needs a revival. It needs it badly! We'll join you."

We stayed in their living room and started praying about 8:30 P.M. All through the night, we took turns praying, reading Scripture aloud, and then praying some more. It was a sweet time of fellowship, earnestly seeking the Lord in the matter of the revival services.

At 3:00 in the morning, the farmer stood up and said, "You know, I just had assurance from God that we are going to have a revival meeting and Brother Nelson is going to preach here. I just feel *sure* about it!"

"Isn't that interesting?" said the pastor. "I just had the same feeling. We're going to have a revival meeting here and we're going to see some fruit out of it."

"What about you, Brother Ed?" they asked.

"I don't have any feeling at all," I honestly replied. "I don't know where you're getting your information, but are you sure?"

"Yes!" they both said together.

"Well, let's go get a little bit of sleep then and we'll get started," I said.

"We can't do anything yet," the pastor said. "Tonight, we have our midweek service. At that time, I'll bring it up to the church and see if they vote for you. If so, we'll have you preach."

We thanked the Lord for His leading and answered prayers and then went back to the house for a short night of sleep.

That night, the pastor got up in front of the congregation. "Brother Nelson is here," he said. "I told him we had canceled the meeting, but he never got the message. Since he is here, I'm wondering if we could still have a revival meeting. After all, he came all this way."

Before anyone could say anything, the chairman of the deacons stood up. "May I say a word?" he asked. "I'm the one who made the motion Sunday night that we shouldn't have the meeting, so we canceled it. The church voted 'yes' on my motion."

"The strangest thing happened," he continued. "This morning, I woke up at 3:00 a.m. from a dead sleep. It seemed that God was telling me, 'You should not have made that motion.' I'm *so* convinced that God spoke to me about it that now I'd like to make a motion that we go ahead and start a revival meeting tonight."

The deacon who had seconded the motion then stood up and said, "Isn't that strange? I also woke up at 3:00 this morning and had the same sense that I shouldn't have seconded the motion. So I second the motion that we have the meeting."

The pastor called for a vote, and the motion unanimously passed to begin a revival meeting starting that very night. Many souls were saved, and the little Baptist church in Altamont, Kansas, saw great revival. I preached for a week and a half and then returned home to Colorado — just in time to spend my first Thanksgiving with Guyla.

Chapter 15

GOD'S MIRACULOUS PROVISION

Following our first Christmas together, Guyla and I traveled across the country holding revival meetings. Most evangelists published brochures and other various advertisements trying to fill their schedules with revival meetings. Amazingly enough, I never once had to publish anything. The Lord took care of us week after week, and our schedule filled up for the entire year.

After a quick stop in Casper, Wyoming, to reschedule the meetings, we drove to Garden City, Kansas, for our first revival meeting of 1950. A family from the church in Altamont had a son attending Fellowship Baptist Church in Garden City. After I had closed the meetings in Altamont, they had immediately written their son suggesting that his church should have me for revival meetings there. After Christmas, that was the first place Guyla and I went.

We spent two weeks in meetings there, and then we traveled from town to town, fulfilling the invitations that kept rolling in. God was taking care of us!

It was a sweet time for us to be traveling together, but it was tough! Guyla was pregnant with our first child. I was still struggling with my Bright's disease. Neither of us knew how long I would last. I had lived a few months longer than the doctors had predicted, but I was in bad shape. I did my best to serve the churches and preach the Word, but it became increasingly difficult.

In February, we received an invitation to Dalton, Georgia, from my former church, South Dalton Baptist Church. I was thrilled to have Guyla meet the people who made up my first church. But I was in a very different condition than when I had been a member there. I was about to die.

Dalton is about 30 miles south of Chattanooga, Tennessee. Tennessee Temple, a Christian college located in Chattanooga, encouraged their students to attend nearby churches every week. Several students from Tennessee Temple attended South Dalton Baptist Church regularly. There was one student in particular that caught our attention while we were there. He had trouble speaking. He would start talking and his mouth would lock up — he could hardly get out one word.

During our week of meetings, this student wrote a note to the pastor:

> *Pastor,*
> *Would you read James 5:13–16? There it says to anoint with oil and pray over the sick. Would you consider anointing me with oil and praying for me? I can't talk, and I would give my right arm if I could talk again.*

The pastor came to me and showed me the note. "I've read this passage, but have never done anything about it. What do you think?" he asked.

"Well, I've read it and never thought much about it either," I replied. "I don't really know."

We pulled out our Bibles and read through the passage together:

> *"Is any among you afflicted? let him pray. Is any merry? let him sing psalms. Is any sick among you? let him call for the elders of the church; and let them pray over him, anointing him with oil in the name of the Lord: And the prayer of faith shall save the sick, and the Lord shall raise him*

> *up; and if he have committed sins, they shall be forgiven him. Confess your faults one to another, and pray one for another, that ye may be healed. The effectual fervent prayer of a righteous man availeth much" (James 5:13–16).*

"What do you think?" the pastor asked. "Should we do it?"

"Well, it is in the Bible," I replied, "so maybe we should."

"Will you help me?" he asked.

"I'm not really sure what to do, but yes, I will help," I said.

We scheduled the special meeting for Wednesday night after the evening service. Three men, former pastors, were members of the church. They were all in their seventies and had retired from their ministries. We asked them to join us, so those in the room were the pastor, the three men, the mute student, Guyla, and me.

On the way to church that night, Guyla and I discussed the situation. "Why are you praying for somebody else?" Guyla asked. "You're very sick too, you know. Very sick. Why don't you have them pray over you too?"

"I don't know. I hadn't thought of that," I said. But as I preached that night, I thought, *Maybe I should have them pray over me too.*

When the time came for us to meet together, I said to the pastor, "You asked me to help you. I'm not going to help you. I am very sick myself and need healing. I have Bright's disease and doctors have given me very little time left to live. Would you pray over me also?"

The men all agreed and both the student and I knelt by some chairs. One of the retired preachers said, "When I was 25, I had a terrible disease. A brother anointed me with oil and prayed over me, and I was healed."

We all took great encouragement from that, especially since the pastor and I had never done this before. They put some oil on our heads, laid their hands on us, and began praying.

All of a sudden, the boy stood up and said, "I can talk!" He looked down quickly and held out his arm. "And I still have my right arm!"

We all got off our knees in a hurry. Several church members were waiting outside. When the boy came out speaking, there was a chorus of "Praise the Lord!" "Hallelujah!" and "Glory to God!" echoing down the halls.

Guyla and I were still in the room with the others. "How about you, Brother Nelson?" the pastor asked.

"I don't know," I said. "I don't feel a thing."

Immediately, Guyla spoke up. "Fellas, I'm going to tell you something. My husband has been healed."

The pastor looked back at me. "What do you think of *that*?"

"Well, I don't know where she got her information," I said.

"You mark it down," she stated emphatically. "Tonight, you have been healed."

Although I was not sure, we gathered around and thanked the Lord for what He had done that evening.

* * * * *

One of the towns we traveled to that spring was right on the border of North Carolina and Tennessee. A church invited me to come for a meeting, so I did.

On Tuesday, the second day of the meeting, one of the church members said, "Would you be willing to come to the factory business luncheon tomorrow? Everybody breaks for lunch, and we'll set it up where you could have an opportunity to preach to the workers while they're eating lunch."

"Yes," I replied.

The next day during lunch, I got up to preach. I had decided to preach on Noah for this occasion.

> "By faith Noah, being warned of God of things not seen as yet, moved with fear, prepared an ark to the saving of his house; by the which he condemned the world, and became heir of the righteousness which is by faith" (Hebrews 11:17).

"Noah was warned by God that serious things were going to happen," I told the factory workers. "The world was in terrible shape. Everything was violent and wicked, and Noah was warned. And so today," I preached, "we need to recognize that God wants to warn us too."

I went on to preach about the sins that God wants us to shun and how we need to realize that we ought to get things right with God.

Somehow, my message brought conviction, and when the service was dismissed at 1:00 P.M., some of the workers did not go back to work. They just left the building.

Later that afternoon, the president of the company called me and said, "You know, when the people left the service at lunch, many did not return to work. Do you know what they were doing? They went home, got tools they had stolen from the company, and brought them back. Something about your message affected them, and thousands of dollars worth of tools were returned."

I was shocked, but I was also thrilled by the working of the Holy Spirit.

"Can you come and preach again tomorrow?" he asked.

After I preached during lunch hour on Wednesday, they asked me to preach during the lunch hour the rest of the week.

On Friday, the president of the company showed up at the service. When I concluded my message, he got up and said, "We appreciate Evangelist Ed Nelson coming and being with us this week. We've had a lot of tools returned! So, Evangelist," he said as he turned to me, "we just thought we'd give you a check for $500 to show our gratitude."

"Thank you for coming," the president said, shaking my hand.

God had provided.

* * * * *

GUYLA WAS due with our first child at the end of June, so after spending the rest of the spring in Kansas and the surrounding area, we returned home to Colorado. The $500 we had received from the factory was spent on traveling and living expenses, so we had very little money left to live on. We rented a small basement apartment in Fort Collins — it was a brick house with an outside entrance for the basement and a little mailbox on the wall next to the door. It was not much, but it was home for the time being.

I picked up a few preaching engagements in neighboring towns where I earned a few dollars to help meet our needs. We were poor; we had no extra money, no money in savings, and hardly enough money to buy groceries for the week. And we were expecting our first baby any day now.

Together, Guyla and I talked about our financial situation. No one knew just how poor we were. We did not know how we were going to pay the hospital bill when Guyla had our baby.

Finally, we decided that we were just going to pray about it, not tell anyone about it, and watch God provide. I knew that if we told any of our family or friends about it, they would probably give us money, and we did not want that. We wanted it to be clear that it was God who had provided. We genuinely believed He would, even though we had no idea how. Over the next few weeks, we often prayed for this secret need to be met.

At the end of June, I scheduled meetings in a school in Ault, Colorado, a small town about 20 miles east of Fort Collins. They did not have a church, so I was trying to start one there. We had a good week of meetings with souls saved. On Sunday, June 25, I preached the morning service. We were closing out the meetings that evening.

That afternoon, Guyla began going into labor. I drove her to the Fort Collins hospital, where they took her to the delivery room. Fathers were not allowed in the room in those days, so I waited anxiously outside for quite some time. I paced the floor, prayed, walked around some more, prayed some more. I guess I was a typical first-time dad.

As Guyla continued laboring, I realized there was nothing I could do to help. The revival meetings in Ault were still scheduled to close that evening, and I was the one running everything — no one could really take my place. So I rushed over to Ault, preached quickly, and raced back to the hospital. I was hoping that I would be back before the baby was born. I made it with plenty of time to spare.

Guyla labored all night long, and sometime on Monday morning, June 26, 1950, we welcomed our first child into the world — a baby girl.

The doctor brought her out to me, and I held my little girl for the first time. "Guyla is doing just fine, and so is this little one," the doctor said as he carefully transferred the baby girl into my arms. I have never forgotten the overwhelming sense of wonder and feeling of awesome responsibility of that moment. I was a dad!

When I was finally allowed to see Guyla, I said, "Hi, Honey. You made it. Our baby girl is so healthy and beautiful! Praise the Lord! What should we name her?"

During Guyla's time at Bob Jones University, one of her dearest friends was named Kathy, so we decided that Kathy would be a good name in honor of her. "Besides," Guyla added, "I want to make her name so short that no one can shorten it."

Guyla's only sister was named Sue. They were very close growing up as they were the only two Pearson girls. Thus, we decided on a name for our baby girl: Kathy Sue Nelson.

I was overjoyed to be a dad, and Guyla, a mom. I felt a tremendous weight of responsibility on my shoulders. Guyla and I now had another person to take care of. And we had no money.

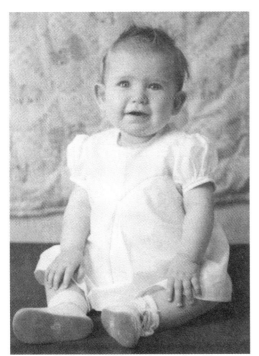

Kathy Sue Nelson, 3 months old

The doctors wanted Guyla and Kathy to stay in the hospital for a few days just to make sure everything was fine. They were still concerned that Kathy might have some difficulties from the effects of Guyla's appendicitis the previous fall.

Tuesday passed. They wanted to keep them still a few more days. "We think they can go home on Friday," they told me. Meanwhile, I was becoming more concerned at the growing bill from the hospital stay. *I just don't have the money to pay the bill on Friday,* I thought. *Lord, please provide for us!*

On Wednesday, Dad called me. "Could you work for us today running the side-delivery rake for harvesting hay?"

I gladly obliged and went back to the farm for the day. At the end of the day, he said, "Well, what do I owe you?"

"Not a cent," I replied.

"Are you sure?" he asked. "Do you have any needs?"

"No, I'm all right," I replied. I was not lying in my answer because we just *knew* that God was going to take care of us. I was trusting the Lord.

The next day, our church in Fort Collins was putting up a tent on the edge of Fort Collins to see if they could start another church out of it. They called me and said, "Are you doing anything? Could you help us put up the tent?"

I had put up many tents at my various revival meetings, so I agreed to help. When it was all set up, they said, "Let's have a prayer meeting."

We went into the tent, knelt down, and began praying. The deacons were there and a number of other men, and I knew that they all appreciated me. When it came my turn to pray, I thought, *I'm going to pray right now about the finances. No, I can't do that. I told Guyla we wouldn't tell anybody. And if I pray in front of these men, they're going to know I have a need, and they're going to help me.*

So I just prayed silently about our financial need and asked God to provide for our little family.

On Friday, the doctor finally let Guyla and Kathy come home. I was to pick them up from the hospital at 2:00 P.M. I worked on the tent some more with the church members and then went home to change clothes before driving to the hospital. My mind was heavy with the burden. *In just an hour, I will need to pay the hospital bill when I pick them up. And I don't have any money with which to pay. Lord, what am I to do? Please provide.*

As I walked up to our basement apartment, I noticed something white sticking out of the mailbox. *That's funny,* I thought. *I already got the mail. What could that be?*

I opened the mailbox and found an envelope without a stamp on it addressed to me. It had the doctor's return address on it. I immediately opened it:

> *Edward,*
>
> *I was surprised today in looking over the books. I've found that we charged you for having the baby and that you paid it on a monthly basis. You have paid it all.*
>
> *I did not know this and somehow, the records got by me. I do not charge preachers to deliver their babies, and I charged you.*
>
> *I just got to thinking, "I should not have done that." So I have returned all of the money to you in this envelope. I thought you might need it right away, so I did not send it in the mail. I wrote the letter, put the check in, and then handed it to a secretary to deliver.*

I took the envelope, got dressed, cashed the check at the bank, and drove to the hospital to get my girls. I was able to pay the bill and even had some money leftover.

We took Kathy and safely tucked her into the car. "Here is a list of items that the doctor said I should get at the drug store," Guyla said as she handed me a piece of paper.

We went to the drug store and bought the items. The money I had leftover exactly paid for the bill. Not a penny short, not a penny left.

We went home and thanked God for His miraculous provision. No one ever knew we had that need. But for the Nelson family of three, God had taken the impossible and made it possible. God had provided our every need. A genuine miracle!

* * * * *

Following Kathy's birth, Guyla and I struggled as new parents. Kathy cried for hours on end, and nothing we did seemed to make anything better. Guyla was up with her all day while I worked on sermons and scheduled meetings. We were close enough to Mother and Dad that often Ken came over to spend the evenings with us. He loved his little niece and called her "Kitty," much to Guyla's consternation. She had chosen Kathy because it was a name no one could shorten, but somehow, Ken found a way. He came in, picked her up, and did everything in his power to comfort his Kitty — rocking her, holding her, patting her back, singing to her, everything.

Once Ken left for the evening, Guyla was so exhausted from the long day of caring for our screaming child, that I ended up watching Kathy all night long. Literally, all night. She did not sleep much, but was up crying, screaming, coughing — you name it. Just when I thought I could put her down and get some rest myself, she would wake and start it all over again.

After several weeks of this, I could not take it anymore. I just *had* to get some sleep! My sermons were suffering. I was falling asleep anywhere I could. It was a real trial. I decided the best way for me to get some sleep was to conduct another revival meeting away from home. Mother came to stay with Guyla, and I left for a week. It was great! I actually slept at night and "caught up" on sleep, just in time to come back and be awake again all day and all night.

Kathy Sue Nelson

Our small little family

We were at our wit's end. Even Mother did not know what the problem could be. After many visits to the doctor, he finally pinpointed the problem: Kathy had a very bad case of colic and allergies. For the colic, the doctor gave us some medicine — a miracle drug for us! He also told us not to feed her any wheat, dairy, or a few other random foods. We tried it and it worked! Kathy stopped screaming, and we *all* were finally able to sleep through the night.

With the colic and allergy situation under control, I decided to continue traveling and preaching the Gospel. Guyla and Kathy traveled with me wherever I went. In August of 1950, we finally made it to Casper, Wyoming, to host the tent meeting. It had taken a year for us to reschedule the meeting that had been postponed due to Guyla's appendicitis, but we were excited to be there, and the people were overjoyed to have us come.

At the beginning of the year, I had driven up to Casper and met with the mayor. He had given me his verbal permission to put up a tent on the north side of town. I never dreamed I would need the permission in writing, but apparently I did.

Guyla, Kathy, and I had driven all day to get there, and I was worn out. I saw the tent company out setting up the tent, so I decided to get a quick nap at the hotel before we began the meeting that night.

When I woke up and went to the meeting site, there was nothing there. No tent. No workers. Nothing. Just the land. I immediately drove to the tent and awning company.

"What happened to the tent?" I asked.

"Well, we were putting it up, but the police came and made us take it down," they told me.

I drove to the police department. "Why did you make them take my tent down?"

"You didn't have permission," they said.

"Yes, I did," I replied. "I talked to the mayor several months ago, and he said it would be fine."

"Well, the mayor isn't here. He's at a convention in Washington, D.C., that President Roosevelt is hosting for mayors. We can try to get in touch with him, but there is nothing on record giving you permission to put up that tent."

They called the mayor but he had no recollection of ever giving me permission and he refused to give permission over the phone. We jumped through some hoops and finally figured out a way for us to legally put up the tent a couple of days later.

While the tent company set up the tent again, I realized I had not checked on electricity. I called the town electric company, thinking it would be an easy fix. There was a power line at the lot, so I thought that we could just get our power from that.

"The voltage is too high," they said when I told them my idea. "You need a lower voltage, and the closest place to get that right now is about two or three blocks away. We would have to run a new line. To do that is going to cost you $1,500 to $2,000."

"Oh," I said. "I can't afford that." I was discouraged. This was not how I anticipated the meeting starting out. I thought I had lined up everything ahead of time. I sat down on a chair to think.

Right then, Virgil Horton walked in. He was an exuberant pastor from Bennett, Colorado. I had forgotten he was coming to help me lead singing for the meetings.

"When's the meeting starting?" he asked cheerfully.

"I don't know that there's going to be a meeting," I responded glumly.

"What? What do you mean, 'no meeting'?"

"Well, we got the tent up, the sawdust down, the chairs set up. Everything is ready. But the electric company can't get us power. It would cost a few thousand dollars and has to come from quite a distance."

"Huh," he said. "I'll take care of it."

Before I could protest or ask what his plan was, he was off across the alley, knocking on the door of the closest house to us. "Excuse me, ma'am," he said politely, "we are hosting a revival meeting but don't have power. Could we plug into your house so we can power our meeting?"

After three "No's," he received a "Yes." He got a long extension cord, plugged it into the lady's house, brought it over to the tent, and just like that, we had electricity.

After that, the meeting proceeded without any problems. People came from all over, and we had quite a crowd. It was thrilling! I had learned from past experience that many charismatic people would come for the emotional high of being at the revival meeting. Therefore, shortly into the week, I preached a message on why we were not going to be a charismatic church. That cut down our crowd in a hurry. But I wanted to be up front and honest with the people, and you cannot build a work on an emotional high. The church must be built on the doctrine of the Gospel.

Even though the crowd drastically dropped in attendance, there were quite a few who stayed and said they would like to see a church started. As we were nearing the end of the meeting, I realized I had another problem: I did not have a pastor to take over the work.

After the close of the meeting on Sunday, Guyla and I planned to leave for Georgia on Monday. I did not know what to do. We prayed hard about it. "Oh, God, what should we do? We have people who want to start a church, but I don't have a pastor for them."

The last day of the meeting came. Before the service started that morning, a young man walked into the tent. He had just graduated from Biola University in Los Angeles, California. "I'm looking for a church now," he said. "I wasn't planning on coming here, but I just got a brand new Chrysler and was driving from Los Angeles to Wisconsin. I fell asleep at the wheel and crashed into a utility pole. I'm waiting for the parts for the mechanic to fix my car, so figured I would come to the service this morning since I'm here."

"What's your name?" I asked him.

"Chester Brock."

"Welcome to Calvary Baptist Church, Pastor Brock," I said as I shook his hand. Of course, I was saying that jokingly. The church would have to be involved in calling its pastor. However, it seemed that God had answered my prayer. Casper, Wyoming, would have a church and a pastor.

> Chester Brock held the church people together for about eight months until he felt called to move on. The church then called John Weidenaar as pastor and began to really grow. Within a few years, they were able to construct a permanent building, establishing Calvary Baptist Church.

I was now free to leave Casper — only I had one more problem. I had incurred some expenses during the weeks there, and I was determined that I would not leave having financial obligations. But we had no money. We had enough for the gas needed to drive from Wyoming to Georgia.

"We will sell our car before we'll leave town with debt," I told Guyla. I had a new Plymouth that if sold, would be enough to cover the expenses. I did not want to give up the car, but I was *not* going to leave town without paying the bills. We prayed about it, and waited to see what God would do.

On Sunday afternoon, we held a jail service. While walking around downtown, a lady saw me and said, "Are you the man who is holding that revival meeting?"

"Yes."

"Well, I want to give you some money," she said as she put a $20 bill in my hand.

A few moments later, another man came up and said, "Are you the fellow over at the tent?"

"Yes." He handed me $20. That went on all afternoon. By the time we returned to the hotel that evening, we had enough money to pay all the bills, and we were able to keep our car.

It was a thrilling time for both of us. In fact, Guyla and I were so encouraged by the fruit the Holy Spirit brought about by this church plant that we made a decision: each year, we would take a month or so, go to a new town or city, and try to start a church.

The result of that decision was life-changing. Over the next decade, God used us to help start churches in Billings, Montana; Leadville, Colorado; Laramie, Wyoming; Pueblo, Colorado; Thornton, Colorado;

Ault, Colorado; and several other towns. Our goal was to provide the believers who were already established in the towns with a local church.

I stayed and preached for the gathering of believers about a month, maybe a little more depending on the town. At the end of my time with them, we had enough people attending the services that they could call their own pastor and be their own independent church. It was exciting to see the hand of God moving among His people, not only in the revival meetings I still held almost weekly, but especially in fulfilling His promise in Matthew 16:18 that Christ **will** build His church.

Following our meeting in Casper, Guyla and I decided to continue traveling in evangelism. I still battled the Bright's disease and often felt very sick, but I had to admit, I was doing better. Not by leaps and bounds, but gradually I was feeling better.

The Evangelical Alliance Mission got word that I was traveling around the country preaching. "If you are well enough to preach," they said, "then you are well enough to be a missionary to Japan. We would like to bring you on again."

We were thrilled and immediately began preparing for the mission field for the second time. We started raising our financial support and began purchasing the items necessary for living in Japan.

Within a few weeks of deputation, I became quite sick again. I was not able to preach; I could hardly get out of bed. *I must have just had a brief time of feeling better. This is not good,* I thought. For the second time, the mission board canceled us as missionaries through them, and we returned to Colorado.

I thought back to when I was anointed with oil and prayed over. *Guyla was so sure that I had been healed! I wonder what God is doing.* I had already lived over a year longer than the doctors had given me. Yet still, the doctors told me I did not have much longer. Every time I went in for a checkup, which was regularly with my condition, I was told I had six months to live. They would show me the x-rays, and I could clearly see that my kidneys were a mess.

For several weeks, I lay in bed trying to recover. To our surprise, I got better — still not completely well, but before long I felt well enough to preach again. Guyla, Kathy, and I began traveling again, and every day, I woke up thanking the Lord for letting me live one more day. I kissed my wife, hugged my baby girl, and prayed that God would see fit to heal me from this disease.

Well, word of our travels got back to the mission board again, and for the third time since my graduation, The Evangelical Alliance Mission appointed us as missionaries to Japan. They say the third time is the charm, but no sooner had we begun raising our support than I became violently ill. I had to cancel my meetings. I could not get out of bed. I was really sick. *Maybe this is the end*, I thought. *I've been living much longer than the six months. This must be close to the end now.*

For the third time, the mission board canceled our appointment to Japan. Again, I began feeling better. Guyla and I realized with new awe that God **really** did not want us to go to Japan as missionaries. Missions was still in our hearts, but as we continued our travels preaching revival meetings (and I continued feeling better), a new burden began to surface — one that would truly change the course of the rest of our lives.

Chapter 16

HOFFMAN HEIGHTS

During my first three years of evangelism, I met many pastors and listened to many problems. I was in a different church almost every week. It was never long enough for me to *really* get to know the people, the problems, or the pastor. I began to feel that I just did not understand the church and the problems pastors were facing with their people. Sure, I had helped start several churches, but I would leave and let someone else be the pastor. I usually never had to deal with any people for longer than a week or two.

Then at one revival meeting, I ran into a fellow evangelist who was a good friend of mine from school. "I just feel bad for these pastors," I told him. "I try so hard to help. They share so many problems they are having, and I just don't know what to tell them. I've never been in their shoes, and I just don't have answers for them."

"I think that in order to really help them adequately," I continued, "I need to be in a pastorate somewhere. I need to spend a little time learning what a pastor really goes through."

"Oh no," the evangelist replied. "That's the beauty of being an evangelist! You can learn all the problems and difficulties of a pastor by osmosis. They tell you about them and you learn how to deal with them. You don't need that experience at all."

I understood his point, but I could not shake the idea from my mind. I really felt that I should be a pastor for a short time so I could then be a better evangelist and a more adequate help to the churches in which I was preaching.

"Lord," I prayed, "take me to a place where it's as low as it will go and can't get any lower. I want to go see a place like that grow up to be a church on fire for you."

Guyla and I prayed for some time and then decided we would leave evangelism and start a church. I had started several churches over the past three years, but this one was different — *I* was going to be the pastor.

This was in the spring of 1952. Guyla was expecting our second child around the end of July, and Kathy was almost two years old. After seeking God's will as to the location of our church plant, Guyla and I decided on an area of east Denver called Hoffman Heights.

We purchased a newly built home in the area, a yellow brick house with burgundy trim, a large front window, a garage, and a small front porch where we could sit and watch Kathy play in the yard. We were thrilled to finally have our own house. Within a few days of closing on the house, I drove to the nearest garden shop and bought some rose bushes, my favorite flower. We planted them beside the driveway leading up to the porch. Guyla decorated the inside with some basic pictures and curtains. It was home.

After settling into our home, we started looking for a place to hold church services. It was such a new area that nothing was available to rent, so we decided to hold our services in the living room of our home until we could find a location.

We printed some fliers announcing the date of our first service, June 8, 1952. I began going door to door every day, inviting my neighbors and others around the area to attend the service. I knocked on every door in Hoffman Heights — all 1,700 of them.

We were not sure what to expect for our church plant. We did not have a church or a group of people supporting us. We had no friends in the area. There were no fellow Christians that we knew of. It was just our little family — me, Guyla, and our two kids (one due in a month).

We had saved up enough money to live on until the church would be able to pay us a salary. We never tried to raise support for this new endeavor; we just believed that God would provide.

The Sunday for our first service finally came. Guyla and I were up early, moving some furniture out of the way. We set up chairs, she put Sunday dinner in the oven, and then we waited and prayed that *someone* would come. We started with a full schedule right off the bat: Sunday School, Sunday morning service, and Sunday evening service.

At 10:55 A.M., a family walked through the door. They lived about five houses down from ours and had just moved in. They introduced themselves as Mr. and Mrs. Harry Warner. They had three children and had recently moved to the area. They were believers and were looking for a Bible-preaching church to attend.

They came in and engaged in small talk conversation until we began the service promptly at 11:00 A.M. We had no pianist, so we sang a cappella. Halfway through, we took an offering, then I got up and preached. At the conclusion of my message, even though there were only eight of us in the room, I gave an invitation for anyone to come to the front and make a decision for the Lord.

That evening, the Warners were back. After the service was over, the husband came up to me. "You know," he said, "I think we'd like to get involved here. We're Christians and would really like to join with you in reaching this community for Christ."

After discussing their faith and finding out that they aligned with us on Bible doctrines, I agreed to let them help.

"We don't have much money to manage as a church," I said, "but I think maybe it would be best if somebody else take care of the money. Would you be able to open a bank account for us and be our treasurer?" I was convinced that the pastor should not be the one to handle the finances of the church.

He accepted the position and then said, "Well, you ought to get some money and have some sort of salary. How much will we pay you?"

After some discussion, we decided that for the time being, I would receive 30% of the offering. He had put in $10 that morning for his tithe, so I would receive $3. The next day, Mr. Warner went to the bank, opened the account, and gave me my salary of $3.00. I had my first pay check as the pastor of a church.

Throughout the next week, I continued knocking on doors and inviting people to come to our services. The next Sunday, the Warners were back and we were thrilled to have a few others join us as well. That week, the offering totaled $15. As we had agreed, I received 30% again — $4.50. Gradually, the church grew. It was amazing to see how people responded to our fliers and door-to-door calls. Some weeks, we had fifty people on Sunday morning. Some weeks, I preached to just Guyla and Kathy. On those occasions, I would go to the front door and look up and down the street for several minutes, just hoping that someone would come to the service. Even on those nights, we sang and I preached, even if two-year-old Kathy did end up sleeping through the message. Thankfully, those evenings became less and less frequent as our church family continued to grow.

It was quite the adventure for us! Guyla discovered very quickly that she could not cook a pot roast or anything hot for Sunday dinner. If she put something in the oven ahead of time, wonderful aromas filled the house about the time I started my sermon. It wrecked the service with the distraction of food. From then on, we ate peanut butter and jelly sandwiches for Sunday dinner.

Within a short time, we began seeing quite a few new converts. It was exciting! Saturday nights, our living room turned into a church auditorium. It was a real church. Our house was by no means big, but we utilized every room of the house for the services. All our furniture was put on rollers and stored in a guest bedroom. Sunday School classes were in the various bedrooms, the service was in the living room, with overflow into the kitchen eating area. One of the bedrooms was used as a nursery for the small children. It was not long before every space was packed to the brim.

One church member jokingly said that there was one more room that we had not utilized yet — the bathroom. "You could have one Sunday School class meet in the shower with the curtain drawn and another in the sink area of the room," he said laughing. For some reason, we just never took him up on his suggestion, but we did have a good laugh.

*****

OUR FIRST service was in June. Seven weeks later, on July 29, 1952, we welcomed our second child into the world: John Douglas Nelson, named after my Grandfather John and my Uncle John.

We were thrilled to have a son, and two-year-old Kathy was delighted to have a new "toy." He was a happy child and within just a matter of days, we could tell that this would be a far different journey than we had experienced with Kathy. John did not have colic, and we were *very* thankful. We actually slept within a few weeks of his birth!

*****

WITHIN SIX months of starting Hoffman Heights Baptist Church, the church began to operate like a church, not a church plant. We were part of the Conservative Baptist Association, an organization that recommended a church leadership structure consisting of a pastor (elder), deacons, and trustees.* We held elections for those officers, and then we began raising money for our own church building. Eventually, we had saved enough to purchase a plot of land a few blocks away, still in the area known as Hoffman Heights. We constructed a temporary building — very basic with a few side rooms, but not much else. It

---

* I later studied this organizational structure and believe it to be Scripturally wrong. The early church had pastors and deacons.

John Douglas Nelson, a few weeks old

worked much better than our house, though. And having our own church building really helped the church grow.

A year into our church plant, I was still receiving 30% of the offering as my salary. The deacons and trustees agreed that I should have a more consistent salary, so they paid me $25 per week. That salary was based on the number of members we had attending and the size of our offerings. But as members kept being added, both the offerings and my salary amount stayed the same, even though expenses increased, the cost of living increased, and the salaries for my congregation increased.

Guyla and I had both been taught to be wise and frugal with our finances, so we tried to make ends meet with our small salary, but it still was not enough to cover the bills. There were several members who came to me suggesting that we raise my salary. We organized a business meeting for a Sunday evening service. I moderated the meeting, and the deacons and trustees ran the procedures. One deacon stood up.

"I move that we raise Pastor's salary from $25 per week to $40 per week," he announced.

The floor opened for discussion and people began asking questions. After a short while, a man stood up. He was one of our trustees and had also been a former pastor.

"You know," he said, "faith is one thing. It's one thing to believe. It's another thing to be practical. I think we ought to raise the pastor's salary, but I don't believe we ought to raise him from $25 to $40. That's too much. I move to amend the motion that we raise the pastor's salary from $25 to $26 per week," he announced.

I could see there was going to be quite the discussion and major problems would break out. I remembered Dr. Bob Jones, Sr., often saying, "The way to keep from having trouble is to have trouble." In other words, deal with the problems right away (a little trouble), rather than letting it go on to create a great deal of trouble. I wanted to avoid the problems if possible, and I also did not agree with the former pastor that my salary should just be raised by one dollar. We would not make it financially on $26 per week.

I knew something about parliamentary procedures and rules, so I stood up and asked, "Is there a motion to adjourn?" Because according to *Robert's Rules of Order,* a motion to adjourn takes precedence over everything else.

Someone made a motion to adjourn. Someone else seconded the motion. The people voted and passed the motion to adjourn. I closed the evening with prayer and dismissed everyone. I had stopped the business meeting.

I immediately went to Guyla who was in the nursery watching the children and said, "Get the kids together quickly and let's go home."

Once the kids were in bed, Guyla and I went to the living room and talked. I told her what had happened in the business meeting, then said, "We started this church trusting the Lord. I've never preached on finances or anything related to money, but tonight showed me that we've spoiled the people. They don't think we need anything, so this man recommended raising my salary just *one dollar* per week!"

We discussed the situation more, and then I said, "I'm not going to visit or do anything else this week. I'm going to study stewardship."

I had never studied tithing or finances or anything of the sort from the Bible, so all week long, I scoured my Bible for what *God* says about giving. I began to realize that the tithe is the Lord's, according to Leviticus, and it belongs to Him. So when you present your tithe, which Genesis describes as 10% of what you have, you are not really giving. You are just letting God have what belongs to Him anyway.

The following Sunday morning, I got up for my message and began with, "About the business meeting last week — I have decided to preach today on Biblical stewardship, and specifically on tithing."

"Each of us should be a tither," I preached, "and then with God's blessing, we would see our church really grow."

After the service, the trustee who moved to raise my salary by $1 came to me. "You really made a fool of yourself today," he said. "Can I see you in your study?"

We walked to my office and he continued, "You said that we ought to tithe. Well, that scares people to death. They think, 'A tithe? Ten percent?!' I've got a better way to do it."

"Oh really?" I asked. "How is that?"

"Why don't you recommend that we give 1%," he suggested. "Everyone gives 1%, and we try that for three months. If it works and everyone is giving 1%, then we increase it to 2%. We'll do that for three or four months, then increase it to 3%. Gradually, you get up to a tithe of 10%, but you don't scare the people."

"That's a wonderful idea," I said, "only I have a problem with it. I read in Malachi 3:8 where it says:

> "Will a man rob God? Yet ye have robbed me. But ye say, Wherein have we robbed thee? In tithes and offerings."

I continued, "That verse says if you don't give the tithe, you're a thief. You are robbing from God. So what you are asking me to do is say to folks, 'I know you're a thief. You haven't been tithing; you've been stealing from God. But I don't necessarily want you to start tithing right away. I'm going to ask you to be 90% of a thief for a while, giving your 1%. You're still stealing, but you aren't as bad of a thief. Then, we'll go to 80% of a thief for a while, giving your 2%.'"

"I am ***not*** going to do that," I told him emphatically. "If you want to do that, find yourself a church that does that. I am going to tell these people, 'If you aren't tithing, you're a dirty, rotten, stinking, good-for-nothing thief!'"

He was angry, but he knew he could not possibly change my mind. He ended up leaving the church, and I continued preaching the truth of God's Word about tithing and giving to the Lord the firstfruits of all increase. The church began to grow. People started tithing the full 10% or more. Money came in. The church was able to raise my salary to $40 per week. And God richly blessed our congregation for faithfully giving and obeying the command of the Lord, specifically in regard to their finances.

> *At each church I pastored after Hoffman Heights, I made it a priority to preach and teach Biblical stewardship. I believe a pastor should constantly challenge people with Scriptural stewardship — not for the sake of raising money, but so each believer can see God's full blessing and provision by simply following God's command to tithe.*

* * * * *

Hoffman Heights Baptist Church was not the only church in the area. There were quite a few other churches of various denominations and beliefs, and together, they made up a council of churches. Every year, they had a Holy Week which began on Palm Sunday and finished on Easter Sunday. On Good Friday, they had a combined service for all the churches to be together.

I had only been pastoring the church for one year. The president of the association came to see me. "We have a meeting scheduled on Good Friday in the theater," he told me. "We have 10 or 12 churches in our association, and we'd like to have you be a part of it too. Would you preach one of the sermons? We have preachers each taking a message on one of the seven cries from the cross. Yours would be, '*I thirst*.'"

I thought about it, prayed with Guyla about it, and finally, after much begging from the president of the association, I agreed to preach the sermon. I warned my congregation that I was going to preach, but I did not want them to come and be in an ecumenical meeting like this. "They begged me to preach, so I am," I told them, "but I don't want you to come. I'm not for what they are doing and how they bring all the churches together, regardless of what they believe."

Good Friday came. The preachers got up one by one and delivered their short sermons, each on one of the cries of Jesus Christ from the cross:

1. *"Father, forgive them; for they know not what they do"* (Luke 23:34).
2. *"Verily I say unto thee, Today, shalt thou be with me in paradise"* (Luke 23:43).
3. *"Woman, behold thy son! Then saith he to the disciple, Behold thy mother!"* (John 19:26–27)
4. *"My God, my God, why hast thou forsaken me?"* (Matthew 27:46, Mark 15:34)
5. *"I thirst"* (John 19:28).
6. *"It is finished"* (John 19:30).
7. *"Father, into thy hands I commend my spirit"* (Luke 23:46).

I had prepared a short message on "*I thirst*," and patiently waited as the other preachers got up and preached about their assigned cry. One of the preachers before me had been given the phrase, "*Verily I say unto thee, Today, shalt thou be with me in paradise*" (Luke 23:43).

Being quite familiar with all of the cries myself, I knew that this was what Jesus told one of the thieves who was hanging next to him on the cross. The thief believed that Jesus was the Messiah, the Son of God, and said, "*…we receive the due reward of our deeds: but this man hath done nothing amiss. And he said unto Jesus, Lord, remember me when thou comest into thy kingdom*" (Luke 23:41–42).

The thief believed, and Jesus, by His statement, was proving that it is not by works that anyone can enter Heaven. It is through faith that Jesus is the Son of God. The thief did not have time to do any good works for God. He was hanging on a cross in his last moments of life; yet Jesus said, "*Today, shalt thou be with me in paradise*" (Luke 23:43).

That is what the preacher **should** have spoken about. However, partway into his message, I was stunned by what I heard him say: "The fact is, Jesus was no better than those two thieves. And those two thieves were no worse than Jesus. There were three deaths that day, and Jesus died just another man. He was not the Son of God."

I was furious at the blasphemy I was hearing. *What am I doing up here?* I thought. *I still have to preach. What am I going to do or say? This is heresy!*

The preacher finished his sermon and after two other speakers finished, I got up. "What is, '*I thirst*'?" I began. "That was the Lord Jesus experiencing Hell in our place. It's the same way Luke 16 describes it:

> "And in Hell, he [the rich man] *lift up his eyes, being in torments, and seeth Abraham afar off, and Lazarus in his bosom. And he cried and said, Father Abraham, have mercy on me, and send Lazarus, that he may dip the tip of his finger in water, and cool my tongue; for I am tormented in this flame*" (Luke 16:23–24).

"It was a picture of the danger of Hell and that Jesus was actually experiencing Hell in our place," I preached.

I continued. "Now, who is it that is going to Hell?" I asked. "Well, let me tell you one person who's going to Hell: any preacher that stands in any pulpit on any platform and says that Jesus was no better than the two thieves and the two thieves were no worse than Jesus — he is going to Hell."

I never did get another invitation to speak in the Holy Week association meetings. But Hoffman Heights Baptist Church continued to grow. And the whole community knew that we stood up for what we believed, and we stood for the truth of the Word of God.

* * * * *

Hoffman Heights was an unincorporated area adjacent to the city of Aurora. In its six years of existence before officially being annexed into the city of Aurora in February, 1956, the Hoffman Heights community faced quite a few battles in court. One of them was my fault.

Our little town did not have a shopping center or much of anything besides the 1,700 homes that were still being built. Therefore, some developers decided to put in a nice shopping center for us. By the time their building project came to light, we had purchased the land for our church building and were meeting in our temporary building. The shopping center was to be built across the street from our church, and the plans stated that there would be a liquor store and a bar with a restaurant.

I vocally and vehemently opposed this. Everyone in the community and surrounding area knew where Hoffman Heights Baptist Church and the Ed Nelson family stood on the issue. I believed that alcohol hurt our community. I have never once seen anything good come from people drinking alcohol. On the contrary, lives have been taken, families torn apart, and many people killed. In my fight against the licensing, I said as much, calling it a "blood business" for the countless lives alcohol had taken.

Knowing what I did about politics and legal battles, I fought the would-be shop owners. I thought I could fight this myself rather than hire an attorney to represent us. Hoffman Heights was a brand new community, and we could go against the trend by not allowing alcohol sales in our community. I was young and did not understand things as well as I thought I did. Not hiring an attorney proved to be a mistake — I did not know how to argue our case like an attorney is trained to do.

Finally, the battle came to a hearing before the county board that dealt with liquor licenses. I petitioned the board to withhold the licenses from the two stores. The owner of the liquor store was Mrs. Estelle Wine, and another man owned the restaurant. She did not like me, but the man was very cordial and understood my position, even though he disagreed with me.

The vote came back from the board: the stores were granted the liquor licenses. I was sorely disappointed. We had lost.

After the hearing, the restaurant owner came up to me. "Pastor Nelson," he said, "You know that I don't agree with you. I am getting that license, but I sure do respect you for saying what you did. You and your family are welcome to come to my restaurant anytime you want and get a free meal."

"Thank you," I said. "That is very kind of you. However, we will never be in there because we're against what you're doing."

"I understand," he said kindly. "However, my offer still stands. I respect you for your stand."

> A number of years later, when I was pastor of South Sheridan Baptist Church, one of my members was seriously ill in the hospital. I went to the hospital to visit him and pray with him and the others gathered in the room. The room was packed. I stood at the foot of the bed, bowed my head, closed my eyes, and began praying.
>
> In the middle of the prayer, I heard some commotion going on around me. I kept my eyes closed and continued praying. When I opened my eyes, there was a man sitting at my feet listening to every word.
>
> "What are you doing?" I asked him.
>
> "Well," he said, "I was walking down the hallway and heard a voice talking. 'That's Pastor Nelson's voice,' I thought. I just had to see if it was you, so I came in and sure enough, here you were praying. I am the restaurant owner from Hoffman Heights. I just had to come and tell you that I got out of that blood business," he said. "That's what you called it: a blood business. I have quit liquor, have gotten saved, and am living for the Lord!"
>
> I was thrilled to learn of this man's salvation and was reminded that our requirement to plant the seed of the Gospel can often lead to salvation in others — even if we never know about it.

Despite the battle we lost over the liquor licenses for the shopping center, our church continued to grow. Before long, we had outgrown the temporary building and needed to expand. We did not have much money as a church, but we had enough to construct a two-story educational building. We purchased the supplies necessary and then primarily used volunteer labor from our church members to build it.

We put up the metal scaffolding poles and put down the wooden planks on which to stand. What I did not realize was that in order to stabilize the scaffolding, we were supposed to nail a cleat along the bottom just outside the scaffolding so it wouldn't slide side to side. Then we were to tie wire to secure it to the scaffolding frame. Instead, we just set the wooden planks on the frames and began working.

My job for the day was to put up soffits by the roof on the second story. We were making this out of plywood, so I held up a sheet of plywood while another church member nailed it onto the overhang. As I held up the first board, the man working with me said, "Being on these heights kind of bothers me!"

I laughed. "Doesn't scare me a bit!" No sooner had I finished talking than the plank I was standing on shot out from under me and slipped off the edge of the scaffolding. Down I went, two stories down, and landed on my bottom. The plywood plank I had been holding landed right next to me, and the scaffolding plank landed on the other side of me. As I hit the ground, I felt something pop in my back. I lay there motionless, not wanting to move at all. I wasn't sure what had happened, but I knew I was badly hurt.

People started gathering around me. The man with whom I had been working quickly climbed down from the scaffolding. Those on the inside came running out. "Nobody touch me," I told them. "Something popped in my back, and I'm not sure what it is. Somebody call an ambulance."

Someone ran inside the church and phoned for an ambulance. The rest of the crowd knelt around me and began praying.

Across the street, there was a Lutheran church. The pastor was out mowing their lawn. He saw us up on the scaffolding working, and the next time he looked over, we were all off the scaffolding down on our knees on the ground. He later told us that he thought to himself, *Isn't that just like those Baptists. One minute, they're working. The next, they're down on the ground playing poker.*

Before long, the ambulance came and took me to the hospital. They gave me medicine to alleviate the pain. X-rays showed that I had ruptured a disk between two vertebrae. The doctors were hopeful that it would heal over time and they would not have to operate on it. They were also amazed that I was not more seriously injured. As I waited for my back to heal, I limited my activities to whatever did not hurt my back too much. Preaching hurt, but I was the pastor of the church, so I kept right on preaching.

A year later, my back was still in bad shape. In fact, it had only grown worse. I scheduled an appointment with the back doctor. A man from the church was kind enough to take me, so we did not have to find a babysitter for the kids. When he dropped me off, I climbed out of the car and froze. I had such a terrible back spasm that I could not walk. I could not move.

The man had driven away already to find a place to park. No one else was around. So I somehow ended up on my hands and knees crawling my way into the doctor's office. The doctor took one look at me as I entered and said, "Surgery."

Within the week, I was under the knife. The doctor repaired the ruptured disk, and after four days in the hospital recovering, I went home. This would be the first of many back issues I was to face in the years ahead.

* * * * *

D<small>URING THE</small> year of "hoping my back would heal," our third child was born. Ruth Ann Nelson entered the world on November 15,

1953, much to the delight of us all. She, like John, was a happy baby right from the start, and Kathy was overjoyed to practice being a mom, even though she was only three years old herself.

For two more years, we continued in the pastorate of Hoffman Heights Baptist Church. Our church family continued to grow — we had between 250 and 300 people attending services regularly. It was exciting!

Not only did our church family grow, but our own family grew again as well. January 12, 1956, we added another boy to the family: David Ernest Nelson. From our perspective, the Nelson family was complete.

Life was a whirlwind for us. Every few weeks, I traveled to hold revival meetings — the invitations just kept coming, and I felt like I could not say, "No." Within the year, I preached at least 10 or 15 meetings in addition to pastoring my church. Guyla stayed at home with the kids, all four of them five years old and under. I was home as much as I could be, but the needs of the church people often kept me out late after dinner on visits to homes or counseling members of my congregation.

Then one day, everything changed.

Ruth Ann Nelson, Age 3

David Ernest Nelson, Age 1

Chapter 17

HARD LESSONS

I SHOULD HAVE noticed the symptoms sooner, but I was so busy with visiting church people, studying for sermons, and just pastoring my church, that I did not see them. Guyla was struggling.

Kathy had just turned six years old, John was almost four, Ruth was two and a half, and Dave was just six months old. In addition to being a mother to our four children (which is a full-time job in and of itself), she was also a pastor's wife. For Guyla, this meant continuous phone calls, people dropping by the house to talk, counseling sessions, hospital visits, and helping me with random tasks. She gave herself to the people of the church, and it consumed her. She thought that in order to be a good pastor's wife, she had to do the counseling, visiting, phone calls, etc. She became a pastor's wife first, and wife and mother took the back seat.

Every day, we had breakfast first thing in the morning. I left for the office at 8:00 A.M., and her day began. By the time I came home for lunch at noon, the breakfast dishes were not even washed. She had been on the phone or answering the door all morning.

She gave so much of her time and energy to the church people that everything else at home was suffering. This had been going on for months. I was so busy myself that I did not see the danger of what was happening to her.

Guyla gradually wore down, and major problems began to surface. She did not want to meet any people. She was afraid to go to church. She was afraid to pick up the phone, or answer the door, or speak to anyone. She was trying to keep it all together — the church, our kids, our marriage — but finally, she broke.

Like I said, I was oblivious to the symptoms. But when I came home for lunch one day, I knew something was desperately wrong. I walked into the house and found children screaming, the phone ringing, and Guyla nowhere in sight. I finally located her — she was hiding in the bedroom closet with the door closed, sobbing.

I quickly found someone to watch the kids, and I took her to the doctor. "Your wife is in a bad way," he said. "She's overdone it. She is quite overworked. I'm afraid you might lose her mentally if you don't change something *now*. I think you really should take some time off from the church. You need to take her somewhere so that she can take time to rest, and maybe she will get better."

I was scared. I had never been through anything like this before, nor had I ever seen Guyla so distraught. I decided right then that I would take the doctor's advice.

I called Mother and Dad and asked if they would be willing to watch the kids for a month. I explained the situation, and they readily agreed that the two of us needed time to be away and completely alone. I told the church, asked some men to preach in my absence, and left.

I rented a little house trailer and we drove to Glenwood Springs. I parked it by a bubbling stream, set up camp, and waited. Guyla slept for days, and I prayed. I prayed like I had never prayed before. I was terrified that I was going to lose my wife to mental illness.

When she was not sleeping, we spent time reading our Bibles together, praying together, sitting by the stream, walking around the mountains. We just took life very easy. We were together, no responsibilities, no people, nothing. Just the two of us.

After much rest and time away, Guyla began to improve. She was not depressed anymore. She began thinking more clearly and rationally. Eventually, she came to the conclusion that she had taken on too much and was bearing all the burdens of the church people on her shoulders. She determined she was going to turn everything over to the Lord.

I was determined to help her. While she had rested for days on end, I had done some soul searching and spent much time in prayer. I began to realize areas where I had been wrong and had helped cause Guyla's condition. *This **must** change,* I thought to myself. *I must change.*

After four or five weeks in the mountains, we returned home different people. The kids were overjoyed to have Mom and Dad back again. Guyla was much better, but she was quite weak. We altered our schedule dramatically. She was going to be a wife and mother, first and foremost. And I was going to be the husband and dad I should be. I cut back on my work and visitation and tried just to be there with her and for her.

As part of that plan, after thanking the church for allowing us the time away to rest and regroup, I announced, "Guyla is not your pastor. I am. She is the pastor's wife. Please do not call her. Do not go by the house to see her. She needs time to gradually step back into the work of the ministry."

Gradually, she got stronger and stronger until she was able to take the full load of mother and pastor's wife again. Kathy and John pitched in as they were able and helped out a lot around the house and with the younger two children. Our family had been through a very dark time; but thanks to much prayer, some life adjustments, and some needed rest, we had come through.

God taught me much during that time. He showed me that time at home was a necessary and valuable thing for me to give my family. By His grace, I learned how to value and honor my wife. I did not always get it right, but I had my wife back, I had my priorities right, and I had a happy, healthy family.

Our wonderful children, 1958

* * * * *

SHORTLY AFTER things started returning to normal and Guyla felt better again, another issue arose. A lady from the church came over every weekday after breakfast to help Guyla with the kids and household chores. Guyla was getting better, but she still required a lot of sleep and spent much of the day in bed. This lady voluntarily cleaned up the dishes, fixed lunch, did the laundry, and helped in whatever way Guyla needed assistance.

I would come home for lunch, and Guyla would typically still be in bed. I visited with her for a while, ate a quick lunch that this lady had prepared, and went back to the office.

One day, I came home for lunch and something was different. The table was set with a nice tablecloth and nice dishes. Everything was nicer than normal, including the way this woman was dressed — fit to kill. As I sat down for lunch, she waited on me hand and foot. I just watched her, growing increasingly uncomfortable by the minute.

She isn't here to help Guyla, I thought to myself. *She's here to get a preacher.*

I finished lunch as quickly as I could, and went straight back to the office. I knew she left our house at 3:00 P.M., so at 4:00, I returned home.

"Honey," I said to Guyla, "that woman can't come here anymore. She's dangerous." And I explained what had happened at lunch that day.

"You must be imagining things," Guyla replied.

"No, I'm not," I told her. "She's trying to lure me away from you. And whether I'm imagining things or not, I'm telling you as the head of this household, she is not coming into this house again."

Disappointed as she was to lose her help, Guyla agreed and backed my decision. I picked up the phone and called the woman. "Thanks for all you've done to help us," I told her. "It's been very kind of you. I've just been talking with Guyla, and we've decided that we'll go it alone. We appreciate your help, but we won't need it anymore. You won't need to come again."

"Oh, Pastor, please, I want to help," she begged. "Please let me come."

"No," I said again. "We appreciate what you've done, but we no longer need your help."

The woman and her husband were hurt and offended. Shortly after the phone conversation, they left our church and moved to Grand Junction, Colorado.

A few months later, the pastor of Pear Park Baptist Church called me and asked if I would come and preach a week of revival meetings in Grand Junction. The church had purchased a big farmhouse, and that was where the pastor and his wife lived. I traveled alone for this meeting, since Guyla was still regaining her strength.

Toward the end of the week, the pastor, his wife, and I were eating breakfast when all of a sudden, there was a knock at the door. The pastor answered it and then came back into the dining room. "Brother Nelson, it's for you," he said. "There is a man at the door who wants to talk to you."

I got up, went to the front room, and found the woman's husband sitting there crying.

"My wife is running off and leaving me," he said. "She's running off with another man."

"Don't tell me who," I said. "I'll tell you who it is. It's the pastor of your church."

"How did you know?" he asked, amazed. "That's exactly who it is."

"Well, I knew you were attending there, and I've had suspicions about his character."

He explained the whole story including how he had discovered the affair. A few days later, his wife left with the pastor, and two families were utterly destroyed.

When I returned home, I told the sad story to Guyla. "I knew on that day a few months ago that she was not here to help you. She was here to get me, a preacher, for a husband. I saw it, and that's why I took the drastic action immediately."

"Praise the Lord that He spared us from that!" Guyla said.

* * * * *

Over the next year and a half, God began working on my heart. Several of my mentors and colleagues had said that I was an evangelist. And here I was, pastoring a church, not out in evangelism. I began to think that I really missed traveling in evangelism. Guyla and I prayed about it and then decided to resign from the pastorate of Hoffman Heights Baptist Church and go back into evangelism.

For a year, Guyla stayed home with the kids while I traveled to churches across the country. I was gone for weeks at a time, but I never heard any complaining from Guyla. It was hard on her and the kids not to have the father figure in the home much. I finally realized that I was needed at home — I needed to prioritize my family. Guyla and I both believed that God still wanted me in evangelism, so we decided to travel as a family. We arranged a schedule with the churches — I would be available during some of the day to help the pastor however I could and then would preach in the evenings. Guyla and the kids would home-school during the day and attend the services at night. Occasionally, Kathy or John would sing or do something with music, but since they were only six and four, that part of the schedule was never set in stone.

It was a difficult year, but we saw much fruit from it. Many churches saw revival, and many souls trusted Christ as Savior. Our travels took us many places, but one town that was particularly memorable was Brush, Colorado.

Often, when we arrived at a church, the pastor selected a couple or family from the church to house our family during our time there. Brush is a small farming town about 100 miles northeast of Denver. "There is a widower in the church," the pastor told us. "He has room for your family. He'll provide your meals too."

We were grateful for a place to stay. The man was an older man who looked like he was in his 80s, a nice gentleman who had been a widower for some time. We enjoyed talking with him briefly, ate some dinner, and then put the kids to bed. The services were to start the next day.

"Those dishes looked filthy," Guyla said in the privacy of our room. "I'm going to stay up and wash them after he goes to bed."

Once we heard him snoring away, we tiptoed to the kitchen, pulled every dish and utensil out of the cabinets and drawers, and began washing. Shortly after we commenced, we heard this awful, raspy cough coming from the man's bedroom. Every 30 seconds or so, there would be a horrible coughing spell. It lasted well past the time it took Guyla and me to finish washing, drying, and putting away all the dishes. "I'm glad we can provide some cleanliness to his dishes at least, given his health condition," Guyla remarked as we put the last dish back into the cabinet.

The next morning, despite the lack of sleep, Guyla was up early fixing breakfast for the kids. She had already fixed oatmeal, but was waiting for the scrambled eggs to finish cooking before serving breakfast. Dave was in the high chair screaming and begging for food.

It was a joy having my family travel with me in evangelism

"Here," Guyla said, as she put down a small bowl of oatmeal in front of him. Dave was now nine months old and still unable to feed himself. Guyla was about to instruct Kathy to start feeding him when our host grabbed the bowl from Guyla.

"I'll take that," he said eagerly. "I'll feed him."

He grabbed a spoon, looked at it and said, "Looks clean enough, but just in case…" He licked the spoon, "cleaned it" with his dirty red handkerchief out of his pocket, scooped up a bite of oatmeal, and stuck it straight into Dave's wide-open mouth before anyone could move.

Guyla was horrified!

After breakfast, I told her, "I think maybe you'd better go home and stay there instead. I have two weeks here, but I'll make it. I'll live."

She readily agreed. "We feel like Ruth was coughing a bit during the night," we told the man (which was true). "Guyla is going to take her and the kids back home and trust she does not get sick."

Guyla and the kids returned home, and I stayed the two weeks. I never got sick, and Guyla was grateful that she did not have to cook with or eat on the dirty dishes in that home.

* * * * *

Our family continued traveling throughout the remainder of the year. Guyla was a wonderful teacher to our kids, and they really learned a lot. Kathy and John were both reading and were a grade ahead for their ages. We decided that Ruth should start with the rest of the children her age. Guyla did not want three children ahead in school. They were good kids, and we really enjoyed the time traveling as a family.

After several months of our grueling evangelistic schedule, Guyla saw something happening to our kids that she did not like. "I think we should stay home and let you travel alone," she told me. "I'm concerned about our kids. I think they are getting proud and entitled just because you go to these churches and you are the special guest. They are the "evangelist's kids" and think that's something special. I don't like it."

We returned to Colorado, sold our home in Hoffman Heights, and purchased a house in Longmont to be closer to my parents. I continued traveling in evangelism, and Guyla stayed home with the kids. In applying for the loan on the house, we learned that there was an Equitable life insurance policy that would bring the interest rate down to 4% if it was combined with house insurance.

I applied for the life insurance and was given a physical examination. Part of that was answering questions about my past medical history, such as: have you ever had tuberculosis? Cancer? Diabetes? And on down the list. Eventually, the doctor asked, "Have you ever had nephritis?"

"Yes," I replied.

"You have?" he exclaimed. "What are you doing sitting here?"

"Well, I don't think I have it anymore."

"That can't be," he said. "Everybody dies from that. You didn't have nephritis."

"Yes, I did," I repeated.

"Well, I am going to hold up your insurance and look at old records. I just can't believe that you had that. Probably a misdiagnosis. Who were your doctors?"

I told him and went home to wait his findings. I knew that I had nephritis — the Bright's disease. It had been eight years since I had been anointed with oil, and I had not seemed to have problems in several years. Although I did not know for certain, it surely did seem as if God had healed me that night when I had been anointed with oil. *Guyla was so certain that night that God had healed me,* I thought. *I guess we will see what the doctor finds.*

Three weeks later, I had some new x-rays done and then saw the doctor again. "I have the new x-rays as well as your previous medical records here," he said. "There is no question about it. You definitely had nephritis, and now you don't. How do you explain that?"

"Well, I had a prayer meeting several years ago, and we asked God to heal me," I told him. "I have been feeling well for years now, but your findings just prove that God completely healed me!"

The doctor agreed.

Chapter 18

SPELLING MATTERS

OVER THE NEXT three years, I continued traveling in evangelism. After that first year of traveling as a family, Guyla and the kids stayed home in Longmont while I traveled alone. I was rarely home, which was quite challenging for Guyla and the kids. But Mother and Dad were nearby and helped out. Guyla and I had prayed much about the meetings I was taking and felt that it was the will of God for me to travel as much as I did. One thing I grew to admire more and more about my wife was that she was completely, selflessly committed to the will of God for our family, even though that often meant she was caring for and rearing the children alone.

However, something began to happen to me as I continued preaching across America. I missed the pastorate. For years, people had told me I was an evangelist. And even though I had pastored a church for four years, I still thought that I was more of an evangelist than a pastor.

But as I thought about it more and studied the qualifications and gifts of a pastor found in the Bible, I began to realize my gifts were more aligned with being a pastor than an evangelist. And I genuinely missed the pastorate. I missed the people, the problems. I missed seeing people grow. As an evangelist, I was only at a church long enough to meet the people and then leave. As a pastor, I had been there every week, seeing people grow, meeting needs, *knowing* about their needs. I missed it.

Guyla and I decided to start praying about getting back into the pastorate. Within a few weeks of earnestly praying for a church opening, First Baptist Church of Danville, Illinois, called me. They asked me to candidate, so I went and preached for them. They phoned me and said they had voted and were calling me to come be their pastor.

"Well, I'll pray about it and see if I should come," I told them. And I did. After a few days, I decided I should go.

I dialed the phone, got them on the line and was going to say, "I'll accept the call," but I just could not say it. The words would not come out. Instead, I said, "I need a little more time to think."

So I prayed about it every day and again came to the conclusion that I should go. I called them up a second time, and just when I was going to say, "I accept," I could not say it. "I'm not sure," I said. "Maybe I better wait a little while."

That happened three times, and they were still waiting for me. Somebody told us that people were saying that I was simply waiting to see whether a bigger church would call me and offer me more money. When the Danville church heard those rumors, they immediately called. "We'll pay you whatever you ask."

"Look," I told them, "money is not the issue. Money has nothing to do with this."

I kept praying about it. Guyla prayed about it. We prayed as a family about it. Every time I had decided we should go and I called the church to accept, I could not get the words out of my mouth. I could not figure out what my problem was. Finally, I called them up for the last time. "I had better turn your offer down," I said. "I am not able to say yes with peace and confidence that Danville is where God wants me."

Once I turned down that offer, I received a phone call from another church, First Baptist Church of Lakewood, Colorado. They wondered if I could meet with the deacons on Monday night and then I was to preach a candidate sermon the following Sunday. The church would hold a vote Sunday evening to see whether they wanted me to become their pastor.

I drove down to the church that Monday night. It was about a 40 mile drive from Longmont to Lakewood, and when I pulled into the church parking lot, I saw about seven of the deacons standing around outside smoking. *Wow, do I want this?* I thought to myself.

We all went inside and began the conversation. "Well," I said after a while, "you need to know something. Wherever I go, I plan to stay 30 years and build a work."

The chairman of the deacons was a successful chiropractor. He was smoking a cigar that night. At my comment, he spoke up and said, "Well, we'd like to have you, but we'd like to let the church know how much it's going to cost. What do you need for a salary?"

"I've never asked for a salary, and I'm not going to start now."

"Well, we'd like to know," he insisted. "We're thinking maybe we ought to pay you what the previous pastor received."

I said, "Well, I don't know whether I can live on it or not. What did he receive?"

"About $8,000 a year," one of the deacons said.

"But," the chairman inserted, "you've got to remember, he received a lot of benefits too. We paid his house payment, we paid his gas allowance, and we paid his telephone bill." As he told me the numbers for each benefit, he also wrote them down so he could do the total calculations.

I had always been quick at math, so with each amount he gave for each particular benefit, I just added the numbers together in my head.

"Now," the man said as he finished his list of benefits, "we'll add this all up. It's quite a bit of money plus the $8,000 salary."

"Oh," I said then, "you don't need to add it. I'll tell you the number." And promptly told him the sum of all the benefits exactly to the last cent.

He looked at me shocked, then quickly added the figures on the paper just to check my answer. "How did you—?

"I just added it up as you went along," I replied. "I think it's a pretty good salary, and I don't think I'm probably worth it."

"But, let me tell you," I continued, "I want you to know something right now. I'm not coming to a church to argue with deacons on matters like this. I'm coming to lead a church and watch God grow the work. And if you're going to fuss about little things like this and be a bunch of penny pinchers, I don't think you want me as pastor."

If he was shocked before, he was even more so with that statement.

"You know," I said, "when I drove up here, I saw 7 out of you 13 deacons outside smoking. If I come here, I won't have you quit smoking immediately after I start. But within a year and a half, we'll not have a deacon on the deacon board that smokes. You need to know that too."

Sunday morning came, the day I was to preach at the church. I got up in front of the congregation and said, "I met with the deacons on Monday night. I told them I'm not here to mess around with little financial matters. I'm coming here to build a church, and if you want to quibble about all those things, you'd better get another man. If you vote for me, it'll be my program that I put in. But if you don't want me, then vote against me."

That night they voted. Seventy-five percent of the church voted against me. That settled that.

So here I was, praying for an open door in a pastorate somewhere. I had now turned down two churches (in one way or another) and had no other leads.

In my evangelistic travels, I had visited southern California a number of times. I had done some preaching in the Los Angeles area over the past few months and had grown burdened for the Thousand Oaks area. It was an area just north of Los Angeles that was undergoing the beginnings of development. They were predicting it would be a large area over time, but at that time, it was literally thousands of oak trees. *What better place to build a church than right in the center of a new town?* I thought.

We prayed about it and decided that this was what God wanted us to do. If I could not find an existing church to pastor, then I might as well start one in a growing area like this.

The first development was just starting to build, so I went to the developers and asked if I could possibly buy a house. "I would like to use it to start a church," I told them.

"Sure," they said. "We'll sell you a house."

I picked out one of the models that would work best for us, gave them the information about Guyla and me, and paid the earnest money deposit. They would send the official papers in the mail. We were to get them notarized and send them back as soon as we received them. It sounded like a great plan to me, so I returned home having bought a new house.

While I waited for the papers to arrive in the mail, I received a phone call from a church in Colorado. It was a church at which I had held revival meetings over the past few years: South Sheridan Baptist Church in Lakewood. It was a small church that had begun as a small group of believers in the 1930s. Over time, they had purchased land on the corner of Sheridan Boulevard and Kentucky Avenue. Though small in number, they had something to brag about. They were the first church in Denver to put up a building for the price of a small house. At just $13,500, the Quonset hut that was built served as the main auditorium for the church for many years.

They were calling to tell me that the pastor had resigned due to health difficulties. "Would you be available to come and candidate?" they asked.

The people had been very friendly and responsive to my messages, but I already had other plans. "No," I said, "I don't think so. I'm planning to start a church in southern California."

A few weeks went by. The papers had still not come, and no other churches had called.

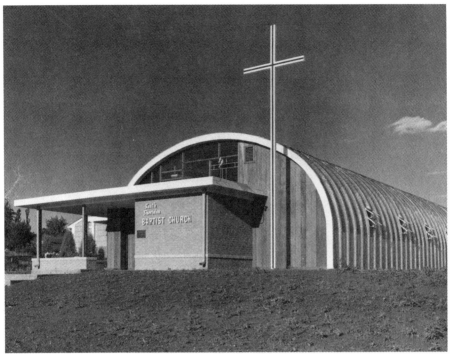
South Sheridan Baptist Church, 1960

South Sheridan Baptist Church called again. "We sure want you to come. Will you please come and candidate?"

"No, I can't. I'm going to southern California."

The papers finally came from the developer. Guyla and I went to the bank and met with the notary. We presented our birth certificates and the man began looking over the papers.

"Something is wrong here," he said suddenly. "They have the names here as Edward J. Nelson and Francis G. Nelson."

"That's correct," I said.

"Well, the spelling on her birth certificate and the spelling on this paper are different," he said.

"You misspelled my name!" Guyla said, looking at me surprised. "It's F-R-A-N-C-*E*-S."

I knew her name was Frances Guyla Nelson, but I never knew there were two different ways to spell Frances. The masculine name is Francis. The feminine is Frances. Guyla explained as much to me then.

"Well, I'll just fix it quickly," I said as I got out a pen.

"Oh, no you won't," the notary replied, pulling the papers away from me. "These must go back to the company. You'll have to contact them to change it. They will make the changes and send it back to us again. I'll return it for you."

He returned the documents, and I notified the company of the mistake. And then we waited. And waited. And waited.

After a few weeks, we still had not heard back from the company. I called them and was told, "We're having trouble finding the documents."

Meanwhile, South Sheridan contacted me a third time. "Will you *please* come and candidate?" they asked.

I finally agreed. I would take questions during the Sunday School hour and then preach the Sunday morning service. Immediately after I preached, someone would rush me to the airport where I would take a plane to California. I had revival meetings scheduled to start Sunday night in Arvin, a small town north of Los Angeles.

Like the other churches where I had candidated, I spelled out my plan to the church people very clearly. The chairman of the deacons at South Sheridan was a good man, but he also smoked. "If I come here, I plan to stay for 30 years and build a work here. And I will tolerate a man on the deacon board smoking for a year to a year and a half, but I'm going to immediately talk to him about it and try and help him out of it. I will not have deacons that smoke or deacons that drink alcohol. Now, if you don't like that, you vote against me."

After preaching Sunday morning at South Sheridan, someone drove me to the airport. Someone else met me at the Los Angeles airport and drove me to the church in Arvin. I made it just in time to preach the evening service.

The members of South Sheridan took a vote that Sunday evening. I received a call from them the next day. "We have voted, and all but two members have voted 'yes.' We are asking you to become our pastor."

I did not give an answer right away. Instead, I drove to the development in Thousand Oaks to find out what had happened to the documents and the housing situation. "We cannot find the papers anywhere," they told me. "We will have to start the application all over again."

"Can I get my earnest money back?" I asked the developer. I had made up my mind.

They returned all of it. Leaving the office, I returned to my hotel room and called South Sheridan back. "I'll come." At the end of the week of revival meetings, I returned home. I was now the pastor of South Sheridan Baptist Church, all because I did not know how to spell my wife's first name.

Chapter 19

BUILDING A CHURCH

MAY 29, 1960, we officially began our ministry at South Sheridan Baptist Church. From my time as pastor in Hoffman Heights, I had learned many things that I was determined to implement with this new church. God's organization on earth is the church, and He wants people in the church. But He does want them to know that the pastor is the leader. At Hoffman Heights and in many of the churches in which I preached in evangelism, there were a lot of people that did not believe the pastor should lead. *They* would lead and just let the pastor preach. But after much study, I learned that it does not work that way. The pastor has to be the leader of the flock and set the tone. So right from the beginning, I told my new congregation that I was going to be the leader. I would listen to advice and listen to what they had to say and make decisions accordingly. I would not be a dictator, but I *would* be a leader.

Some people did not agree with that. "I've watched you," a lady and her husband told me. "You're an evangelist, not a pastor. How long are you going to stay?"

"I'm going to stay at least 25 years, maybe 30 or 35," I replied.

"Oh, you're not going to do that," she said. "I'll give you two years and you'll be gone."

And I said, "Well, you watch and see. I won't be."

Two years later, she was gone, and I was not. It seemed that many in the congregation had the same attitude as that lady — "He's an evangelist, not a pastor." In fact, years later, I learned that the two negative votes I had received when they voted to call me as pastor, were because the two individuals (who later became dear friends) thought my preaching was too evangelistic and too much of a fire-and-brimstone type of preaching — not what they were looking for in a pastor.

As a result, I really tried to become a pastor. I went to the hospital to visit people who were sick. I was there when their babies were born. If they needed counseling in the middle of the night, I was there. I loved it, and I really started becoming a pastor.

It was not long, though, before the criticism and complaints started rolling in. "You're not meeting my needs." "I don't like the way you preach." "I don't like how you comb your hair." "You said this, and I don't agree with that."

I did not know what to do. Finally, I decided that instead of preaching the topical messages I preached as an evangelist, I should learn expository preaching — preaching through a passage of Scripture or a book of the Bible as a whole. I would let God's Word meet the needs of my people rather than try to meet their needs on my own.

It changed me and the way I preached. It changed the church. We all began to grow, and the criticisms became less. I began writing a book to help new Christians. I called it, *Growing In Grace.* We *all* began growing in grace and in the knowledge of Scripture, and the Lord began adding people to the church.

But those first years were not without their problems. During the question and answer time while I was candidating, a church member, John Gray, had stood up. He was a mailman, and he and his wife were godly people. "Now, Brother Nelson," he said, "I've heard about your preaching, and you do seem to be pushing missions. I've heard that in *many* of your revival meetings, you always emphasize missions. Are you going to work hard to support missions when you come to this church?"

Building a Church

I did not know exactly what he was asking until later, but I had responded, "John, this church should be a missionary church. If I take this church, I plan for it to become a strong missionary church. I won't push it too hard at the start though. We need to get out of that little Quonset hut and get a permanent building. And the church needs to grow big enough so that we can support missions."

Two weeks after I began pastoring, I discovered that the missionary budget totaled a measly $1,000 a year. But I also learned that the former pastor had not paid the missionaries in over three years. I was to receive a salary of $80 each week and I had already received the money for the first two weeks. But when I discovered that we had missionaries that were unpaid for *three years*, I put my foot down.

"I will take no salary until the missionary support is all caught up. It is wrong what you have done to them," I told the church. "I will take no salary, *and* we will pay no bills until the missionaries are paid in full."

The offerings had been running about $200 per week. The Sunday after I announced the financial changes, the offering jumped to $700. For several weeks, the offering increased, and after three weeks of no salary for me and no bills being paid, we had the $3,000 to pay the missionaries in full.

I really could not afford the lack of salary, but God provided for our family and blessed my efforts to see our missionaries paid.

About the same time, I learned that the church had significant debt. The previous pastor had received a salary, but there was not enough money left to pay all the bills that the church owed. The church had borrowed money for three months, paid the bills, but then would owe the lender money. They would borrow money from someone else to pay back the three months' worth, but then not have enough to pay that person. It was a vicious cycle that had landed the church in thousands of dollars of debt.

There was one wealthy man in particular who attended a different church, but whom the pastor had borrowed from the most. He claimed to be a Christian and had been called to preach, but he told the Lord, "I'll preach, but I want to work in the world until I have $25,000 in cash in the bank. *Then* I'll step out and become a preacher."

Well, $25,000 turned into $50,000, which turned into $100,000, which turned into $1 million. He never did surrender to preach. The church had borrowed thousands of dollars from him and many others all over town, and had not paid them back.

This had to stop. I created a list of all the debts we owed and I visited each lender. "Would you be able to discount this loan?" I asked them. Everyone except the non-preacher-millionaire agreed to discount our loan. This man said, "No, you'll pay me every penny you owe me." So we did. We began putting money aside from the weekly offerings and cut as many expenses as we could in order to pay off these debts.

Some people in the church had also loaned some of their own items to the church. One day, a lady called me and asked me to visit. She and her husband had something they wanted to discuss with me.

"The church needed a typewriter, and so I bought one and loaned it to the church. It cost me $200," she said. "Now that the pastor is gone, I've been looking for the typewriter, but I can't find it. Do you know where it is?"

"I don't know anything about it," I told her.

"Well, I want that typewriter back," she said.

It was lunchtime, so I excused myself saying Guyla was waiting for me for lunch and that I would do some checking on the situation.

I returned to church and made a few phone calls. I found that the pastor had sold the typewriter and pocketed the money. At home, I told Guyla the situation. "What if you and I give her $200 for the cost of a new typewriter?" I suggested to Guyla.

She agreed, even though we could not afford the $200. I wrote out a check to the couple and drove back over to their house. "The typewriter has been sold, and we can't find it," I told them. "I don't know how much it was sold for, but here is a check for $200. I'm paying you for it."

"I won't accept it," she said.

"Ma'am," I replied firmly, "you either accept this or keep your mouth shut."

"Well, I'm not going to talk about it."

"I don't want you to bring it up ever again. You can have the $200," I tried again as I handed her the check.

"I won't take it!"

"Then just be quiet," I said.

The lady and her husband left the church the next Sunday.

For three years we sacrificed and put money aside from each week's offering. We did *not* sacrifice on the missions budget, but kept that consistently paid. And after three years, we were debt free.

* * * * *

South Sheridan Baptist Church met in what was called a Quonset hut, also known as an Arch Building due to its shape. It was the cheapest option for the struggling church to be able to put up a building, but it was far from ideal.

During the summers, it was scorching hot. We installed a makeshift cooling system that helped take the edge off. We ran three sprinkler hoses down the middle of the roof and had them spray the top of the steel roof. The water would run down both sides of the building and helped to cool the inside a few degrees. We also had huge fans by each door to circulate the air. The noise from the fans made preaching incredibly difficult.

I fought those fans each Sunday and Wednesday for months. One day, I completely lost my voice. The doctors could not seem to help me get it back and suggested I leave the church for a while. I did not leave, but I did take some time off.

I was put on strict vocal rest. I did not speak to anyone including my family for two months. I communicated solely by writing notes or using hand motions. Other men filled the pulpit during my vocal absence.

Two families in the church came together and offered to pay for my family to enjoy a two-week vacation in Seattle, Washington. We took them up on the offer and had a wonderful (silent) time as a family. The rest helped me a lot.

After we returned from the vacation, my voice gradually came back, but it never did return to what it had been in college or my days in evangelism. I returned to preaching over the noise of the fans, but I was much more careful and recognized the limits on what I could handle without ruining my voice any further.

Whenever it rained (or hailed), we had to stop the service until the storm passed. We could not even hear ourselves sing above the din of the pelting rain on the metal roof. Oddly enough, our organist, Mrs. Gray, kept right on playing through the storms — even though no one could hear her.

In the winters, the Quonset hut was exactly opposite from the summer months: it was frigid. Most of us wore our overcoats, overshoes, hats, and gloves inside because it was so cold.

I discovered that the salesman (the previous pastor) who had sold the building to the church advertised that it was "easy to cool, and easy to heat." He was not kidding either! It was very easy to heat in summer and very easy to cool in winter.

After a year of preaching in this building, and because many people had been added to the church, I knew we needed a new building. We had maxed out every space available to us. There was a children's Sunday School class that met in an old chicken house that we rented each week. The owner of the chicken coop lived about half a block from the church. It seems crazy to think about it now, but our 4th–6th grade children walked each Sunday morning to their classroom — an oversized chicken coop of all places.

Most people could not tell it was a chicken coop until it rained; then, *everyone* knew what it was. There was a house on the corner of the church property that we rented for the teen and adult Sunday School

Groundbreaking for the Miracle of '61

classes upstairs, and the younger children's classes downstairs. Another house was used for church offices, and the Quonset hut doubled as both an auditorium and an adult Sunday School classroom.

Even though we were still in debt at the time, I knew we needed to spend a bit of money in order to grow. I prayed and challenged the people to give what they could and then trust God to provide for this building. We called our first building project, "Miracle in '61."

The plan was to build an educational building that could get the children's classes out of the rented chicken house. We also needed a nursery and better office space. We decided we could survive in the Quonset hut for a while, but the children absolutely needed a better place for their classes.

I still do not know how the money came in. People just gave and before long, we were able to start the project. We put up most of the building ourselves with volunteer labor. Kermit Larew, a member of the church, was a building contractor and built houses for a living. He knew quite a bit about construction and headed up our project.

Slowly but surely, the building took form. I checked on the progress daily and helped wherever I could, although I did not know much about construction. Thankfully, there were other men in the church who knew much more than I did.

One day, Mr. Alexander, one of the deacons and a volunteer laborer on the project, came to me. "Pastor Nelson," he said, looking somewhat distressed, "I cannot find the building plan anywhere! We've been looking everywhere but can't find it."

"Well, where was the last place you remember it?" I asked.

He thought a minute, then put his hands on his head and groaned. "I nailed it on some of the framing boards."

"Well, I guess we had better take off the drywall and find those plans then," I replied.

Sure enough. After taking apart some of the walls, we found the plans nailed to the inside.

Fortunately, we had no major setbacks and at long last, the educational building was completed and we did not owe one dime on the project. It was paid in full: the Miracle of '61.

In the middle of all this excitement around the church building, we had some excitement of our own. For the past year, we had been living in Longmont, about 40 miles away. It made for very long days and long commutes to the church office. After a year of the long drive each week, we decided to sell the house in Longmont and build a house in a new neighborhood five minutes away from the church. It made things *much* easier for our family of six. Then one day, Guyla came to me with a shocked look on her face. "We are expecting a baby!"

Chapter 20

CONTROVERSY

CHRISTIAN ORGANIZATIONS ARE nothing new. Conflict is nothing new. Since before the Pilgrims first landed in America, Christian organizations had existed and experienced divisions. Division was the major reason the Pilgrims came to America in the first place. They wanted to separate from the Church of England so that they could be free to believe and practice what the Bible said, not man-made religious traditions and doctrines.

Over the next 300 years, Christianity in America took on many forms as more and more people immigrated to the country bringing their religious beliefs and traditions with them. Various groups arose, each in accordance with its particular belief system and denominational organization.

For the Baptists, the first major organization of churches was in 1707 with the formation of the Philadelphia Baptist Association. Through the efforts of the five churches that had started this association, Baptist churches multiplied exponentially across the States.

In the 19th century, the Baptists in America began cooperating in national organizations formed for specific purposes — mainly overseas missionary work. Adoniram Judson and Luther Rice were two of the first missionaries to go out under the General Convention, which later became the American Baptist Foreign Mission Society. When the Civil

War disrupted the unity of the country, it also divided the nation's religious organizations. In 1845, Baptists in the South formed the Southern Baptist Convention. Although the Baptists in the North continued on for many years with the missions societies and organizations they had founded, in 1907, the Northern Baptist Convention was formed.

From that time forward, theological controversies divided the Baptists and became the catalyst to starting several new Baptist groups. The reasons were as varied as the men and women that made up the new groups: church organization structure, converts among new immigrants, dissatisfaction with the Northern Baptist Convention, and issues with interdenominational and ecumenical bodies, to name a few. While each of the new organizations had begun as a conviction of separation, it was not long before the Baptist conventions and associations faced a real problem: compromise.

Within the realms of Christianity, particularly within the Northern Baptist Convention, a system of thought called "modernism" (now known as "liberalism") began to grow. It started simply with questioning the authority and inerrancy of the Bible. Suddenly, instead of a literal interpretation of Scripture, a variety of interpretations arose. The Bible could now mean whatever the interpreter wished it to say. Once the absolute truth of the Word of God is removed or questioned, mankind has nothing on which to anchor his soul or faith. From the modernist mindset came the questions and doubts of many fundamental doctrines of true Christianity.

Social reform became a major concern. World War I and the Great Depression were over. World War II was looming. Communism was a real threat. As a result, many churches began reinventing their doctrine in order to accommodate and appeal to the social issues of the day.

Modernism, however, was not confined to the United States. Under the auspices of its missions society, the Northern Baptist Convention sent out missionaries who adopted and actively promoted the liberal doctrine. These missionaries, along with the leaders who sent them, were denying the fundamental doctrines of the Christian faith: the inspiration of the Word of God, the virgin birth of Christ, the deity of Christ, the resurrection of Christ, and salvation by grace through faith in the shed blood of Jesus Christ alone.

Conservative pastors within the Northern Baptist Convention tried many times to rein in the theologically liberal association, but it was to no avail. Finally, they decided to take a stand. Dr. Bruce Shelley, a long-time professor of church history and historical theology at Denver Seminary, wrote, "In 1943, after renewed but frustrating efforts to create theological tests for the Northern Baptist Convention's missionary program, several hundred conservative churches joined in the call for the creation of the Conservative Baptist Foreign Mission Society."

This newly formed mission society determined it would only send evangelical missionaries to the field. Three years later, a national fellowship of churches was formed, creating the Conservative Baptist Association (CBA). And that is where I enter the picture.

In 1944, I accepted Christ as my Savior at a service in the First Baptist Church of Fort Collins. Immediately after my salvation, that church became my church. In 1947, it was one of the many churches that joined the newly-formed Conservative Baptist Association. It was a good, Bible-believing church that really helped me to grow in my walk with God.

The church in Adairsville, Georgia, where I pastored as a student was part of the Southern Baptist Convention. Unlike the Northern Baptist Convention, this group of churches had remained true to the fundamentals of the faith and rejected modernistic views.

As the modernist movement gained more and more followers, and as I grew more in my understanding of Scripture, I began to notice some issues within the various Baptist organizations. I really began to study and figure out what *I* personally believed. When I started the church in Hoffman Heights, we made the decision to join the Conservative Baptist Association. That was in 1952. Just three years later, issues began to arise.

Two distinct groups began forming within the Conservative Baptist Association: the "hard core" and the "soft core." The issue? A new school of thought known as New Evangelicalism.

I was part of the hard core group. We were labeled with titles such as "militant," "scribal," "fundamentalists," and "separatists." Along with the titles, we were labeled with characteristics such as arrogant, uncooperative, and evaders of social problems. The words painted an extremely ugly picture of us in the minds of many around the world. Yet in our minds, we believed we were right.

The soft core group began compromising the Gospel. The whole mentality of the New Evangelical movement was to hold to the conservative doctrines, but to partner with the non-Christian world in order to share the Gospel with more people. They were different from the modernists in that they still believed that the Bible is the inerrant Word of God and salvation is through Jesus Christ alone. But they compromised by questioning some of the application and interpretation of the Bible. In the book *The Young Evangelicals,* Richard Quebedeaux wrote a chapter titled *The New Evangelical Orthodoxy* where he stated, "They [New Evangelicals] acknowledge that the Bible is the word of man as well as the Word of God…. The old concepts of infallibility and inerrancy are being reinterpreted to the point that a number of Evangelical scholars are saying that the *teaching* of Scripture (i.e., matters of faith and practice) rather than the text itself is without error."

Science was another point of discussion. It seemed that the New Evangelicals wanted one foot in the Bible and the other in the scientific world. Later in the same chapter, Quebedeaux expounds on the ramifications of such ideas and theology when he names some evangelical scholars who were adopting the Theory of Evolution because it was "seemingly more compatible with the findings of biology and geology than the traditional creationist view had been." Topics such as these fueled some incredibly heated discussions.

As the arguments continued, more and more pastors from the soft core were willing to partner with those who did *not* believe the fundamentals of the faith. Ecumenical Evangelism became a major dividing point between the two sides. In practice, these pastors held evangelistic efforts both with Bible-believing churches and with churches that did not believe the fundamentals of the Christian faith.

Our association was supporting para-church organizations and evangelists who hosted revival meetings and included leaders on the platform or in the crusade who openly denied the deity of Jesus and even refused to pray in His name. This cooperation with unbelievers is direct disobedience of Scripture. The Bible clearly states, *"Be ye not unequally yoked together with unbelievers" (2 Corinthians 6:14a);* and *"Wherefore come out from among them, and be ye separate, saith the Lord" (2 Corinthians 6:17).*

The whole mindset of the New Evangelicals was that churches needed to change in order to be more appealing, more concerned about the social impact of preaching and teaching, and more concerned with *experience* than with *doctrine*.

Missions was another topic up for debate. Our association missionaries were preaching and teaching along the lines of the soft core. They, too, were compromising.

In Colorado, I took a stand. Leading the fight with me was a pastor in Durango, Colorado, Wayne Van Gelderen, Sr., who was a fellow alumnus of Bob Jones University and one of my best friends. Missions was the heartbeat and at the forefront of both of our ministries. We could not stand by and let this association disobey the Word of God.

I talked with several other pastors and I sought the advice of my most-esteemed teacher at Bob Jones University, Dr. Monroe Parker. The issues bothered all of us who were part of the hard core group within the CBA. Finally, we decided to take some drastic action. In September of 1961, a group of pastors met in Chicago, including Earle Matteson, Monroe Parker, Ernest Pickering, Paul Seanor, Arno Weniger, Sr., John

Weidnaar, Bryce Augsburger, Lee Long, several others, and me. After much prayer and discussion, we voted to start a missions agency of our own: the World Conservative Baptist Mission. In the documents we drafted on that historic day, we wrote that it was formed "to be a consistent fundamentalist and separatist mission agency without any compromise with New Evangelicalism." In June of 1966, we changed the name to Baptist World Mission.

* * * * *

ARGUMENTS CONTINUED at the annual meetings of the Conservative Baptist Association of Colorado. The discussions were vicious. We tried to negotiate, but that was disastrous. The deeper we got into the fight, the more hostile the two sides became.

During some of the meetings, our side asked Pastor Jack Hyles to speak for us. At one of these meetings, several professors from Denver Seminary (a CBA school that was also compromising) attended. As soon as Hyles opened his mouth to speak, the professors grabbed newspapers they had brought with them and noisily read and rattled them around. It was a great disturbance.

Many times, the discussion was moderated in a debate format. The hard core speakers were lined up on one side of the room, the soft core on the other. We alternated speakers — one hard core, one soft core, then back to the hard core. At one of these debates, I was in line to speak next for the hard core. The man speaking for the soft core was a good man whom I respected. But he stood with the soft core because he did not like the perception of being a fighter. When he finished speaking, he looked down at me, standing at the head of the hard core line. He said, "Nelson, are you speaking next?"

"Yes, I am," I replied.

"Honey," he said, turning to his wife in the audience, "pack up your things. We're leaving. I can't *stand* to hear that man speak!"

The meetings took a toll on my family. Late one night after a particularly long, difficult day of discussion, Guyla asked me, "Do you have to go to any more meetings? I am sick and tired of the constant back and forth, the bickering, the fighting. I'm just tired of this."

"We will come to a decision soon," I reassured her. And we did.

In 1962, the battles finally came to an end. The Conservative Baptist Association of Colorado took a vote. Who would stand with the CBA and the New Evangelical theology, and who would stand with the Fundamentalists?

I believe there were 92 churches that were members of the Association in Colorado. My church, South Sheridan Baptist Church, was one of them. The vote came in: 30 to 62. Sixty-two churches voted to leave the Conservative Baptist Association of Colorado and stand for the fundamental truths of the Word of God. Within a few years, about 200 fundamental churches across the nation left the Conservative Baptist Association of America.

Chapter 21

Church Split

T HE YEAR 1962 began with a bang for our family. Our church had just voted to leave the Conservative Baptist Association. Guyla was due in just about a month with our fifth child. And my back had grown much worse. The doctor said I needed surgery again. And no, I could not wait a few months until after Guyla had the baby. It needed to be done immediately. So one week before Guyla's due date, I underwent a second back surgery.

"You aren't to preach or do anything for nine weeks," the doctor said. "No exceptions."

A week later, on February 20, 1962, our youngest child was born. I was lying on the couch at home, per doctor's orders, and was watching the television coverage of John Glenn orbiting the earth when I received the phone call: "It's a boy! Mom and baby are doing well."

"Well, great!" I replied. "John Glenn is successfully orbiting the earth right now. Maybe we should name him Orbit!"

Guyla disagreed, although we had a good laugh at the suggestion. We wanted all our boys to have Bible names, and someone from church had suggested we name him after me, Edward. Finally, we decided on a combination of the two ideas: Timothy Edward.

While we thought our family was complete without him, once he was born, we could not imagine life without Timmy. He was the best surprise that could have happened to our family. Kathy, eleven years old, and Ruth, now eight, were both delighted to practice being "Mom" yet again. John and Dave, nine and six, were thrilled to have a new toy to play with, although they spent much more time playing baseball with each other.

While Guyla kept the house and adjusted to life with a newborn, I followed the doctor's orders and rested for nine weeks — well, almost nine weeks. A problem came up before the recovery time had elapsed. A *big* problem — one that would define my ministry for the rest of my life and that needs a brief explanation.

* * * * *

P<small>ART OF</small> the growing tension among Conservative Baptists in Colorado began in the 1950s. As a result of the New Evangelicalism and modernist philosophies, many colleges, seminaries, churches, and pastors began to compromise and thus taint the truth of the Gospel they were teaching and preaching. One such school was Denver Seminary.

Having begun in 1950 as the Conservative Baptist Seminary — the first seminary to come from the CBA — there were high hopes and expectations for the pastors it would train to go forth into the ministry. However, as the CBA began accepting more of the liberal mindset, the school went right along with it. Board members resigned

Timothy Edward Nelson, age 5

and those who were for the softer position theologically took their place. Within a few years, they changed the name to what it is now: Denver Seminary.

Many of us from the "hard core" side were opposed to it, and even after separating from the CBA, I and many fellow colleagues were vocally opposed to the school. We refused to support or recommend the school since it had compromised the Word of God and the truth of the Gospel, and the professors were now teaching *many* pastors to do the same.

In 1962, the school had a tremendous push in churches across the state to get an ecumenical crusade to come to Denver — one led by Evangelist Billy Graham. As Graham gained more popularity, he began holding revival meetings with religious leaders of the Baptist, Catholic, Methodist, Lutheran, Jehovah's Witness, and any other religious denominations who wished to be involved. It did not seem to matter that many of these pastors on the platform refused to pray in the name of Jesus. Some of the crusades had co-chairmen who were leading politicians who openly stated that they did not believe that Jesus was the only way to Heaven.

After watching the movement gain popularity during the previous few years, I saw the danger of it. Even though Billy Graham still preached the Gospel, his crusades included a wide variety of religious denominations and people who did not believe the same doctrines he was preaching. There was a total lack of standing for the truth of the Word of God. He was compromising and I wanted nothing to do with it. I based my beliefs and actions upon passages I found in Scripture:

> *"Look to yourselves, that we lose not those things which we have wrought, but that we receive a full reward. Whosoever transgresseth, and abideth not in the doctrine of Christ, hath not God. He that abideth in the doctrine of Christ, he hath both the Father and the Son. If there come any unto you, and bring not this doctrine, receive him not into your house, neither bid him God speed: For he that biddeth him God speed is partaker of his evil deeds" (2 John vv. 8-11).*

Based on that passage, I firmly believed that what Billy Graham was doing was wrong because he was associating with those who did not hold to the doctrine of Christ — that Christ is the Savior of the world and that there is *no* other way to God except through Him.

In March of 1962, one of the crusade leaders held meetings preparing for the crusade scheduled in 1965. I had told our small congregation that we would not be supporting the movement and would not be attending the meetings. However, I was flat on my back still and had five more weeks of immobility.

Before all this transpired, our church had called a man to be the song leader for the church. In interviewing him, I had said, "Before you join, there are some things you ought to know. Number one, you have come from a church that doesn't hold the same position we hold. So I want you to know that we'll never support a Billy Graham crusade."

His reply was, "I hope Billy Graham never comes to this town!"

I interpreted that as, "I am against it." His meaning, however, was, "I don't want a fight."

And then I said, "We won't support Denver Seminary either."

"I wish Denver Seminary had never come here," he said.

That did not mean he did not like it. It meant that he did not want to fight about it.

With just a few more weeks left of my recovery, I was resting in bed one day when I received a visit from Ed Byrd, the current chairman of the deacons. "Pastor," he said, "you know that I don't agree with you about Billy Graham. I kind of think we ought to support his crusade. But I do believe we ought to back our pastor. And you said that as a church, we were not going to support him.

"Now, this man, Jim, who is leading the singing," he continued, "he is leading the church to turn against you. And I don't believe that's right. He said, 'Pastor Nelson isn't the one who decides these things. We do. We're the church, not him. He's just the pastor. We ought to have a vote.'"

"Wow," I said. "My doctor told me not to preach for nine weeks after I got out of the hospital, and it's only been four — so don't say anything to him! But you announce to the church that on Wednesday night, I will come and speak to everyone about why South Sheridan is not going to support the Billy Graham crusade."

I prepared hard all week and studied as best as I could while resting. Wednesday night came. Ed Byrd set a chair on the platform for me to preach from, and then I spent the entire evening explaining where Billy Graham stood, what he stood for, and that we believed he preached the Bible and people got saved. "That is good!" I said. "Where we do *not* agree with him is joining hands with Jehovah's Witnesses, Methodists, Catholics, and any other denomination that does not stand for the Word of God and salvation through Christ alone.

"Now, I heard that some of you have said that the church ought to vote. I agree with you. It ought to vote. But the fact is, you *did* vote when you called me to be the pastor. When I was a candidate, I said, 'I will not support an ecumenical evangelistic crusade, and I will not support Denver Seminary.' And you voted to call me anyway. So you voted. We don't need to take another vote."

The question was lingering in the air: now what? "Well," I added, "if you cannot agree with what I've just said, you should go find another church."

Immediately, 10 families, including the song-leader Jim, rose from their seats and walked out of the auditorium. I cannot put into words the heartache and discouragement I felt in that moment. I knew I was standing for the truth of the Bible, and I was willing to pay whatever that cost. But I did not think it would cost quite so much. Half of my congregation had just walked out the door.

Chapter 22

MISSIONS AND GROWTH

OUR SMALL CHURCH had just gotten even smaller. We had an educational building now and had already paid all the bills for it. We were putting the finishing touches on the building when those 10 families walked out. By the time I was well enough to preach again after the surgery, we were ready to open up the new building. It was exciting for our little group that was left.

Our church attendance grew slightly, but our finances remained tight. It was tough, but each one of us knew that this was the right stance to take. "We are going to trust the Lord and keep doing what the Bible says to do," I told my people.

And trust the Lord we did. We made no financial or staffing changes. We continued our tithes and offerings. We consistently paid our monthly bills and within one year following the church split, all the previous debts had been completely paid. Most importantly, we had continued to support all of our missionaries. We had a handful of missionaries that we were supporting at $10-$25 per month. I thought it was a piddly amount, but that was what we could afford at the time. *Give it time and we will increase that minimum amount of support*, I thought.

From what I had found in Scripture, missions is to be at the forefront of the church. The Bible says, *"Go ye into all the world, and preach the gospel to every creature" (Mark 16:15)*. Matthew reiterates this command in Matthew 28, *"Go ye therefore, and teach all nations, baptizing them in the name of the Father, and of the Son, and of the Holy Ghost: teaching them to observe all things whatsoever I have commanded you: and, lo, I am with you alway, even unto the end of the world. Amen." (Matthew 28:18-20)*

The Great Commission appears in Matthew, Mark, Luke, John, and Acts — five times in the New Testament, followers of Jesus Christ are commanded to go. Before He ascended into Heaven, Jesus told His disciples that they would be witnesses of Him in all the world.* So if we were going to have a church that wanted to see God's blessing, we needed to be involved in missions.

We had faced problems at the beginning of my pastorate with missionaries not being paid. But we had gotten that caught up within the first few months and had not looked back — the people kept giving to missions, small as our congregation was.

Once the missionaries were completely caught up and were being paid on a consistent monthly basis, I said, "Now folks, we are supporting our missionaries at the rate of $1,000 per year. I want us to start praying. We are going to ask God to help this church grow to the place where we give $1,000 per *month* to missions."

Their jaws dropped. "Oh, how can we do *that?*" they asked. But I encouraged them to trust the Lord. We were small — half the size we had been. But I firmly believed that God would bless our efforts in missions and our stand for truth. And He did.

* * * * *

THE BILLY Graham crusade came to Denver in July of 1965. We did not support it and I preached another message on why we would not support the Billy Graham crusade and ecumenical evangelism.

I did attend the crusade one evening with my son, John, to see what it was like. John went forward at the invitation. I thought it was be-

---

*But ye shall receive power, after that the Holy Ghost is come upon you; and ye shall be witnesses unto me both in Jerusalem, and in all Judaea, and in Samaria, and unto the uttermost part of the earth (Acts 1:8).

cause he desired to get assurance of salvation. He had accepted Christ as Savior at a young age, and I thought maybe he was having some doubts. Later, he told me he went forward just to see how they handled an invitation. They had asked John what denomination he was from and led him to meet with a man who was also Baptist. At the end of the conversation, the man asked John to fill out a card with his information and church preference.

Even though our church had not supported the crusade at all, I received many cards just like John had filled out, with the names and addresses of individuals who had listed South Sheridan Baptist Church as their church preference. I took the cards and went to visit each individual.

One day, as I was making visits in Englewood, I noticed another man across the street who had cards that looked like mine. I went over to see him and discovered he was a Jehovah's Witness. Billy Graham's team had sent him cards just like mine. That confirmed in my mind that I had made the right decision about not supporting the crusades. Jehovah's Witnesses do not even believe that Jesus is God.

The cost was great in opposing the Billy Graham movement. It cost me many friends in surrounding churches — I endured much criticism. It also cost me family relationships. When my Uncle John found out I was not supporting Billy Graham, he ceased all gifts to my family. He used to send us $250 every Christmas. When he heard Billy Graham was coming to Denver, he wrote to me, "You get behind him." I wrote him back and said, "No, I can't back that meeting. I will not support it." He said, "Well I'm not sending you any more money," and he didn't, because he disagreed with me. We were still friends, and he was a godly man, but our relationship changed forever.

Standing for the truth will cost you, but it is worth the cost. After the crusade left town, our church grew faster than any other church in Denver.

* * * * *

It took a while for us to hit our goal of $1,000 per month for missions — seven years, to be exact. In the sixth year, we still had not reached our goal of $1,000 per month. We had acted in faith and raised the missions support minimum to $100 per month for each missionary, but I wanted our church to do more.

I had heard about Faith Promise giving. The idea was that each member of the congregation would promise the Lord and the church to give a specific amount to missions each week over and above their regular tithes and offerings. After studying Faith Promise, I believed this was the program to follow.

I announced that we would have a Faith Promise Conference. "Our goal is $12,000 for missions this year," I said. "That's $1,000 per month."

It would be a sacrifice. Many in our congregation had no idea how they were going to afford their tithe, bills, *and* the Faith Promise. I encouraged them to trust the Lord and He would provide for their every need.

We prayed toward that end, and we exceeded our goal. When the totals came in for what the people were promising to give, we were all astounded. Our first Faith Promise total was $19,000 for the year.

It is one thing to promise an amount. It is another to act on the pledge. So we bought poster board and made a giant paper thermometer. Each week, when we counted the money given for missions, we would color in a little more red on the thermometer. We had quarterly goals that were written on the sides, and we had a special time of thanksgiving and praise when we reached each mini-goal. At the end of the year, we had fulfilled our $19,000 promised to the missions fund. God had provided once again.

From that point forward, we used the Faith Promise method for our missions giving. In 1968, we raised our goal yet again. We raised the minimum support amount to $200 per missionary per month and set the Faith Promise goal for $24,000 ($2,000 each month). It was not long before we hit that goal too.

Missions and Growth

The Missions Globe

Over the next decade, we raised the missions budget every time we hit a new goal. We went from $2,000 per month to $1000 per week — $52,000 in missions giving for the year. Still using the thermometer, we worked hard for a few years and then finally hit our goal. After hitting the goal of $1,000 each week, we raised the goal to $2,000 each week, and we came up with a new way to track our Faith Promise giving. An artist in our church, Linda Anderson, built a monstrous globe which we hung from the ceiling on the left side of our auditorium near the piano. On the band around the equator line, we installed 52 light bulbs. Each light bulb represented a week in our giving year. Every week that we met our Faith Promise goal of $2,000, we lit a light bulb. If a week passed that we did not meet the goal, the light bulb stayed unlit. Occasionally, we would have a week where we failed to meet our goal and we would be unable to light that bulb. I encouraged the people to continue giving and to catch up reminding them of the importance of missions. Once the money was all caught up, we would light all of the light bulbs to signify that we were back on target. At the end of the year, we reached our goal — $104,000 given to missions, and all 52 light bulbs were lit.

Our church was growing — with our missions budget as well as our church membership. Our congregation had started out with 10 families — less than 50 members. The year of my 15th anniversary as pastor of the church, we pledged $146,000 for missions and saw over 1,000 people regularly attend our services.

By the time I resigned from the pastorate, South Sheridan Baptist Church was giving nearly $250,000 for missions every year. Each time we raised the goal, we wondered, "How are we going to make it? There is no way we can give that much money this year!" But God always provided, and He blessed our efforts to obey His command. We were sending out hundreds of missionaries all over the world to preach the Gospel and make disciples — just as we were doing in our own mission field of the greater Denver metro area.

Chapter 23

A Trip Around the World

Early in our ministry at South Sheridan Baptist Church, a student from Denver Baptist Bible College visited the church. This man was José Lazo, a Filipino native who had come to America to get some training for the ministry so that he could return to the Philippines as a missionary. He told us all about his plans and goals to reach his people for Christ, specifically training pastors in Baguio, a mountain town in the Philippines. We were thrilled and immediately wanted to support him as a missionary. He seemed to have a personality that would do very well on the mission field.

Our church supported him and formed a mission board which helped him raise the rest of his support. We sent him out from our church and even purchased a brand new 1964 Ford Station wagon for him. We also paid for it to be shipped over to the Philippines.

After he was in the Philippines for a while, I began to wonder if José Lazo was on the level. I would read his reports and ask myself, *"Have we made a mistake?"* I talked to the deacons and then the church and they decided that I should go check out José Lazo's ministry. We determined that I would go to the Philippines in January of 1965.

My good friend, Wayne Van Gelderen, was pastoring in Durango, Colorado, at the time. He phoned me and said, "I hear you are going to the Philippines."

"Yes."

"May I go with you? I'd love to go."

"Well, sure," I said.

"I've checked, and the airfare to the Philippines is $1,000 round-trip. A fare around the world is only $1,300," he said. "So for only $300 more, we could go all the way around the world. Why don't we do an around-the-world trip and visit several missionaries? I want to go to Japan anyway," he added.

"Well, I don't want to go to Japan," I said. "Every time I have tried to go to Japan, I get sick."

"It will be fine," he reassured me. "We'll go in one day, and we'll be out two days later. I've got a missionary in Japan that I'm wondering about, too, and I want to go check on him."

Finally, I agreed to go. We would fly into Japan on a Friday and leave on Monday. Before we left, another friend, Charles Homsher, called. He was the founder and director of Neighborhood Bible Time, headquartered in Boulder, Colorado. "Are you going to the Philippines?"

"Yes, a trip around the world, actually," I replied.

"May I come too?"

"Of course!" I replied.

So the three of us, Wayne Van Gelderen, Charles Homsher, and me, began our seven-week trip around the world.

We flew west from Denver, stopping in California and Hawaii before continuing to Japan for a few days. Wayne visited his missionary there, and amazingly enough, I did not get sick! After Japan, we flew to Korea and spent a few days there visiting missionaries. From Korea, we traveled to Taiwan, and then to the Philippines, visiting missionaries at each stop.

We landed in Manila and met our missionary, José Lazo, and his family. It did not take us long to realize the guy was a fake. He was living more extravagantly than any of the other Filipinos. The car we had purchased for him was comparable to what the president of the Philip-

Charles, Ed, and Wayne — Honolulu, Hawaii, 1965

pines was driving. José had one of the best vehicles in the land! That made him attractive to all the preachers in the Philippines because he would have money to help them. He had quite the following. But it was a fake following and we saw right through it.

Right then, I decided that when I returned from our trip, I would recommend to my church that we should drop him from our missionary support. He was not winning any souls. He was not building anything. He was just living it up on *our* money and the money from other churches who also supported him. That was not and is not something any missionary should ever do.

Despite the shocking discovery of José Lazo's extravagance, we had a wonderful time in the Philippines. Well, wonderful except for a few meals. In each country we visited, we ate at local restaurants or with the missionary families. That proved to be an interesting experience. At one home, I was given a Filipino delicacy: balut. Balut is a developing bird embryo (usually a duck) a few days from hatching that is boiled and eaten from the shell. The hostess had cracked the egg shell for me and to my surprise and horror, I looked at the plate and saw the skeleton of the bird, cooked, inside the shell. It was swimming in a broth with the boiled yolk next to it. I knew it was an honor for them to give me one of these treats, but I could not get past the smell or the look. There was no way that I would ever be able to get that into my mouth and actually swallow without losing everything I had eaten that day.

Fortunately, the hostess understood my predicament and offered to give it to her servant. I was beyond grateful and gladly handed the plate with the egg on it to the servant. She promptly went into a dark closet, shut the door, and came out a minute later licking her lips. Apparently, the way to eat balut is in the dark.

A few days later, one of the churches decided to prepare a feast for us. At that time in the Philippines, dog meat was considered to be a delicacy, so the church prepared a dog meat feast just for us. Wayne and I decided to embrace the culture and eat the special food. How bad could it be? Plus, as a five-year-old boy, I had promised Mother that I would eat anything on my plate and say it was good.

Homsher, however, was not so brave — a wise move on his part. Wayne and I put the first bite of dog in our mouths and immediately gagged. It was the worst taste I have ever had in my mouth. It was truly all we could do to put a bite in, grab a swig of water, and swallow each bite whole. Even then, the flavor, if you could call it that, was so horrendous that every bite threatened to bring lunch back up with it.

It was not long into the feast that Wayne quit eating the dog. He just could not stomach it. I was determined to try to keep my promise to my mother, so I continued. Several times, the meat got caught in the back of my throat. The ladies who had prepared the meat had not gotten all of the hair off the dog before cooking it, and I could feel the bristles hitting the back of my throat. I poured a lot of water into my mouth, grabbed the edge of the table, and swallowed as hard as I could. It went down, bristles and all.

We ate as quickly as we possibly could and immediately headed to Clark Air Base, which happened to be in the same town, Angeles

Balut

City. On the base, we found the first place that served ice cream sundaes and promptly inhaled an entire large ice cream sundae with *lots* of chocolate. The taste of dog was still in our mouths. We ordered another sundae. "More chocolate please," we asked. Within minutes, those sundaes were also gone. Yet still, the taste lingered. "No ice cream. Just chocolate," we said.

The chocolate finally did the trick and we were able to mask the taste of the dog meat. It was terrible, though. Wherever we walked, we saw stray dogs. In alleyways, we would see people grab a stray dog and kill it for dinner. The dogs were rarely more than skin and bones — literally. They had hardly any meat on them whatsoever and they were filthy. Yet dog meat was considered a delicacy.

We decided we liked America's version of delicacies better.

* * * * *

After our extended stay in the Philippines, we went to the mainland of Asia and visited missionaries in Hong Kong, Thailand, Burma (now Myanmar), and East Pakistan (now Bangladesh). One of the missionaries we stayed with was Viggo Olsen (Vig), with whom I had previously had some contact. He was a missionary under the Association of Baptists for World Evangelization (ABWE) and was very involved in the politics and medical aid in Bangladesh. The governor of Bangladesh really liked him because Vig did many things for the government. They liked him so much that they asked him to build a village to take in refugees.

While we were there visiting him, Vig was told there was going to be a big elephant hunt. Vig was also a photographer, and the natives asked him to come to the hunt and photograph the event for the country.

"How would you like to go watch an elephant hunt?" he asked us.

"We would love that!" we replied.

Also invited to go on the elephant hunt were a man and his wife who had moved from California to help Vig build a hospital. They had brought their old pickup truck with them in the move and volunteered to use their truck to transport us to the location of the hunt.

The day came for the hunt. Vig had already left in his vehicle, so it was the five of us in the old pickup. The man, his wife, and Wayne climbed into the front seat. Homsher and I sat in the bed of the pickup. Unfortunately, there was no tailgate — the bed was wide open.

As we drove, we came to a deep gorge that required us to drive across a rickety wooden bridge. As we went over the bridge, I looked down. It looked like it was about 2,000 feet to the bottom of that gorge. We made it across just fine and continued on our way to the elephant hunt.

When we arrived, we saw a huge field with fences all around the perimeter. The elephants were on one side of the field, and there were other fences that had been erected in strategic places that would help the men catch the elephants. The goal was for the men to herd the elephants between the fences and into the big enclosure where they could then capture them to ship to America for the zoos.

We had a prime vantage point for the whole ordeal. They had constructed a stand where we could be above the danger of the hunt and where Vig could take his pictures. It was fascinating. We watched the elephants come barreling into the enclosures while the men quickly

The Elephant Hunt

closed off the opening so they could not escape. It was quite the experience!

After the day's activities had ended, we climbed back into the old pickup and began the journey back to Vig's home. Again, Homsher and

I were in the back, without any tailgate. We drove over the same rickety bridge with the 2,000 foot drop beneath us. When we were almost to the other side, the bridge started to creak and crack and make terrible noises. The man driving sped up and barely got the front wheels on the ground when the bridge beneath us started falling. It was a front-wheel drive vehicle, so the man gave it everything he had to get all four wheels on solid ground. No sooner had the back of the truck hit land than the entire bridge collapsed into the ravine, all 2,000 feet down.

We just sat there, still hanging on for dear life. If the bridge had collapsed a second sooner, the back end of that truck would have been pointing straight down into the ravine and all of us would have fallen to the bottom of that gorge. We were miraculously delivered.

* * * * *

AFTER OUR exciting, near-death experience in Bangladesh, we flew to India, visiting Calcutta (northeast coast), Madras (southeast coast), and New Delhi (mid-north). We visited several missionaries in each town as well as a Christian college that had recently been started. It was encouraging for all of us to see believers from the other side of the world who were studying the Scriptures and preparing to reach their own people with their native languages.

It is one thing for an American to go to a foreign land and reach people for Christ. It is entirely different when a natural-born citizen who already speaks the language and knows the culture reaches his own people. Language is important to the Indian people — and it was quite the communication barrier for us.

There was one situation we found ourselves in, however, that had no barrier whatsoever for us to understand the people. While we were in a main town, a riot broke out against Indians using the English language. Wayne and I were out walking around a short distance from our hotel when we came upon this riot. Men, women, and children were shouting, chanting, and breaking things. It was terrifying.

The Taj Mahal

Suddenly, someone from the crowd spotted us, two obviously American English-speaking individuals. They pointed and shouted, and immediately the whole crowd turned and began running straight toward us. They were not pleased to see us, and they looked as if they were going to kill us!

Wayne and I took off running as fast as we could. We ran back to the hotel, threw open the doors, ran inside, and closed and bolted the doors shut. Amazingly enough, the riotous crowd did not try to break down the hotel doors. Once we made it into the hotel, we were safe and the riots continued without boasting of two American deaths.

From India, we were relieved to have no near-death experiences as we traveled to Iran, Greece, and Lebanon. After a few days in each of those countries, we met up with Dr. Bob Jones, Jr., in Egypt and participated in the Bible Lands tour he was leading. This tour included Egypt, Jordan, and Israel. I had never been to the Bible Lands, so I soaked up every piece of information I heard and saw. I saw the pyramids in Egypt, the ones that the Israelites had built under Pharaoh when they were slaves in the 14th century B.C. In Israel, I saw what is believed to be the Upper Room, the place where Jesus and the disciples ate the Last

The Great Pyramids and Sphinx of Giza — Egypt

The Colosseum — Rome, Italy

Wayne Van Gelderen and I near Westminster Abbey & Big Ben — London, England

Supper before Jesus was arrested and crucified. It was amazing to visit the Garden Tomb where Jesus had been buried. It was empty — and still is empty! Jesus is alive!

After the tour of Israel and Egypt, the three of us flew to Rome, Italy; Paris, France; and London, England, visiting local missionaries in each country. We estimated that during our seven-week excursion, we visited over 100 missionaries in 17 different countries.

The Lord taught me many lessons on that trip — lessons about missions, lessons about travel, lessons about miraculous protection, lessons about the providence and sovereignty of God. I was a different man after that trip, and I was excited to get back to my church where I could share with them the lessons learned and the clearer direction for the future.

At last, the day came for us to return to the United States. All of us were sad that our trip around the world was coming to a close; but at the same time, we were ready to be home with our families. Seven weeks was a long time to be away.

We had a direct flight to Chicago. From there, we were to fly to Denver, but our international flight was incredibly late. By the time we landed in Chicago, our flight for Denver had already left. We boarded a later flight, which was fine for Homsher and me. But Wayne still had to fly to Durango. We thought there was no way he could still make his flight that evening; but over the two-hour flight from Chicago to Denver, we had a tailwind and made up a lot of lost time.

Our flight to Denver arrived at the same time Wayne's flight to Durango began boarding.

"Wayne," I told him, "there is a chance you *might* still make that flight. You just go, get off the plane as quickly as possible and run to your gate. I'll grab your bag and send it to you on the first flight to Durango tomorrow."

He agreed that was a good idea, so as soon as we were off the plane, Wayne took off running to Concourse A while Homsher and I went to the baggage claim. Wayne's bag was one of the first to arrive on the carousel, but before I could grab it, Homsher had it in his hands and took off running — straight toward Concourse A.

I ran after him, leaving our bags on the carousel to pick up once I caught up to Homsher. "Wait!" I yelled after him. "What are you doing?"

He did not listen to me, nor did he stop to even acknowledge he had heard me. He just kept running, right up to Wayne's gate, security guards following as quickly as they could, and me close behind. The door to the tarmac was still open, but the plane door was closed and the plane was beginning to taxi away from the gate.

Homsher ran out onto the tarmac, Wayne's suitcase still in hand. He ran in front of the airplane to where the pilots could see him. He held up the suitcase with both hands and began yelling and waving it around.

To my amazement and utter shock, the plane stopped. They let down the stairs, grabbed the suitcase from Homsher, put the stairs up again, and continued on their way.

The security guards had finally caught up to Homsher by this point and ushered him back into the airport concourse.

"What were you doing? What were you *thinking*?" I asked.

He calmly replied, "I just wanted him to have his pajamas."

Chapter 24

"Honey, We've Got a School"

Several years before I became the pastor of South Sheridan, a fellow pastor and evangelist, Harvey Springer, had started a Christian school in the state of Colorado. It was a grade school, kindergarten through 8th grade. While there were many students who attended this school, his dream was to start a Bible college to train people for the ministry.

He already had a college of sorts at his church, First Baptist Church and Tabernacle in Englewood, but he wanted to expand it to an organization that involved other churches too. At that time, he had only three students in his college.

So Harvey decided he would like to have a board of pastors to organize this college. He contacted me along with about 10 other pastors in the western region and asked us to help. The others decided to make me the chairman of the board. I was to work with Dr. Springer as he provided land that he already owned as well as the funds for the buildings of the college.

But the day before we were to meet and organize the new college, I had come to realize that I could not work with Dr. Springer. He and I disagreed about the method of handling finances. I believed in open accountability.

So at a board meeting, I said, "Men, I'm resigning from this board. My idea about handling finances and Harvey's are completely different, and I think it is wise for me to step down."

We were sitting in Harvey Springer's office that day and he was sitting in his big swivel chair behind his desk. As soon as I finished speaking, he swung around and said, "We accept your resignation. Paul Seanor," he pointed at the man, "you will be the new chairman."

"Yes, sir," Paul said.

And so I was out and Paul was in. However, as the meeting continued, Paul Seanor said, "We don't need a college. We need a high school."

Paul already had his own grade school, too, kindergarten through 8th grade. He made the case that his students and other Christian families needed a Christian high school for their children. "It would prepare them well for the future," he suggested.

Everyone else agreed, so the board began working on starting a high school. It was March of 1964 and they worked hard at it. I honestly was relieved to be off the board and not working on the issue.

Harvey Springer had already purchased an old school building on Bannock Street in Englewood. He rented it out to the board and within a few months, they were able to open up Silver State Baptist High School, grades 9–12.

Our oldest daughter, Kathy, was 14 that year, and since she had begun school a year early, she was going into the 10th grade. We decided to take her out of the public school and enroll her in this new school. She was one of 30 students that year.

That school year proved to be a mess. All of these students had been in public schools, and many of them had learned the rebellious behaviors of the worst of the public school kids. The teachers and board members thought they could handle the Christian school like a public school, but it did not work. Elmer Jantz, an assistant pastor at South Sheridan, became the principal of the high school. The school year did not go very well. Our daughter, Kathy, did learn a lot academically, however, and she really grew spiritually in spite of the rebellious students in the school.

Halfway through the school year, the board members asked me to come back on the board, so I agreed. We began planning for the second school year. Within the first few board meetings, I learned that the current teachers and faculty had not been paid at all. There simply was not enough money to pay them.

This was not right. I went home and told Guyla. Together, we decided to take out a personal loan from the bank and pay each faculty member's salary.

The planning continued for the 1965–66 school year. We decided to expand the school to include 7th and 8th grades in addition to the high school. In September of 1965, we had 120 students enrolled, including my three oldest children. This was the first year not in a public school for both John and Ruth, and I saw changes in their lives also. In looking at my kids, I saw that being in a Christian school really had spiritual benefit for children.

Unbeknownst to me, the rest of the board members held an informal meeting in the spring of 1966. A few weeks later, they called a formal board meeting that included me.

Harvey Springer got up and said, "The other members of the board have met without you. We have decided we must close the school. It is not working financially, so we are going to close the school."

"Oh, please don't close the school," I interjected. "It has meant so much to my daughter, Kathy, and this year, to John and Ruth as well. We *must* keep it open."

"I did not finish," Dr. Springer continued. "We decided we have to close the school, *unless* you will become president and be the one who leads the school."

Someone else added, "We've all agreed that if Ed Nelson will become the president of this school, we'll go with him. If he doesn't, we're going to close it down."

"No, I'm not going to do that," I replied. "I already have seven holes in my head, I don't want anymore. I won't do it."

"Well then, men," Harvey turned to look at the other board members, "let's have a motion to close the school. He's refused."

They made a motion, someone seconded it, and Harvey said, "All in favor, say—"

"Don't vote for that!" I cried. "Don't vote to close the school! It can be such a blessing to so many!"

"Okay, then will you be the president?"

"No."

"Let's have the vote then. All in fav—"

"Don't vote for it."

"Will you become the president?"

"No."

This happened four times. The fourth time, I said, "Okay. I will be the president."

I had no idea what I was getting myself into.

I went home and said, "Honey, we've got a school."

"A what?!" she exclaimed.

"A school. At the school board meeting today, they made me president of the school. They wouldn't take no for an answer, and I finally accepted because they were going to close it down. I don't know what to do. You have to help me."

"I think I can help you," she said. "I think we can do this."

* * * * *

THE 1966–67 school year was interesting, to say the least. I was now the president of Silver State Baptist School, grades 7–12. We met in Harvey Springer's old school building every day. I preached chapel messages daily. There was quite the mix of kids. All of them had come from public schools and had learned many tricks. They tested out this new authority figure *many* times that year — including during one memorable chapel service.

Every morning, the entire school would gather together for a chapel service. We sang a few hymns and then I would preach. Because the weather is very dry in Colorado, speakers often need water during their speech or message. There was a glass of water on a shelf in the pulpit. I began preaching and before long, I needed a drink. I took a drink of the water only to discover it was not water. It was urine. Fortunately, I was able to subtly spit the urine back into the glass and not make a scene. I never said a word about it. I just kept preaching. I was almost sure I knew who had done it, but I figured the best way to handle the situation was to ignore it and keep on preaching as if nothing had happened. I must admit though, it was a horrible thing to put into my mouth. Although I never did find out for sure who played the trick, both of the boys I suspected of the mischief grew to be godly men who lived for the Lord.

Now, not every student was rebellious or mischievous. There were several who really loved and followed the Lord. But every day, I approached the school with apprehension. No one ever knew just what was going to come next. Every kind of rebellion that the students had learned and gotten away with in the public school, they decided to try with us.

We learned many lessons over the course of the school year. Perhaps the biggest lesson we learned, however, was that you really should not start a school at the 7th grade. You need to reach the kids *before* they get to junior high school. They need a solid foundation both educationally and spiritually to build upon in the upper grades.

That is not to say that we had no impact or influence on the high school students, or that they did not learn anything. Many made decisions for Christ and went on to serve Him with their lives. We had many bright, capable students, but from the educational standpoint, we needed something different — something taught at the elementary level.

We needed an elementary school. I presented the idea to my church and we established Sheridan Baptist Elementary School. Our opening enrollment for the 1967–68 school year was 80 students, kindergarten through 6th grade, and our youngest son, Tim, started in that first kindergarten class.

For one school year, I was quite torn between the two schools. I was president of both the elementary school and the high school, and they were meeting at two different locations.

Each morning, I would drive to Harvey's old school building on Bannock Street just in time to start the school day at 8:00 A.M. Then about 10:30 A.M., I would drive back to South Sheridan and start to do my work there, both with the pastorate and with the grade school. These two locations were about 20 minutes apart — it was exhausting.

The following year, Silver State Baptist High School faced a difficult problem. Harvey Springer did not want his old school building anymore and he wanted to sell it to the school board. Several of the men wanted to buy it, but I had never liked the building at all. "Well, let's check it out," I said.

The next day, I went to the state and asked, "Could you come check out this school building and see the condition of it — whether it meets your standards?"

They came and inspected it, then told me the results: "It's condemned. Nobody can be in this building any longer. It's unsafe."

So now, we were faced with an even bigger problem. The school year was quickly approaching, and we were being forced out of the building in which we held classes.

The school board met and decided that the best immediate solution was to use the educational building at South Sheridan Baptist Church. It was a tight squeeze between the high school and the elementary school, but we made it work.

South Sheridan Baptist Church now had two schools meeting on our church property. And each year, the enrollment grew drastically. In 1970, Sheridan Baptist Elementary School had 250 students enrolled. Within just three years, we had tripled in size.

At the rate both schools were growing, changes in policies and board members were required. In 1971, the board of Silver State Baptist High School voted to ask the church if they would be willing to take the school as a ministry.

Silver State Baptist High School *and* Sheridan Baptist Elementary School would both be our schools. "If we vote yes to accept the offer," I told my congregation, "then that means we have to run it." The church voted yes.

On June 18, 1971, the board of Silver State Baptist High School voted to dissolve. Both the board members of Silver State and the South Sheridan Baptist Church deacons were present at this meeting. One board member of Silver State resigned; then the rest of us elected a new board member who was a deacon of South Sheridan. Then another Silver State board member resigned and another South Sheridan deacon was elected to take his place. This process continued until all of the Silver State board members had been replaced by deacons of South Sheridan Baptist Church. That day, the school formally became a ministry of South Sheridan Baptist Church.

We made one other change that day. We merged Silver State Baptist High School and Sheridan Baptist Elementary School. We now had one school in one location, kindergarten through 12th grade: Silver State Baptist School.

Chapter 25

Building a School

Silver State Baptist School proved to be a great blessing. That does not mean we did not have problems. We did. In fact, I told many people that if I found out a pastor was planning to start a Christian school, I would send him a sympathy card. Although we had our challenges, God worked all of them out according to His sovereign plan.

One problem that repeatedly arose was this: students who transferred into Silver State from a public school often would have difficulty reading. The teachers struggled with ways to help those students catch up to the rest of the class.

Guyla thought that there must be a simple solution available to help with remedial reading, so as the Curriculum Director, she ordered sample materials from every publisher she could find, looking for the solution to the problem. She quickly narrowed her list down to phonics-based language programs, and from there she carefully reviewed each program to see if it could help to solve her problem.

One by one, she eliminated each program until she had nothing left, and still no solution. Though each had good qualities about it, none of them taught the American English language in the way she wanted it taught. She took copious notes on what she liked and what she disliked. She knew that there had to be a better solution; so she started thinking back to how she first learned to read, and then she began the unthinkable — reading dictionaries.

In her "spare" time, she read through dictionaries looking for one-syllable words that fell into word families — e.g., cab, dab, fab, gab, lab, nab, tab. Using a typewriter, she compiled list after list of these words and their definitions.

After compiling these word lists, she then looked for commonalities among the words. She eventually settled on six broad categories for all the one-syllable words. She then published the *Phonics/Spelling Manual, Part 1,* which was the result of her years of work categorizing the language.

One of the observations Guyla had made when reviewing the curriculum of various publishers was that they spent an enormous amount of time going over the letters of the alphabet. Time would be spent learning the names of the letters, the various sounds the letters would make, how to write the letters, etc. — but words were not being put together until the students had spent most, if not all, of an entire semester learning the letters.

Guyla knew that students could learn more material in less time if the material was presented in a comprehensive and coherent way. Her goal was to teach children how to read, write, and spell in the most easy and organized method, and in the least amount of time possible. She believed that the best way to accomplish her goal was to have a holistic method that used the same rules to teach a child to read, write, and spell at the same time. And of course, her ultimate goal was to enable children to read the greatest book of all — the Bible.

Once the basic outline of her new phonics curriculum was set, Guyla began working with Saundra Scovell, the kindergarten teacher at Silver State, to develop student materials based on the *Phonics/Spelling Manual.* Together, Guyla and Saundra began introducing the letters in an entirely different format from the traditional alphabetical order.

After just six weeks of kindergarten, the students had learned the basics and began reading the first of six readers, which correlated with Guyla's six broad language categories. This method ensured that children were never reading above the lessons they had learned for phonics and spelling.

Since the mascot for Silver State was a patriot, we named the curriculum the *Little Patriots Series*, published by our newly created company, Mile-Hi Publishers (MHP).

> *Other Christian schools began using both the phonics curriculum and the readers. Each year, we received more and more orders. In 1984, Guyla received a call from Alpha Omega Publications in Tempe, Arizona. Alpha Omega had already developed an alternative curriculum to compete with that of Accelerated Christian Education (ACE), but they had failed to create a beginning reading curriculum. The following year Alpha Omega entered into a distribution and licensing agreement with MHP, and the Little Patriots Series became widely distributed among the fast-growing home school movement.*

The results using the *Little Patriots Series* were amazing. Because students were taught the American English language in a comprehensive and integrated way, they had a solid foundation for all the academic subjects. The academics in our school were outstanding — and that was all thanks to Guyla, her vision for education, and the dedication of our outstanding teachers.

* * * * *

At Silver State, we carefully screened our teachers before we hired them. Later, we realized just how good our teachers were. One teacher who was a tremendous help to the school was Omer Perdue. When he and his wife Carolyn first came to the school in 1969, we saw immediately that he was an excellent teacher. His classroom was handled with discipline and grace — two difficult things to combine. Students in his classes were rarely sent to the principal's office. They really seemed to be learning.

After two years as a teacher, we asked him to become the principal of the Junior-Senior High School. Omer joined with Guyla in leading our school through those early years, securing the right faculty, and developing the right curriculum program. The decision to make Omer Perdue the principal was one of the best decisions we ever made. He was disciplined. He knew how to lead the faculty. He was committed to discipleship, not just disciplining the students. He insisted on a strong academic program and required excellence in all facets of school life. He embodied our goal of teaching the students the Word of God which helped the students grow both academically and spiritually. Omer Perdue *made* our school what it was.

Omer Perdue, Principal of Silver State Baptist School 1971-1990

The school grew rapidly. Before long, we had completely outgrown our facilities — again. In 1971, I learned that the Lowry Air Force Base was selling some old barracks that they did not need anymore. We bought five of them and moved them to the church property.

John, who was now 19, worked with Tom Hagan, a builder from our church, to build the foundations for the barracks. Tim still claims that he worked on the project too. John and Tom paid him a penny for each nail he pulled out of the old wood. All summer long, John and Tom built and renovated the old barracks, turning them into adequate classrooms for our ever-expanding school. The goal was to have the entire project completed by the beginning of the school year. And they made it. All the foundations were built and the buildings were completely renovated and furnished by the time we started classes in fall. I was amazed and so proud of John and what he had accomplished.

Word about the spiritual and academic excellence of the school spread throughout the area. Many students from other churches began enrolling. By 1974, we had enrolled about 875 students. Tim was in 7th grade that year and was part of the largest class in the history of the school — nearly 100 students.

One day, we realized that there were a number of Mormon and Roman Catholic students in our student body. They felt they could attend chapel and hear the messages, but not believe the Gospel we were preaching and teaching. Omer came to me and said, "We are enrolling students that are compromising our spiritual position. It could be that within a year or two, the school will have grown so much that we lose the testimony and effectiveness of our school."

At that time, 30% of the student body came from South Sheridan Baptist Church. That meant 70% of the students were from other churches in the area — some of which did not believe or preach the Gospel. We announced a new program: we would enroll no new students unless their families were members of South Sheridan.

Within a short time, the enrollment dropped to about 500 students. The spiritual atmosphere improved with these changes. The standard of excellence only increased. Over time, however, we began to notice a problem among our church youth and the students at the school. They had become spiritually apathetic.

Chapter 26

REVIVAL

I HAVE HEARD many preachers say, "I have never seen a genuine revival." It is true that many times we are guilty of using the word "revival" in an improper way. Revival meetings often endeavor to bring new life to a church, to improve it, and to help it grow deeper than ever before.

True revival, however, cannot be announced in advance. It cannot be planned or scheduled. People might be praying and working toward revival in a meeting, but it is completely the work of the Holy Spirit moving among His people that brings genuine revival.

Some people confuse revival with evangelism. In my years of traveling in evangelism, I called the special services "Revival/Evangelistic Meetings." Revival happens only among the saved people. Evangelism is the work of reaching the unsaved. It is true that real corporate evangelism will require saved people to get right with God so He can effectively do His convicting work in the lives of the unsaved. But evangelism is not necessarily revival. Some unsaved people may accept the Lord in a revival/evangelistic meeting without real revival coming to the church, and without dealing with the sin of lukewarmness or particular sins in the lives of church members.

I personally have not seen genuine revival very often. In fact, as I look back over my ministry in churches, I can only remember four times. That does not mean that the result of my ministry did not bring revival. I believe revival came to many churches, but I am saying there were only four specific times when I saw definite results of real revival ministry. One thing I know: I did see two life-changing and ministry-changing revivals come to our church through the ministry of our school.

The first one took place in the summer of 1973. South Sheridan Baptist Church sponsored a revival/evangelistic meeting with Dr. B. R. Lakin, a well-known evangelist. In that meeting, one of our high school juniors, Levi Robinson, surrendered his life to the ministry and to become a soul-winner. His life was dramatically changed.

As the quarterback of our football team, Levi was a popular young man in the student body. With his outstanding athletic ability, he had led the team to several victorious seasons and had gained a great deal of respect from the students. Our son, Dave, was in the same class, and he and Levi became best friends.

When school began that fall, Levi was still the quarterback; but something was very different about him, and all the students saw it. He unashamedly confessed Christ and lived a changed life — one sold out and on fire for God.

Among the majority of students that fall semester, however, there was an attitude of rebellion toward the administration. It climaxed and came to an ugly head over one particular issue: Homecoming.

Each fall, our school hosted a homecoming weekend. It included a spirit week during the school days of the week before, a football game, and a special banquet to close out the week. Instead of hosting a dance, like most of the public high schools, we held a banquet that gave the students an opportunity to fellowship, dress up, and have an enjoyable evening. As part of the homecoming celebration, we had the students elect a Homecoming King and Queen for the event. It was considered a great honor to be elected to one of these positions. Not only did the two students get their pictures and names displayed in the yearbook, they also received special honors at the Homecoming Banquet.

In the fall of 1973, we held the election, and the king and queen were chosen. However, before the homecoming weekend arrived, we discovered that the elected Homecoming Queen had been involved in sin.

As president of the school, I was faced with the tough decision of proper discipline. After much discussion with the deacons and school administration, we decided that one of the consequences the girl would face was that we would remove the Homecoming Queen title from her. She would not receive any of the special honors and she would not be named or pictured in the yearbook as queen.

When the students found out, the rebellion in the school multiplied. Parents were furious and lashed out against us, and me in particular. Students vocally and loudly protested that the punishment was too severe. The most vocal of them all was the former queen's sister. She led the students in a vicious attack on me and my reputation as pastor of the church and president of the school.

Despite all this backlash, we held our ground. The former queen herself agreed with our decision, although the rest of her family did not. All of us on staff were greatly concerned about the lack of spirituality in the school. We prayed often for a change and for revival in the school. Then one day, it came.

For our daily chapel messages, I often had staff members or guest speakers preach, knowing it was a great opportunity to have the students hear some wonderful messages from servants of the Lord. Occasionally, we had a student chapel — one with a high school student bringing the message. However, when this rebellion broke out, I decided I would preach the chapel services every day for a while; no guest speakers, staff members, or students.

I remembered what Dr. Bob Jones, Sr., had advised us in the Preacher Boys class in college: "If the rats of sin take over in the ministry, just start shooting down the rat hole with the preaching of the Word of God until the rats come out." So for two weeks, I preached daily on sin and its consequences and the need for repentance and obedience to Jesus Christ.

Finally, I decided that it would be a good idea to have a student chapel. I asked Levi Robinson to preach. He readily accepted and prepared a wonderful testimony of what God had done in his life that summer. I had what I thought was pressing work to accomplish, so I did not attend the chapel service that day. I just went straight to my office.

I was busy working when my phone rang. It was a faculty member who had been in the chapel service. "You need to get over here right away," she said. "Something very unusual is happening."

I ran from the office building over to the school building where the chapel service was taking place. As I entered the door, I was shocked to see the rebellious sister who had so viciously attacked me standing on the platform beside Levi. She was weeping and telling the students how wrong she had been in her rebellion.

When I entered the auditorium, she saw me come in and ran from the platform to meet me. She stopped before me, and with tears flowing down her cheeks, she asked me to forgive her for her rebellion. I immediately forgave her completely. Behind her, a line was forming. There were many other students that came and asked my forgiveness, which I readily gave. Students went to each other asking forgiveness for wrong actions, attitudes, and words spoken about them. Students sought out teachers and told of their need for forgiveness for cheating on tests and homework assignments.

I stood at the back of the room and watched this time of confession, forgiveness, and restoration take place for hours. Chapel was in the morning. By lunch time, everyone was still in the auditorium with no thought about food or classes or anything but seeking forgiveness and praising the Lord for what He was doing.

All the teachers knew that this was *much* more important than the class lectures they had prepared for the day. Classes were canceled and the teachers and administrators stayed with the students in the auditorium. Near the end of the school day, I asked two faculty members to go buy ice cream and cookies for the students to eat before they went home.

After the last student had left, I returned to my office and meditated on what had happened that day. God had miraculously changed the hearts of the hardest of students and had brought repentance and true revival.

The next morning, some students came and asked if they could use one of the rooms during the lunch hour for prayer. We granted them permission and announced it to the students. At lunch that day, many students ate quickly and then went to the separate room to pray. I decided to join them. I saw students in small groups — three or four girls in one place, three or four boys kneeling in another place. The room was filled with small groups of students praying. The revival had not stopped after one day. It was changing our school.

When the church found out about it, it changed the church too. Many surrendered their lives completely to the Lord. Others asked for forgiveness. Others repented of sin and made it right with the people involved. And best of all, the girl who was supposed to be the Homecoming Queen also confessed her sin and asked forgiveness.

* * * * *

OFTEN AFTER a time of great revival in the lives of believers, the fire diminishes and lukewarmness and apathy set in. Such was the case for Silver State Baptist School. A few years after the revival of 1973, the school once again lacked spiritual fervor.

Each year, our school sponsored a tour for our school choir. This particular year, our music pastor, Bob Fox, planned a tour to churches in Colorado, Kansas, and Oklahoma. He asked the youth pastor, Dan Dickerson, to go with the students and have daily preaching for the choir members. When they returned, I could see that something was different. Pastor Fox and Pastor Dickerson both told me what had happened. There had been a revival that had broken out among the choir members.

I asked the choir to sing for Monday's chapel service. We then gave them the opportunity to give testimonies about the trip. During the testimony time, I noted that there was a real movement among the student body as they realized that the choir members really had something happen in their lives while on this trip. Pastor Dickerson preached and gave an invitation at the close of his message, and the students flocked to the front. They knelt at the altar confessing sin and getting right with God. Then many went to teachers and other students and asked forgiveness, telling them of the wrongs that had been done. For the second time in the history of the school, we saw genuine revival.

Again, the chapel service went through the lunch hour and ended with everyone enjoying ice cream and cookies, as well as hearts right with each other and God as they went home from school. And again, our school administration, faculty, and church members marveled at the goodness of God and the work of the Holy Spirit in bringing revival to Silver State Baptist School and South Sheridan Baptist Church.

Chapter 27

BUSES, RADIO, & A LITTLE BIT OF CRAZY

THERE IS NO doubt that God brought revival and blessing to the school and the church, and we got to be part of it.

As we continued to grow in size, our ministries grew, our activities grew, and we were able to offer many more programs in which people could be involved and serve.

We added a deaf ministry in addition to our normal Sunday School classes. As the name portrays, this was primarily for the deaf or hard of hearing. Having grown up with a blind brother, I was very sensitive to making whatever provisions were necessary so that *everyone* could participate in the church. The next ministry added was one for people with special needs, including intellectual disabilities and mental health disabilities. Then we added a Spanish ministry. While each ministry had its own Sunday School class, everyone came together for the morning service — even those in the Spanish ministry. Becasue many of the Spanish-speaking people struggled with English, a man from the church volunteered to translate our services into Spanish. Each Spanish-speaking individual was given a headset linked to a microphone that we set up in a separate room where the man translated the service. It was such a blessing for the people to hear the Word of God in their own language.

When we added the bus ministry, our goal was to reach people, primarily children, in poorer communities, minority communities, and entirely unchurched communities, providing a way for them to hear the Gospel and accept Christ. Our hope was that the children would return home and share the Gospel with their own families and friends.

When we started, volunteers from the church would go into the communities on Saturdays and develop relationships with the people they met. Then they came back with their personal vehicles the next day and offered rides to anyone who wanted to attend Sunday School and the morning service. Before long, the church was able to purchase a few 15-passenger vans that were used instead of the personal vehicles. Little by little, we added to our fleet until we had 17 school buses, three 15-passenger vans, and two pickup trucks. All were used every Sunday on the various bus routes, sometimes multiple times each Sunday just to be able to bring everyone to church who wanted to come.

We started by bringing the bus children into the Sunday School classrooms with the children of our church members. That did not work out as we thought it would, so we quickly moved to separate Sunday School classrooms for the church children and the bus children. We had designated volunteers to work in the bus ministry.

The entire program was a huge success. Each week, we had more and more children come to church. To try and reach more people, we held regular promotional days, such as:

> "World's Strongest Man"
> "World's Largest Ice Cream Sundae"
> "Old-Fashioned Sunday"
> "Roundup Sunday"
> "World's Longest Hot Dog"

The children kept pouring into the church and many accepted Christ as Savior. The largest crowd we recorded was in May of 1975. We had

Old-Fashioned Sunday

a total of 3,238 attend Sunday School — 1,717 in the bus ministry, 1,521 in the other Sunday School classes.

As the years continued and the culture changed, we began to realize that the bus ministry was no longer the most effective way for us to reach our community with the Gospel. Hundreds of church members had faithfully served in the bus ministry; however, we made the difficult decision to stop running the buses and shut down our bus ministry.

Many of the bus children and some of their parents did receive Christ as Savior. Our church had grown as a result of the changed lives, and we had gained many more members. Many people, both adults and teens, were faithful servants in the bus ministry and learned skills that aided them in their future ministries. Two such men were Steve Pettit and Mathew Thomas.

✶ ✶ ✶ ✶ ✶

STEVE PETTIT came to our church in 1977 as a new believer who had just surrendered his life to the ministry. As a rising senior at

The Citadel, the military college in South Carolina, he was one of a handful of our young adults who was not attending a private Christian college like Bob Jones University. But he was growing as a Christian and showed great potential to be used by God. During Christmas break, I suggested he consider returning to Denver after graduation to intern at our church the following summer.

The summer of 1978, Steve interned at South Sheridan Baptist Church. It did not go according to his plans. His parents lived about an hour from the church, so during his summer internship, he lived with Dickie and Sandy Sharbaugh and their two children. Dickie ran our bus ministry and was a ball of energy, *much* different than the military demeanor Steve was used to, so it was a challenge for him. For the first few weeks that Steve lived with the Sharbaughs, Dickie pestered him trying to get him to join the bus ministry. Steve wanted nothing to do with it, but I knew that the bus ministry was an amazing opportunity for people to serve and grow. In many cases, it required serving with little or no thanks from the people being served. I figured that was just the place to have Steve serve and gain some understanding of his very energetic host. So one night after church, I walked up to Steve and told him that I wanted him to be a bus captain. In true military style, he responded with, "Yes, sir!" and began working in the bus ministry the next Sunday. He did not enjoy it, but by the end of the summer, he realized how much he had grown and how God had used the children in those buses to help shape him to become more Christlike. He had really learned how to work with children and serve sacrificially.

Of course, the bus ministry was not the only work Steve did for his internship that summer. I had him spend time in door-to-door visitation; he came with me, Chuck Crabtree, and other pastors or deacons for hospital visits; he preached for junior summer camp and for several Vacation Bible Schools; and he did many other ministry-related jobs.

At the end of that summer, Steve was a different man. We had given him many leadership opportunities. Although he did not always like the task, he still completed it and learned to humbly serve, even when no one else noticed or gave thanks.

That fall, Steve began working on a Master of Arts in Pastoral Studies at Bob Jones University. After graduation in 1980, he was both ordained and married at South Sheridan Baptist Church. Steve and his wife Terry began their ministry in Michigan, and then traveled in full time evangelism for 29 years before he accepted the position as the President of Bob Jones University in 2014.

* * * * *

MATHEW THOMAS was an entirely different story. Mathew, his wife Saramma, and their two girls, Sophie and Sumi, lived in New Delhi, India. In the 1970s, the United States was experiencing a shortage of nurses and requested foreign nurses to come and help fill the void. Saramma was a nurse in India and saw this as an opportunity to make a better life for her family. In 1974, Saramma immigrated to America and began working as a nurse in Denver. She was able to stay with an Indian family who "happened" to attended South Sheridan.

Since neither Saramma nor Mathew had been to America before, Mathew kept his job in India until Saramma felt it would be all right for her husband and the girls to come. Within a year, Mathew and their two daughters, Sophie and Sumi, joined Saramma in Denver.

Just a few weeks after being reunited in Denver, the Thomas family attended a service at South Sheridan. Saramma had been attending with the Indian family and quickly told Mathew, "I think this is the real thing. They preach the Bible here — the whole Bible, not just the Psalms like they do in our church in India." Saramma's father was an Eastern Orthodox priest in India. While that religion is one of the Christian religions in India, they did not profess Christ as the only way for sins to be forgiven and for people to get to Heaven.

The next Sunday, the whole family was back at South Sheridan. Over the course of the next few months, the Thomas family was very dedicated and faithfully attended our services. We were overjoyed when one by one, Mathew, Saramma, Sophie, and Sumi all professed faith in Jesus Christ alone as their only hope for eternity in Heaven and were baptized in obedience with Scripture.*

I never saw a more dramatic change in a man's life than I saw in Mathew Thomas when he accepted Christ. He immediately became a man of prayer. They had already made their basement into a prayer room — now they prayed directly to the God of Heaven and had a personal relationship with Him. At 5:00 every morning, Mathew and Saramma began their day with prayer. They began to live the Christian life with a real zeal for Christ. They attended all the services we held each week — Sunday School, Sunday morning, Sunday evening, Wednesday prayer meeting, Thursday visitation, and any other special services we held. The whole family enthusiastically jumped into almost every church ministry and activity that we offered at the church.

Mathew's first ministry that he joined was the bus ministry. He loved sharing the Gospel and inviting others to attend our services. He became a real soul-winner, and he became one of the biggest advocates for the bus ministry.** He began as a bus captain, but wanted to do more. So he got his license to drive our buses and became a bus driver. His daughter, Sophie, became the bus captain on his bus, and they brought people to South Sheridan to hear the Gospel.

About a year after Mathew accepted Christ, his brother became very sick in India. Mathew decided to make the long journey to India to visit his brother and his other family still living there. When he came back, he told me, "I led my brother to the Lord, but there is no Bible-preaching church for him to attend like we have here. Let's pray for a man to go to India."

---

* Baptism is a huge step in Eastern religions. Whenever someone professes Christ as Savior and is baptized, that person is shunned from and sometimes killed by his or her own family.

** This is where I got the story a little confused. Mathew Thomas was *so* involved in the bus ministry, that I began to think that he had come to South Sheridan as a *result* of the bus ministry. For years, I incorrectly believed and stated that Mathew Thomas was probably the greatest fruit we saw from the bus ministry. That was not the case.

I agreed to pray with him. We knelt down right then and prayed that God would send someone to meet the family's spiritual need.

That very week, Mathew was assigned to go on visitation with Herb Schaeffer. An older couple, James and Joyce Garlow, had attended our service the previous week. Mathew and Herb were asked to visit the couple.

When Mathew and Herb knocked on the door, Joyce answered. She did not even wait for them to introduce themselves or get out one word. Instead, she looked at Mathew and exclaimed loudly, "You are an Indian!"

Mathew and Herb just looked at each other, not knowing what to say or do. Quickly, Joyce recovered her manners and invited them in. But as she led them to the sitting area, she yelled up the stairs, "Honey, come down. An Indian is here."

James immediately came down. Mathew and Herb finally were able to introduce themselves and explain the reason for their visit. James told them that he and his wife had just returned from India. They had been Baptist missionaries there for nearly 50 years, but had been forced to leave the country due to new governmental restrictions on foreign missionaries.

Mathew then told them about his recent trip to India where his brother had accepted the Lord. "There is no church in the area," Mathew said. "Will you join me in praying for God to send someone?"

James quickly answered, "No, I won't."

"Why not?" Mathew asked, taken aback by the man's response.

"Because God already called someone, and he didn't accept the call."

"Where is he? I'll go see him right now!" Mathew anxiously replied.

James pointed his finger at Mathew and said, "You are the man. You should go."

That really troubled Mathew. The next morning around 8:00, my phone rang. It was Mathew. He told me what had happened.

"Last night after talking with the Garlows, I went home and headed to the prayer room in my basement. Saramma came home from work and found me down there on my knees praying. When I told her what had happened, she said, 'Isn't that strange? Today at work, I felt that maybe we should be the ones to go as missionaries.' She joined me and we prayed downstairs for a long time. I do not know what to do. May I come to see you?"

He came to my office, and after a time of prayer, we sat down to talk. "I am afraid that man is right," he said. "But if I am to go, I want to know I have a call from God."

As we continued talking and praying together, Mathew finally said, "You know? I believe it is God's will for us to go."

That settled it. Over the next three years, Mathew went to school and received Bible training. He applied to Baptist World Mission, but made an unusual request — he told them he would not need as much money as an American missionary because he was used to the culture in India already. He could live like the Indians. Mathew and Saramma went on deputation and raised support to return to their native land and start a church there.

On November 5, 1988, Mathew and Saramma Thomas officially left America and moved back to India to become missionaries to their people. Sophie was in her second year at Bob Jones University, and Sumi was a student at Silver State. The Delo family from our church graciously took in both girls and became like a second family to them. Mathew and Saramma wanted their girls to finish their education in America while they began their missionary work in India.

Commissioning Mathew Thomas — missionary to India

I visited Mathew and Saramma many times throughout my world travels, and our church supported them financially and through prayer. It seemed that every few years, we heard about another church that Mathew had started in Kerala, India. It was thrilling. He ended up starting, planting, or helping over 20 Bible-preaching churches in the predominately Hindu country of India.

After Sophie graduated from college, she returned to India and married Santhosh George, a native from India. Together, they began working with Mathew and Saramma, especially by establishing ministries for children such as Vacation Bible Schools and summer camps. They also worked on church outreach activities designed to draw people to the churches in order to hear the Gospel. What Sophie and Mathew had learned in the bus ministry was bearing fruit on the other side of the world.

As her parents aged, Sophie and Santhosh slowly took over the ministry. It was amazing for us to watch and be part of the work God had done. He had used our church to reach a family who had surrendered to the truth of the Gospel and ultimately surrendered to the will of God in reaching the nation of India. And God had used our bus ministry (and really, all the ministries of the church) to help prepare them for meeting the needs of the Indian people.

* * * * *

While the deaf ministry, special needs ministry, Spanish ministry, and bus ministry were all growing and reaching people with the Gospel, our church branched out even further to reach a greater number of people. We did this in a few ways.

The first was through the radio ministry. In 1965, I started a daily five-minute broadcast on the Christian station KLIR — 990 AM. The program was called "Five Minutes with an Open Bible." Before long, I realized that five minutes was not long enough for me to preach my short sermon, so I expanded the program to be ten minutes. That still was not long enough. When KLIR made station changes and switched to KRKS, I made some changes too. We purchased air time on KRKS from 11:45 A.M. to noon Monday through Saturday and called our program, "The Wonderful Life Hour."

When we first started the radio program, I would have to stop whatever I was doing and drive to the local station to broadcast live from their studio. Eventually, we worked with the station to develop a more convenient way for me to broadcast. We built a mini studio in our church offices. It simply had a small table, a little microphone, and the appropriate "ON AIR" lights. The walls were built much thicker than normal and were carpeted in order to deaden echoing, feedback, and any other sounds. My signal would transmit directly to the station where KRKS would take it live at the designated time. It was great! I could be having a conversation at 11:44 A.M., step into the studio, and be broadcasting live at 11:45 A.M.

In the 1970s, we added another radio element — we began broadcasting our services live each Sunday from 11:00 A.M. to noon. It was quite challenging the first few times we tried it, because our timing had to be perfect. But once we all got used to it, no one thought anything about it. At 10:59 A.M., Chuck Crabtree led the congregation in singing the hymn "To God Be the Glory." Then, at exactly 11:00 A.M., the program manager at KRKS would say something like, "And now, we join the following service in progress..." and would fade into our ongoing service.

I quickly learned how to pack a lot into my sermons because I had only 45 minutes until the red light in the back of the auditorium would turn off, meaning that we were off air. Even with the time constraint, I managed to memorize and quote a poem about the Bible each week of 1979. One of my favorites is titled "The Greatest Book."

> This is the greatest Book on earth,
>   Unparalleled it stands;
> Its author God, its truth divine,
>   Inspired in every word and line,
> Though written by human hands.
>
> This is the Volume of the Cross,
>   Its saving truth is sure,
> Its doctrine pure, its history true,
>   Its Gospel old, but ever new,
> Shall evermore endure.
>
> This is the solid Rock of Truth
>   Which all attack defies;
> O'er every stormy blast of time,
>   It towers with majesty sublime;
> It lives and never dies.
>
> —Author Unknown

The radio ministry proved to be a tremendous blessing for many who did not normally attend church or who were unable to attend church due to sickness or age.

Another way we reached others was through *The Mile-Hi Evangelist*. For years, it was a weekly four-page publication full of articles, poetry, upcoming church or school events, reports on the past week's events, goals, verses, pictures, and more. We eventually changed to publishing it monthly because much of the weekly content was already covered in our Sunday bulletin.

The Mile-Hi Evangelist was distributed throughout the country. We sent it to our church members, other pastors, missionaries — anyone who requested the publication received it in the mail.

We also developed materials to help our church grow spiritually. Sparky Pritchard, our associate pastor, wrote an excellent series on the life of David that we used in our adult Sunday School classes. I wrote a daily devotional that we published monthly called, *My Morning*

Manna, to encourage our congregation to read through the Bible each year. The booklets included poems, hymns, passages of Scripture both for personal devotions and family devotions, and a short devotional explaining the passage for the given day.

It was a lot of work, but I loved it! It seemed that God had given me an uncontainable amount of energy. Sometimes, I felt as if I could burst with how much energy I had flowing through me. My days were full of ministry, writing, meetings, radio broadcasts, school chapel messages, hospital visits, home visits, family time, ball games, and other random things that came up. To me, it was not just a job, it was what God had called me to do. To others, it was a little bit (or perhaps a lot) of crazy.

Chapter 28

THE SHENANIGANS OF THE NELSON KIDS

Most people have the perception that the pastor's children must be perfect little angels. Surely they must never act up, misbehave or disobey their parents. Although we worked diligently to train our children to love and follow the Lord and to obey us as parents, we knew our children were sinners. They often showed their sinful nature in their actions and suffered the consequences. We were, after all, just another normal family — and sometimes our kids were just kids.

#1: "Boy, were we ever surprised!"

When I was a little boy, I *fervently* believed in Santa Claus. Every Christmas Day, I was the first one awake and rushed to see what Santa had left in my stocking and what presents I had received. It was magical!

I discovered, however, just three weeks after my 7th birthday — at Christmas — that Santa was actually my dad. I was utterly devastated. Dad was the most honest person I knew. He *never* told lies. I could always trust him to tell me the truth. And he had **lied** to me about Santa Claus!

The discovery of Dad's deception left such a horrific scar on my childhood brain that when Guyla and I found out we were expecting our first child, I told Guyla, "We will *not* have anything to do with Santa Claus. Our children will know from the very beginning that he is not real."

The day Kathy came home from the hospital, I carefully placed her in her crib and whispered, "Kathy, there is no Santa Claus."

Three years later, Kathy and I went to JCPenny in Aurora. I wanted to show Kathy some Christmas decorations and festivities. We were walking around the store looking at the toys when suddenly, Kathy stopped and refused to move. When I asked her what was wrong, she said nothing and just pointed straight ahead.

I looked, and saw Santa Claus walking down the aisle toward us. He stopped and said, "Hello, little girl."

Kathy remained mute.

"What do you want for Christmas, little girl?"

Nothing. Not even a peep.

Eventually, Santa gave up and continued on to a more receptive child. When he had turned the corner and was out of sight, I felt a tug on my pant leg.

"Daddy," Kathy whispered anxiously.

"What is it, Kathy?"

"Boy, were we ever surprised. We thought there was no Santa Claus, but really, there is!"

#2: Footprints of Jesus

During our early evangelistic meetings, when Kathy and John were young, I brought the family to as many meetings as possible. I thought it was good for the people of the churches to meet my family and for my family to be involved in our ministry. Guyla was a tremendous blessing to many ladies along the way. And the kids — well, they were kids.

In one particular meeting, we had just finished singing the last congregational hymn, "Footprints of Jesus," and everyone began to sit down — everyone except Kathy and John who were standing on the pew in the front row. As I began walking to the podium from my chair on the platform, Kathy (4) and John (2), at the top of their lungs, belted out the hymn chorus, "Footprints of Jesus that make the pathway glow" one more time.

Apparently, my beloved children thought the singing should continue — not my preaching.

#3: Mashed Potato Curls

On our 8th wedding anniversary, Guyla and I decided to take the whole family out for lunch with us to celebrate. It happened to be on a Sunday, so everyone was dressed up nicely. Both girls were in beautiful lace-trimmed dresses with their hair in pretty curls. The boys were wearing their Sunday best, hair slicked back and shoes shined. I must admit, I had good looking kids. We went to the Blue Parrot Inn, a nice, sit-down restaurant. We did not eat out often, so this was a special treat!

We had been late getting out from the church service and the kids were famished. Dave was just 17 months and Ruth was 3½ years old. The two of them had not quite learned patience while waiting for food. Ruth was whining and crying because she was so tired and hungry.

After being seated, we asked the waitress to bring us some mashed potatoes and gravy as soon as possible. She brought them immediately, and we set them in front of Ruth so she could begin eating while the rest of us waited for our entrées to come. Much to our chagrin, Ruth promptly picked up the bowl and dumped it on top of her head. Mashed potatoes and gravy slowly dripped off her blonde curls and fell to the floor.

Needless to say, we did not take the children with us for our next anniversary dinner.

#4: "They Just Tasted Good!"

After we left Hoffman Heights, Guyla and I bought a brand new house north of Denver in Longmont. It was a cute little house with large front windows, wood floors, and enough bedrooms for all of us with our family of six.

Shortly after moving in, Guyla discovered some strange marks on one of the front window sills. After examining them more closely, she saw that they were actually teeth marks. The marks were on every single window sill — right at the perfect level for a small child. Kathy and John were missing some of their front teeth, so she knew they were not the culprits. Dave was too little. Ruth — it must be Ruth. We sat her down and asked her about it. Her response?

"They just tasted good, and it was right at the level of my mouth. I just had to!"

#5: Elevator Scare

As a family, we visited my parents' farm often. We made a point to let each child stay for a week or two alone with my parents each summer. The children loved exploring the farm and seeing the animals. Their favorite part of the farm, though, was the big equipment. My dad (a.k.a. Grandpa) loved to take the kids with him on the tractor or have them ride with him in the truck as he fed the sheep in the feed lots.

The new grain silo at Dad's farm

One summer, when John was staying at the farm for his week, he and Grandpa were in the new grain silo that was used to store the food for the sheep. My dad had just installed a new elevator system that allowed him to have access to any part of the silo at any time. The elevator was a type of pulley system. One end of a rope was weighted, and the other end held a platform on which a person could ride up to the top. The person on the platform had to adjust the weights at the other end of the rope according to his weight. If a heavy person used the elevator, he needed an equal amount of weight on the other end of the rope. If a lighter person then came along, he needed to adjust the weights on the other end before climbing onto the platform. Failure to do so would be disastrous and could be life-threatening.

John was small and unaware of the dangers of the improper use of the elevator. He just thought it was cool. My dad told him repeatedly, "Do *not* go near that. Don't climb in that unless I am with you."

John, being a typical boy, did not heed the instructions or warnings. While my dad's back was turned, John climbed in and released the rope that held the elevator car in place. Immediately, the elevator shot to the very top of the silo. It had been weighted for a grown man, not a young boy.

John screamed and my dad wheeled around from what he was doing. John was already at the top and was covered with grain dust. It was a miracle that he was not killed that day. There were many people who did not follow the proper procedures with elevators like that and were thrown to the roof and killed instantly.

Grandpa called Ken who climbed a tall ladder on the outside of the silo. At the top, Ken climbed through a window that was almost the height at which the elevator was keeping John. With Ken's weight on the elevator, they were able to slowly bring it back down to ground level.

John learned a valuable lesson that day — listening to and obeying Grandpa.

#6: "Just as rebellious as ever"

I am a firm believer in disciplining children. It is biblical to do so. Particularly, it is biblical to spank children for disobedience. Guyla and I just could not deny the truths we found in verses such as:

> *"He that spareth his rod hateth his son: but he that loveth him chasteneth him betimes" Proverbs 13:24.*

> *"Foolishness is bound in the heart of a child; but the rod of correction shall drive it far from him" Proverbs 22:15.*

> *"And, ye fathers, provoke not your children to wrath: but bring them up in the nurture and admonition of the Lord" Ephesians 6:4.*

Verses like these guided our decision to spank our children for lying, stealing, or direct disobedience. However, our discipline was **_not_** done in anger and we would **_never_** mercilessly beat the child. We gave a few swats, then turned the child around and talked with him or her. If the child was not repentant, he or she received additional swats and additional talks until there was finally a spirit of submission to the authority of the parents and repentance to God for the sin they had committed.

Each one of our kids knew this method of child-rearing from an early age. So when Dave directly disobeyed Guyla, it truly was not a surprise for him to hear me say, "Go to my room."

Once in my room, I told him why I was spanking him. "The Bible says you are to *'obey your parents in the Lord: for this is right' (Ephesians 6:1).* You disobeyed your mother and that is sin. God commands you to obey."

Yelling in his rebellion still, I bent him over the bed and spanked him. When I turned him around to talk with him and see if his spirit was broken and repentant, Dave yelled, "I'm just as rebellious as ever!"

After more spankings, he thankfully looked at me and said, "I don't think I'm so rebellious anymore, Dad."

#7: "Listen to her, Dad!"

Like my dad, I was a firm believer in hard work for my children. An old proverb says, "An idle mind is the Devil's workshop." So once our children got to a particular age, we required them to have some sort of job. For the girls, it was usually babysitting or housekeeping. For the boys, they chose something a little more active.

John chose to deliver newspapers for his job. Every afternoon, he would pile the newspapers into a basket on his bicycle and deliver papers to the surrounding areas. On Sundays, however, the paper needed to be delivered first thing in the morning. John had a large route to cover, and we had church responsibilities as well. So each Sunday, I would take the car and drive him around to deliver the papers instead. I also insisted that Dave help so we could be finished in time for breakfast and to get to church.

John did his job well and was very considerate of his customers. I was proud of him. He thought that to be a good paper boy on a snowy day, he should put the paper on the porch, not just toss it on the sidewalk or driveway. One particular Sunday, it was snowing quite heavily. As was his custom in this sort of weather, he walked each paper up to the porch. Dave did not have the same convictions or care.

John said, "Dave, don't do that. Don't throw it on the sidewalk. Walk it up to the front porch."

"I throw it on the sidewalks," Dave retorted.

"Well then, quit helping," John replied. "I don't want that. I want it on the porch where it will be easier for people to get."

"I won't do it!"

I saw the argument taking place, so I got out of the car and said, "Dave, do it. John told you and it's his paper route. You need to do what he told you."

"You just can't please that kid," he muttered angrily. "You just can't please him."

"Bend over," I said sternly. Every child of mine knew what that meant — a spanking.

There was a lady across the street who was out on her front porch sweeping off the snow with a broom. "You quit that!" she yelled from across the way.

"He's my son, not yours," I yelled back.

"Dad, listen to her!" Dave yelled in between swats.

I could see that Dave still had his rebellious attitude, so I gave him another swat. The lady saw that and came flying off her porch, broom in hand. She marched across the street, and as I began to give Dave one more swat, she hit me over the head with the broom and knocked me over.

Dave doubled over laughing. "Dad, I'll put them on the porch," he said sheepishly.

A few weeks later, the lady and her husband came to church and became members of South Sheridan. Apparently, she did not remember (or recognize) that I was the one she had clobbered over the head with her broom. A few years later, I ended up preaching both of their funeral services.

#8: BABYSITTING GONE WRONG

Tim was three, and wow, was he ever an active three-year-old. He loved to run around the house making noise and annoying his siblings. But one of his favorite activities as a happy three-year-old was riding his tricycle.

One summer evening, Guyla, Kathy, Ruth, and I had to leave for a school meeting. We left John (13) and Dave (9) in charge of Tim.

"Give him a bath and then put him to bed," Guyla told them.

So they did — kind of. They filled the bathtub, gave him some toys, and then went outside to play basketball with the next door neighbors.

Tim yelled and hollered for help and for someone to get him out of the tub, but no one was there. He had observed his siblings do so many things that he was convinced he could handle this. So he took matters into his own hands, got out of the bathtub and dried himself off.

Then he proceeded to throw the towel over his shoulder and ran outside, stark naked. He climbed onto his tricycle, threw the towel over the handle bars, and rode up to join his brothers. They were not as impressed as he was about his "accomplishment," but they did have a good laugh.

Tim loved his tricycle

#9: "You're ruining my fun!"

I tried to spend time with my family whenever I could. Being involved in the ministry is very busy work, but I believe that family is important too — very important. So as often as I could, I would take the boys (and sometimes Ruth) hunting.

There was a 10-year gap between John and Tim, six between Dave and Tim, so it was difficult to take all three of them at the same time. When Tim was young, I let him come with us but often left him in the car to stay warm while the rest of us hunted. He was a very talkative kid and would have scared the animals away anyway.

When Tim was five, John, Dave, and I went pheasant hunting and decided to take Tim with us. I left him in the car to warm up with the engine running. We were in the middle of the plains in eastern Colorado, near a small town called Wray. We had parked in a field and there were a few other cars nearby, and the drivers of those vehicles were also out hunting with us. It was perfectly safe — so I thought.

After our hunting party had walked through the field hunting for pheasants, we headed back to the cars. When we were in sight of our car, we got the shock of our lives. My car started moving and was headed toward the other cars, and it looked like no one was driving it!

John, David, and I out hunting

I took off running toward the vehicle, convinced it was going to crash into the other cars, with Tim inside. Much to my surprise, my car drove around and between the other cars. When I got closer, I could see the very top of the head of a very blonde child at the steering wheel. Tim pulled up right where I was and stopped the car. I jerked open the door, made sure the vehicle was in park, and grabbed Tim out of the car.

"What were you doing?" I asked him.

"I was coming to pick you up!" he said cheerfully. Apparently, he did not want us to have to walk so far, so he decided to "help."

"Bend over."

"But Dad," he cried. "You're ruining my fun!"

#10: Where there's smoke, there's fire

Tim had an unhealthy fascination with fire and matches. It was thrilling for him to watch things burn. One day when he was just three, he was playing in our living room and started a paper bag on fire. Not knowing what to do, he dropped the bag — onto the newly carpeted floor. The bag burned a hole in the carpet and would have kept burning had not Mrs. Anderson, our housekeeper and daytime babysitter, come to the rescue and put the fire out.

A few years later, he still had not learned his lesson. Ruth and Tim had gone to the nearby mall. When Tim disappeared (which he often did), Ruth got frustrated and drove home. After a while, Tim waited for his sister outside the JCPenny entrance, but Ruth never returned — so he started walking home.

He had seen some kids earlier that week start a fire in a field and thought it looked like fun. For some reason, (we are not sure just how or why), he had matches with him. While walking through the field on the way home, he lit a match. It caught the dry grass and ignited a fire immediately. It was a windy afternoon and a gust of wind took the fire and spread it before he could stomp it out. He had started a prairie fire.

Not knowing what else to do, he ran away and continued toward home. I was on my way home and saw him walking on the side of the road. I stopped and picked him up, not knowing what he had just done. Tim climbed into the back seat of my car.

"Look at that fire," I commented.

Tim said nothing.

As we turned a corner, I saw a vintage car drive by. "Oh," I said, "I'm going to follow him and ask if we can use his car for our Old-Fashioned Sunday in a couple of weeks."

I quickly turned our car around and followed the old car. When it stopped in front of a house, I pulled up next to it. Before I could say anything about using his car, the driver saw Tim in the back seat.

"You!" he said pointing his finger at Tim. "You're the kid that started that fire!"

Shocked, I turned around and asked, "Is that true?"

His face said it all. Instead of asking about the vehicle, I simply thanked the man and drove straight to the fire station. "You will tell these men what you did," I told Tim.

Sheepishly, he confessed to lighting the matches that set the field on fire. The fire chief accepted his apology, but he also wanted to teach him a lesson. He assigned Tim the task of writing a 15-page paper on the Beneficial and Detrimental Uses of Fire.

From then on, we had significantly fewer fires in the house and neighborhood.

#11: SHOPLIFTING

Pastors' children are not exempt from the temptations and difficulties that other children face. Lying, running, hiding, blame-shifting — all are natural reactions when a child steals, whether it is cookies, candy, or in Dave's case, bubble gum.

When Dave was nine years old, he was riding his bike with a neighbor boy. While out and about, they decided to stop by a 7-11 convenience store two blocks from our house, just to look around.

Dave often tried to copy his older brother or John's friends so that he could be "cool" like the older boys. Some of John's friends had told Dave that it was really easy to steal from a convenience store. So when Dave and his friend rode up to the store, Dave told him, "It's really easy to steal here."

They both wandered around the store and picked up a few pieces of candy. Dave subtly grabbed a piece of bubble gum and shoved it into his pocket. His friend was not so discreet. He shoved the gum into his pocket right in front of the watching manager.

The manager did not say a word; he just waited to see what they would do. Both boys grabbed a few more pieces of candy and took them up to the cash register to pay for them. The manager took their money for the items they put forward. When they walked out the door, the man followed them.

"Are you boys going to show me what else is in those pockets of yours?" he asked pointedly.

Sheepishly, the boys pulled the stolen gum out of their pockets.

"Follow me," the manager said, and walked back inside. The boys reluctantly followed.

"We'll pay for it!" they repeatedly offered.

"No, no," the man replied. "My boss told me what to do with boys who steal." He led them to a cooler in the back of the store. "I am to lock you in here and call the police."

And that is just what he did. The police came, let the boys out, and an officer told them, "Get on your bikes and ride home."

The boys immediately obeyed, the patrol car following behind them.

The house of Dave's friend came first, so the officer got our address from Dave and sent him home while he dealt with this boy and his parents.

Dave rode home and saw John out in the driveway folding newspapers for his paper route. He did not say a word to any of us about what had happened. He just quietly started helping John fold the papers.

About 30 minutes later, a police car turned down our street. Dave saw it and immediately ran inside.

I was at home when the police car pulled up in front of our house. "Mr. Nelson," the officer said, "your son stole some bubble gum from the 7-11 convenience store."

As the officer patiently waited, I searched for Dave. I found him hiding behind the couch. "Is this true?" I asked him.

"Yes."

"Thank you for letting me know," I told the police. "I will deal with my son and make things right with the manager of the store."

As the police left, I turned to Dave. His face showed the remorse he felt. "What you did was wrong," I told him. "You know that. Get your money. We are going back to the store. You will apologize to the manager and then pay him for the piece of gum that you stole. And you will not be allowed to have any of the candy you purchased."

"I'm sorry, Dad. I promise I won't do this again," he said sorrowfully.

He quickly obeyed and got his money. When we returned to the store, he sincerely apologized to the manager for his theft and paid for the bubble gum.

Shortly after Dave and I returned home, the other boy's father called me on the phone. He was furious, but not with his son. "Lock a boy up for stealing just one piece of bubble gum? It's such a small thing! Why would they do something like that?" he yelled.

I had an entirely different perspective. "Because what our boys did was wrong!" I told him. "We believe stealing, no matter how small, is stealing. It's wrong. So yes, they deserved to be locked up and then some."

To my knowledge, Dave never did steal anything ever again.

* * * * *

THERE ARE many more stories I could share about the Nelson children and their mischievous "adventures" or sinful disobedience. They were and are sinners, just like the rest of us. And while I did not always get the parenting right, Guyla and I worked hard to instill respect, obedience, and love for God and others in the lives of our children. We definitely had some shenanigans, but I thank God for the privilege of being Dad to some of the best kids in the world.

Chapter 29

THE FAMILY GROWS UP

We had good children. Yes, we had our "moments" with each of them, but really, God gave us five amazing children. From the time they could talk, they were serving with us in the church, traveling with us in evangelism, folding bulletins before the services — they were a help in so many ways and were an integral part of our ministry. It was not simply "Dad's and Mom's jobs" — church was a family activity that required each family member to be a part of it. It strengthened our family as we served side-by-side to build God's church and share His Gospel with as many people as possible.

One of the biggest ways the Nelson children served churches was through music. Starting with the days at Hoffman Heights, Guyla was adamant that our children would have the opportunity to learn an instrument. When Guyla was a little girl, her daddy had saved up enough money to purchase a piano for the family. Guyla had played a little, but between working to help provide for her family and her schooling, she did not have much time to practice. She was determined that our children would learn piano and make time for practicing.

One of our church members at Hoffman Heights told us we should give Kathy piano lessons because she was picking out all the hymns and Sunday school songs on the church piano. "If she doesn't take lessons right away, she will never be able to read music and will be handicapped musically her whole life," the lady told us.

Neither Guyla nor I were very musical, so we did not know how unusual it was for a four-year-old to be able to "pick out" the tunes and play them on the piano. She had that special gift of being able to "play by ear" — she could hear a hymn tune and play it on the piano. We listened to the concerned church member and started Kathy on piano lessons with a widow lady from the church, Beulah Jones. Kathy learned how to read music amazingly well, even though she still picked out new hymns by ear during her practice times.

The music lessons went so well with Kathy, that we decided the rest of the children should take piano lessons too. All of our children continued piano with various teachers until at least high school. Well, all of them except Tim. Tim's piano teacher died after six years of lessons — and that was the end of his piano career.

In addition to piano, the girls both tried stringed instruments. When we moved to Lakewood, Kathy and Ruth both took violin lessons. Kathy really complained about the teacher. She just did not like her. I knew that the teacher probably was not a great teacher, but I also did not want our children to disrespect authority. I believed (and still believe) that parents should support the position of the teacher and make their children respect authority. So I told Kathy that the teacher was right and she needed to submit and obey, and fix her attitude.

She did fix her attitude, but the problems with the teacher continued. Kathy became convinced that the problem must be the violin, so she switched to cello and finally the flute, which she loved.

Ruth tried violin for one year but, like Kathy, decided that she enjoyed flute better as her second instrument. Both girls really loved playing the piano and excelled at it. Kathy and Ruth played both the piano and the organ at church, and regularly played for church services and evangelistic services whenever I traveled.

Kathy began piano lessons at 4 years of age

Ruth tried violin for a short time

Dave was excellent at trumpet

The boys also branched out with their musical abilities. All three of them took trumpet lessons from Byron Jolivette, the director of the Denver Junior Police Band, and they really learned to play well. He was a demanding instructor who was a stickler for technique.

Music came naturally to John, and he excelled at anything musical that he set his mind to. Dave had to practice a bit more, but took his practicing very seriously. He was usually the first child awake, and used that to his advantage. He took great pride in perfecting his bugle call at 6:00 A.M. every morning — inside the house and directly below our bedroom! Early morning bugle calls were *not* appreciated by his siblings!

Tim also played in many trumpet groups at school and became proficient on the instrument. However, his trumpet career ended just like his piano career had. After six years of trumpet lessons, his trumpet teacher died — and that was the end of his musical career. We joked that no one would take him for any other instrument or vocal lessons because after six years, he or she would die.

In addition to music, most of our children enjoyed sports — the boys particularly. John especially enjoyed playing baseball, but he also played basketball and soccer in junior high and high school. Dave loved anything that included "ball" in the name — football, basketball, baseball — and Tim played basketball and football. Every Friday or Saturday, there seemed to be some game to attend. Guyla went to every single game. I went as often as I could, but many times, church responsibilities held me up and I was unable to be there for the games. It became easier to go to the games once we included sports in the activities of Silver State Baptist School.

John loved baseball

John had started playing baseball in his elementary school years and developed into an incredible player — first base was his favorite position. He worked extra hard to earn his place on teams because they were determined by grade, not age, and he was a year younger than most of the boys on his team. He absolutely loved baseball. Once he reached junior high, however, the games were scheduled on Sundays instead of on Saturdays, so I insisted that he quit the team. Sundays were for resting and worshiping God, not for playing baseball games.

Despite all of the crazy activities with ball games, music lessons, music practices, church activities, and homework, we made time for some key family activities. The boys' favorites were downhill skiing, hunting, and fishing. Ruth even joined us on a few of the hunting trips!

On one particular hunting trip, we had a bit of a scare. I was with John and a few other men up in the mountains near Steamboat Springs. It was elk season in mid-October, so we loaded up our rifles, rented a few horses (so we did not have to walk so far), and set up camp. On the first day, we rode around looking for the elk and saw some roaming in the trees. John and I rode our horses toward them, but John got ahead of me. I called to him, but he was too far ahead to hear me. Finally, the timber got so thick that I stopped, tied my horse to a tree, and started walking back toward where we had seen the elk. I could hear the animals around me, but I neither saw nor heard any sign of John. Every once in a while, I heard the elk rushing and saw glimpses of them, but I never saw them clearly enough to take a shot. I figured John was nearby and that was why the elk were rushing. So I just kept following the elk back into the forest, waiting for a chance to get off a shot.

All of a sudden, I realized that I was all alone. John was gone, and no one else in our hunting party was nearby. *I should head back to camp,* I thought to myself. I was high enough on the mountain that I could see the lake where we had set up camp. So I set off in that direction and started walking back.

Without warning, I hit a dead end. I was stuck in a box canyon with no way out but up. Right about that time, it started snowing. I was bundled up with a hat, gloves, and a nice warm winter jacket. I looked up the face of the box canyon and started climbing. It was exhausting. I had to stop several times, and by the time I reached the top, I was sweating profusely. Somewhere, I had heard that it is extremely unwise to take off your coat in cold weather when you are perspiring. Apparently, the sweat will freeze and chill the body, and eventually you can do nothing anymore because you are so chilled and fatigued. So I kept on my coat.

I finally made it back to the place where I had tied my horse. He was gone. I could see the lake again off in the distance, so I kept walking. I walked and walked and walked. I do not know how far I walked, but I finally made it to the edge of the lake. A man saw me and said, "Where are you going?"

"We have a camp up here somewhere in that area over there," I said as I pointed. By this time, I was not really sure exactly where the camp was, but I thought it was in that direction. I was so exhausted I could barely stand.

"Get in my car, now," the man said.

I got in, and we drove in the general direction I had pointed. Sure enough, there was the camp. John, Levi Robinson, and all the others were circled up around the fire. John heard us drive up and jumped to his feet.

"Where were you?!" he cried. "Where have you been?"

"I was lost up there—" I started.

"You're white as a ghost," he interrupted. "You need something hot in you *now!*"

"Here," he said as Levi handed him a mug of hot chocolate. "Drink this now."

I obeyed, despite my dislike for chocolate. I was too weak and exhausted to argue.

John turned to Levi and said, "We need to get him to lower elevation immediately. Can you take my dad back to Denver? Since I'm in charge of this hunting trip, I feel like I need to stay with the rest of the group."

Immediately, I was helped into Levi's truck, and we drove the four hours back to Denver. When I arrived at the house, Guyla rushed me to a hot bath and insisted I drink *lots* of fluids. After five days, the color finally returned to my face, and I was able to be up and about. When John came home with the rest of the men, he told me that someone had found two other men who had gotten lost that same night. They had taken off their coats and frozen a bit. They were not able to get out until the next morning, and by the time someone found them, one man's legs were so badly frozen that they had to amputate them.

When I heard that, I realized just how close I had come to death. And John, with his quick, level-headed thinking, had saved my life.

* * * * *

Our family dentist and his boys taught John and Dave how to ski in the late '60s and they loved it. Every time it snowed, they were begging me to take them up for a day on the slopes. There was only one problem: I did not ski. However, it was a great excuse to spend time with my kids, so I would drive them up to a resort — the favorite was Winter Park — and while they skied, I studied in the lodge. Sometimes, they finished skiing before I finished studying, so they would have to wait for me.

We did this for a couple of years, but eventually I decided that it would be a good idea to try and ski *with* the boys, not just take them. It was quite comical as they watched their 45-year-old dad taking a ski lesson at Arapahoe Basin. I have always been a tall, lanky guy with very long legs. The boys frequently doubled over laughing as I fell and rolled head over heels. After my one lesson, the boys picked up the teaching and within no time at all, I was zipping down the intermediate slopes. I loved it! It was a wonderful way for me to unwind and relax from the various stresses of ministry. I found that when I was skiing, I could not think of anything else besides where I was going to turn next.

I loved spending time with my kids. I loved listening to them play their music and watching their ball games. I did *not* enjoy listening to them complain about the practicing, and I often encouraged Guyla to let them quit their instruments. She refused, however, and I am glad she did.

* * * * *

EACH OF our children accepted Christ as personal Savior at a young age. There was no greater joy than to know that no matter what happened in the future, each child would be with our Lord in Heaven when death came. And there were several times over the years when some of them almost *did* die.

Easter Sunday, 1968, was one of those times. On most Sundays, we drove two vehicles to church so that Guyla did not have to wait on me after each service. After the evening service on that particular Easter Sunday, I took Dave and Tim with me in my car. Guyla was following us in her car with Ruth and John. Kathy was already in college and was not there.

Dave had recently broken his leg while skiing, so he was in the back seat with his casted leg stretched out on the car seat. Tim sat in the front next to me, even though he was only six. Seat belts were add-on options in all vehicles until 1965. Our car was much older than that, and like most families at that time, we considered seat belts non-mandatory for us or our kids.

To get home, we only had two right turns: one from Ames Street onto Mississippi Avenue, and one from Mississippi to Upham Street. Ames Street was one block away from Sheridan Boulevard — it was a little shortcut that we took each week. I pulled up to the stop sign at Ames and Mississippi, and Guyla stopped directly behind me on Ames Street. I looked both ways. There were no cars coming in either direction, and the traffic light at the intersection of Mississippi and Sheridan was red. I made the right turn onto Mississippi.

No sooner had I turned into my lane when two vehicles, racing side-by-side on the two-lane road, ran the red light at Sheridan and sped straight toward my car. They were drag racing and had no intention of stopping for me. One of the trucks slammed at full speed into the back of my car. The force propelled my car across the ditch into a huge tree on the opposite side of the ditch. The impact was so great that the car actually bounced back across the irrigation ditch and landed on the shoulder of the road. The trucks did not stop or even slow down — they continued racing down the road.

Guyla, Ruth, and John watched all this transpire as they waited at the stop sign on Ames. Horrified, they quickly drove the 200 feet to where we had landed.

Since none of us in my car had been wearing seat belts, all three of us had been thrown around the inside of the car. Dave had been thrown into the front seats and ended up on the floor in the back seat. Although he was moaning and holding his leg, he seemed to be okay. Tim had been thrown onto the floor and squished under the front glove box and had been knocked unconscious. I had hit the bridge of my nose on the steering wheel and was bleeding quite profusely — but I did not know I was bleeding. I leaned over and picked Tim up. He was covered in bright red blood. "Lord, no! Please, no!" I cried. "Please spare my son!"

Guyla rushed up just then. "Look at Tim — he's unconscious and bleeding to death!" I cried.

There was a bar across the street. "Honey, go in there and call an ambulance," I told Guyla.

"I do *not* go in places like that," Guyla said emphatically.

"But Honey, Tim will bleed to death if you don't! Go call the ambulance."

"I will *not* go into that bar!" she exclaimed.

Just then, a man walked up to the scene. He had overheard the last part of the conversation. "It's okay, ma'am," he said kindly. "I have a phone in my car. We can use that."

This was 1968. **No one** had phones in their cars. To this day, we do not know whether that man was an angel or an actual man, but we did use his car phone to call an ambulance. The emergency personnel came and looked at Tim and then at me. "He's just fine," they told me as they took Tim. "You're the one who is bleeding. Looks like you broke your nose!"

Tim, Dave, and I all rode by ambulance to the hospital and got checked out. Dave had re-broken his leg in the accident. Tim had a concussion, so he missed school for several weeks. I had, in fact, broken my nose and also had a minor concussion. Our car was totaled, but we were all alive and made complete recoveries.

Someone else had seen the accident happen and had followed the two trucks to get license numbers. The drivers were held accountable for the whole ordeal.

* * * * *

Although our kids faced a few near-death experiences, I must say that I probably had more of them than most people ever knew. Sometimes, being the preacher is a dangerous job!

One snowy Saturday in 1975, I received a phone call from a lady who attended our church. She was a believer, but her husband was not. They were having some marriage issues and she wanted me to come to visit them at their home.

I picked Tim up from his basketball practice and told him that I needed to make a stop at this couple's house before going home. This was nothing new for any of my kids — they were used to waiting for me while I made last-minute visits.

We pulled up to the house and I left Tim in the car listening to the Denver Nuggets basketball game on the radio. I rang the bell and the door opened about two inches. I was staring straight down the barrel of a double-barrel shotgun. "Come in," the man holding the gun said.

I obeyed.

He motioned to a seat and commanded me to sit down. So I sat. I figured I should carefully follow instructions with someone pointing a gun at me — even though I really did not think the gun was loaded.

I calmly asked the man and his wife some questions. The man did not like that. "I should just kill him right now," he said, carelessly waving the gun around as he spoke.

"Oh, don't do that," I said. "It would leave an awful mess. And I would very much like to live."

He calmed down slightly, so I asked another question. Again, I got the same response: the suggestion that I be killed on the spot. I was not scared because I was convinced that there were no shells in the gun. Yet, I could not be completely sure, so I just did as I was told and tried to convince the man to sit down and have a rational conversation.

Meanwhile, Tim was still in the car, oblivious to anything happening inside the house.

We were getting nowhere. Finally, I suggested that we call Ed Byrd. He was a good friend, a deacon in the church, and, best of all, he was an officer with the Denver Police Department.

"Fine," the man grumbled. I picked up the phone and dialed the number. The man jammed the gun into my back. "But you tell him no lights! I don't want any lights or sirens going when he comes."

"Hi Ed, this is Pastor Nelson," I said when Ed Byrd answered the phone. "I'm sitting here with a man who is holding a gun on me. We'd like you to come help us out. No lights or sirens. Just come." I gave him the address. Then we all sat down and waited.

The room in which we were sitting had windows that were higher up than most — you could not see out of them from a seated position. The curtains were closed on the rest of the windows in the house. Pretty soon, flashing lights start reflecting on the ceiling.

"I told you to tell him no lights!" the man jumped up shouting. "I'm going to kill you right now!"

"Wait!" I responded. "I did tell him. Let's just look out the windows and see what it is."

We both peered out the windows. It was a snowplow driving by with its orange oscillating lights going. I breathed a deep sigh of relief.

A few minutes later, Ed Byrd showed up — without his sirens or lights. The man slowly calmed down. Pretty soon, Ed Byrd said to him, "You know, I really don't like this situation at all — the gun pointed right at the preacher. Why don't you let me have it?"

To my amazement, the man handed the shotgun right over. At the end of the brief conversation, I told Ed, "Break open the gun. I don't think there are any shells in it, but why don't you check?"

He broke it open and two shells hit the floor. That is when I really got scared. I never did get into the marital counseling session with them. But after that scare, I really did not mind. As much as I enjoyed helping people, I also enjoyed coming home to my wife and family.

* * * * *

One by one, the kids left home for college. Kathy graduated from Silver State Baptist High School in 1967. That fall, she enrolled in Bob Jones University to study piano performance. We were sad to see her leave home, but overjoyed at her decision to further her musical abilities for the Lord. It was definitely different around the house without her. Tim started kindergarten that same fall, becoming part of the first kindergarten class at Sheridan Baptist Elementary School. Kathy's absence left a big hole in the music at the church, but Ruth, as a freshman in high school, took over the piano playing at church.

Two years later, in 1969, John began his freshman year at Bob Jones University. At that time, the school did not let students have two majors, so he declared his major as Bible but took all the courses needed to major in music with a trumpet principal.

In the spring of 1971, Ruth graduated from Silver State Baptist High School as valedictorian, and Kathy graduated from Bob Jones University. That fall, as Ruth began her studies in piano performance at Bob Jones University, Kathy began work on her master's degree. She was also working simultaneously on her MRS degree. During her senior year, she had met a man who piqued her interest. They met the same way Guyla and I had met — as host and hostess at a dinner table. His name was Sparky Pritchard. Two years after dating, they were married at South Sheridan Baptist Church in the summer of 1972. I had the wonderful privilege of officiating the ceremony.

A year later, John graduated with his degree in Bible and shortly thereafter married Gale Shallenberger, a girl he had met while at school. I had the privilege of marrying them in her church in Greenville, Southside Baptist Church — the same church where Sparky and Kathy were members. John and Gale stayed in Greenville for a year, but then in June of 1974, John, Gale, and her mother Frances, moved to Lakewood and became staff members for South Sheridan. John took over all the music for the church and many music classes in the school. Gale and Frances both worked in the offices of the church and school. It was a true delight to see how they were being so greatly used by God and were such a blessing to us and our ministry.

In April of 1975, we were delighted to welcome our first grandchild into the world: Alana Pritchard. We were even more delighted when a year later, Sparky, Kathy, and Alana moved from Greenville to Denver to a house a few miles away from us. Sparky had agreed to become an assistant pastor at South Sheridan. His primary role was leading all Sunday School activities, overseeing the Bus Ministry, and teaching the Calvary Class — the largest of our adult Sunday School classes.

Both of our children and their spouses did a tremendous job serving the people of South Sheridan Baptist Church. It truly warmed our hearts to be serving side-by-side with our grown children. Tim, only 14 years old, thought his niece was the greatest thing ever — and vice versa. When the Pritchards moved two doors up the street from us, Tim

Sparky and Kathy Pritchard, 1972

John and Gale Nelson, 1973

frequently walked over to watch or play with Alana. We all loved doting on the first grandchild.

The same year Alana was born, Dave was finishing his freshman year at Bob Jones University. He decided to study accounting as he did not feel like God was calling him into full-time ministry. I was completely fine with that. I did hope that one day God would call him to be a pastor, but I also knew plenty of businessmen who were very active in their churches and engaged in ministry. Ministry is something every Christian should be involved in, not something only for pastors. Besides, if God had not called him to be a pastor, I was definitely not going to push him to be one. That would be going against God and His revealed will for my son.

Out of all the kids who attended college, Dave was the most faithful and diligent in writing letters home. Nearly every week, we received a letter from him. Of his own accord, he mailed us his tithe check to place in the offering each week.

For the first few years, Ruth had even surpassed Dave with the letters she sent home. But school got busier for her, and the practice hours demanded more and more of her time. She was required to practice over 14 hours every week in addition to her other classes. She still wrote letters as often as she could, and we loved to hear how God was using her and growing her spiritually and educationally.

One January, I was speaking at a Stewardship Banquet in Muncie, Indiana. I met the young man who was leading the singing. His name was Fred Coleman, and he did an excellent job with the music. After one of the services, he came up to me and introduced himself.

During the course of conversation, I discovered that he was going to be auditioning to enter graduate school at Bob Jones University, hoping to begin that fall.

"Oh, I have a daughter there," I told him.

"Yes, I know!" he replied eagerly. "Kathy Pritchard. She's supposed to be playing for my audition."

Fred and Ruth Coleman, 1977

Dave and Robbi Nelson, 1979

"No, no, no," I said, shaking my head. "I have a *single* daughter there, Ruth. You need to look her up when you get to Bob Jones."

He took my advice and two years later, they were married at South Sheridan. They started off their marriage by working at Grace Baptist Church in Muncie, Indiana. Fred was the music pastor there and also taught music in the Christian school.

Two years later, the Nelson family grew again. Dave had met a southern girl from Georgia who had stolen his heart. He finished school in just seven semesters, graduating in January of 1979. While he waited for his fiancée, Robbi Wilcoxon, to finish the school year, he took a job with an insulation manufacturing company in Indiana. That summer, we all headed to Lebanon Baptist Church in Roswell, Georgia, where I was delighted to perform Dave's and Robbi's wedding ceremony. After their honeymoon, they moved to Colorado where Dave had accepted a position at an accounting firm.

In addition to the wedding that year, we were delighted to have two more granddaughters enter the world — Alyssa Pritchard and Kristin Coleman.

The following year, Tim graduated high school. He was one of seven students who were the first to attend Silver State Baptist School from kindergarten all the way though 12th grade.

Tim also went to Bob Jones University and followed Dave's example studying accounting. He finished his bachelor's degree in just three years, and despite the many attempts of girls to turn his head, he graduated unattached. From there, he went on to further his education at Duke University School of Law. Tim graduated from law school in 1986 and returned to Denver where he began working as an Assistant Attorney General in the appellate section of the Colorado Attorney General's office. Because of a budget funding fight with the Colorado legislature, the Attorney General's office lost funding and was forced to cut positions in 1987. As the newest attorney hired, Tim was one of the first to be cut. At that time, Guyla's company, Mile-Hi Publishers, was requiring more full-time attention, so Tim took over the operation of the company and helped her fulfill her dream.

The same year Tim was cut from the Attorney General's office, he met a girl. In 1986, Monica Stoeckmann moved from Wisconsin to Colorado to take a 4th grade teaching position at our school. Tim and Monica both attended the singles class at church and got to know each other. Two years and many dates later, they were married at South Sheridan. The end of the school year is very busy for everyone, teachers especially. Monica decided to throw a wedding into the craziness — they were married the day after school ended for the summer. It was our fault, actually. We told Tim and Monica they had two choices: have the wedding ceremony without us, or have it the last weekend of May. We were going to Russia for a month and could not postpone the trip. So, the end of May it was — and what a beautiful time to get married in Colorado. I had the privilege of performing this ceremony too, complete with Tim sweeping Monica off her feet for the kiss and promptly holding out his hand for the bribe his best man, Dave, had promised him.

It was a joyous time for sure and we were delighted to welcome Monica into the Nelson family. Yet there was an unspoken pain from four years prior — a pain that had changed our entire family.

Tim and Monica Nelson, 1989

Chapter 30

FAMILY MATTERS

ONE OF THE hardest years of my life was 1985. All of our children except Tim were now married with families of their own. Kathy and Sparky lived two doors up the street with their three girls, Alana, Alyssa, and Ashley. John and Gale were living in California with their son, Chad, and Gale's mother, Frances. Ruth and Fred and their two children, Kristin and Miles, had recently moved from Michigan to Illinois. Dave and Robbi were living about 15 minutes away from us with their girls, Aimee and Alli. And Tim was in his second year of law school at Duke.

It had been a rough few years for Guyla and me. Now that we were in our sixties, things that used to be easy for us became a little more difficult. We did not slow down our activities or responsibilities, but it seemed that some things just took more time to accomplish than they had before. We stayed extremely busy with the church and school. I was active in the politics of the county, state, and country. The curriculum that Guyla had written was starting to be widely distributed. Every day, she received dozens of phone calls either ordering curriculum or asking advice on how to homeschool children. It was a lot for us to handle, and that was just on the work side of things.

On the family front, we had our children and eight grandchildren whom we wanted to visit as often as possible, even though they lived in three different states. At the same time, we also became increasingly busy caring for my parents. In 1983, my Dad turned 90 years old and finally retired from working on the farm. The responsibilities had grown to be too much for him, and all of us boys insisted he take better care of himself. He frequently battled colds and pneumonia, going to the hospital many times.

Shortly after Christmas of 1984, the doctors discovered a gallbladder problem that required surgery. The surgery finally took place after the new year, but he did not survive the operation. He died on Thursday, February 28, 1985, at the Poudre Valley Hospital.

We held the funeral service for him at First Baptist Church of Fort Collins. It was an incredible honor to preach my dad's funeral, but that day was one of the most difficult days of my life.

Two hours before the service was to begin, John and Gale asked if they could meet with Guyla and me in their hotel room. We were hopeful that this meeting would help us repair the tension that had been present in our relationship over the past few years.

John and Gale had moved to Denver in 1974 in order for John to assume the leadership of the music program in both the church and the school. Gale's mother, Frances, had also relocated to Denver to be near them. Both she and Gale were a great blessing to the ministry.

John was one of the best music directors we ever had. Under his leadership, the students excelled: the choirs, the brass, the pianists. He was amazingly gifted in both music and teaching.

Over time, however, we began to realize that there was tension developing in our relationship with John and Gale. We were not quite sure why. Guyla and I were so busy that it honestly was very difficult to make time for family — something I regret to this very day. I never appreciated what I had until it was taken away from me.

In 1980, Guyla and I were privileged to help John and Gale adopt our first grandson, Chad. He was a delight to all of us, and John and Gale were overjoyed to have a child of their own.

We were thrilled for them and saw them as much as we could. But the underlying tension continued to increase. Within six months of Chad's adoption, John accepted a teaching position at a school near San Diego, California, and moved his family there.

During the next several years, we wrote letters back and forth, but we did not see them. Our hearts ached and longed for restored fellowship. We just did not understand what was going on. We had not seen them since they had moved to California.

We longed to hear from them and were overjoyed whenever a letter would come. On several occasions, John wrote long letters sharing the blessings God was pouring on his family, the lessons he was learning through his time with God in prayer and devotions, and the information he was studying as part of his master's degree. It thrilled our hearts to hear of the growth he was experiencing as God continued to work in and through him and his family.

But the letters also included sharp rebukes — which I needed! Over the 30 years in which I had been preaching, I had seen firsthand, preachers who did not accept criticism, but instead became defensive. As a result, the preachers had become hard and unteachable — not a Scriptural attitude at all. Thus, early on, I had determined that I would accept any and every criticism and not become defensive. Whether the advice was given graciously or poorly, I was confident that there was something I could learn from it. This was no different with the rebukes I received from my son.

This difficult situation had been going on for five years and had only gotten worse as time had passed. Now, two hours before the funeral, we arrived at the hotel room hoping for restoration. Instead, they completely severed all ties with us and later with the rest of the family. They told us, "Don't write us, don't call us, don't visit us — nothing!"

Thirty minutes after hearing this, I got up and preached my dad's funeral. It was the hardest sermon I have ever preached. I saw my mother overcome with the grief of losing her husband of 64 years. I watched Ken weep over the loss of the strongest man he had ever known, and Don sorrow over the protector Dad had been for him throughout the years.

The tributes to Dad were sweet. Many friends and family members shared how incredible he had been. When I got up to speak, I shared how Dad had always been a moral person, but how as a child, he had given his life to the Lord and placed his trust in Jesus Christ alone for the hope of eternity in Heaven. I told how Dad, in his later years, had come back to his childhood faith and had been active in the church, First Baptist Church — the very church in which I had been saved.

Following the service and burial, the extended Nelson family, including John and Gale, gathered at the farm house where Mother still lived. John and Gale informed his siblings that they were cutting off all communication with Guyla and me and that they did not want communication from his siblings either. No one knew what to say.

Since that night, neither Guyla nor I have seen John or Gale.

* * * * *

WORDS CANNOT express the agony of losing a son, not to death, but to his conscious choice to disown his family. What could I possibly have done differently? Was I so blind to my own sin that I had pushed John and Gale away?

The tears would not cease to flow. Memories flooded our minds. Guilt over things we should have done differently as parents was at times overwhelming. We cried out to God through tears and prayers like we had never done before. In the distress of our souls, we found comfort in verses such as Romans 8:25–28 and Psalm 109:4.

> *But if we hope for that we see not, then do we with patience wait for it. Likewise the Spirit also helpeth our infirmities: for we know not what we should pray for as we ought: but the Spirit itself maketh intercession for us with groanings which cannot be uttered. And he that searcheth the hearts knoweth what is the mind of the Spirit, because he maketh*

> *intercession for the saints according to the will of God. And we know that all things work together for good to them that love God, to them who are the called according to his purpose.* —Romans 8:25-28
>
> *For my love they are my adversaries; but I give myself unto prayer.* —Psalm 109:4

We wanted desperately to know what the outcome would be of all this. We prayed for John, for Gale, for Chad. We longed to see them, to speak with them, to just hear their voices, to see Chad grow up. We begged God daily for the opportunity to be reconciled.

I began writing letters, though never sending them per John's instructions. Five days after Dad's funeral, I wrote the first letter.

> *Dear John, . . .*
>
> *I just want you to know we love you. That will never change. . . .*
>
> *You are right — I need to grow. I have believed that I had grown in recent days. But this has driven me to prayer and the Word where by His grace I shall grow more. . . .*
>
> *All day long my mind has been racing back to fond memories with you as a boy and a young man. They are such fond memories. Oh — how we enjoyed you — how you were a blessing to us in so many ways! Thanks! Thanks!*
>
> *You seemed to love to hear preaching of the Word of God. You were able to grasp Scripture truth, often — so quickly. My heart is lonely for you today — but thank God there are blessed memories. And I guess we will live with just them for sometime to come — but be sure we will cherish them. Thanks for having blessed our lives — even if now you have broken that relationship — I suppose we will sit often as I am doing now crying and remembering. But we love you — I cannot find it within me to grow bitter.*
>
> *We are concerned. I hope someday we will have fellowship here again. Whenever you want to open the relationship again — our arms are wide open.*
>
> *Love,*
>
> *Dad*

I continued writing letters and stored them in a file folder, hoping that one day I could hand the letters in person to John, Gale, and Chad. But as the days turned into months, then years, then decades, the file simply continued to grow. Almost every day, Guyla and I prayed for our children and grandchildren by name, asking God to bless them and keep them. We also asked God to restore our relationship with John and his family — something that God has chosen not to do.

I made so many mistakes as a father, and through this experience with the disunity of my family, I realized that the biggest mistake of all was that I had just been too busy — too busy for my kids; too busy for my wife; too busy for my grandkids; I was so focused on the ministry that I missed the greatest ministry in front of me: my family.

It was a tremendous wake up call for me. I altered my schedule. I was still busy, but I became more intentional about spending time with those around me. We made it a priority to visit our children and grandchildren.

I will forever regret the time I did not spend with my most beloved family. I wish I could go back and do it over again — do things differently. Yet, God does not allow us that privilege sometimes. Sometimes, we do not get second chances.

March 4, 1985, was a day that forever changed my life. It was the day I buried my dad and lost my son. It changed my ministry. It changed my family. I was humbled like never before that day. Broken. But the Lord sustained me and grew me through that time.

My heart still aches for my son. I long to see him, to be reconciled and have fellowship restored. I have prayed for John and his family often and consistently since the last time I saw them — that God would bring reconciliation. Yet God has not seen fit to answer that prayer for 35 years now.

* * * * *

Following my Dad's funeral, my brothers and I deliberated how best to help Mother. For the time being, we determined that she could stay in her house at the farm. Ken and Donetta lived about one mile up the road in their own house, so they could check in on her frequently.

That worked fairly well for a little over a year. During that time, she was in and out of the hospital with aches, pains, broken bones, and other age-related problems. Despite our incredibly busy schedule with the school and church, Guyla went up to the farm once a week and spent a day or two with Mother.

As Mother's health declined, we brothers talked again. Before he died, Dad had made me promise to take care of Mother — and she did *not* want to be in any sort of assisted living facility. Guyla and I decided to have her come to live with us.

She moved into our Lakewood house in early December 1986. She was recovering from surgery to repair a broken hip, and we simply took her to our home from the hospital. Dave, Robbi, Tim, and some friends from church helped us move much of our furniture into Tim's house and our garage. Then, we all drove up to the farm to bring Mother's furniture down and move it into our house. It was an exhausting weekend, especially for us 63-year-olds! But by the end of the weekend, our house had a new "normal" with Mother's furniture in place for her to enjoy.

She was a delight to have in our home. Guyla took such good care of my mother and treated her as her own mother. We all knew that Mother would likely die within the next few years given her failing health. Guyla's biggest fear was that she would be alone at home and find Mother dead in bed. She prayed earnestly that that would not be the case.

One morning, about two months later, Mother got up, baked cinnamon rolls with Guyla, and reconciled her checkbook. Then she went for a walk around the inside of the house with Guyla at her side. While walking, Mother told Guyla that she was very tired and wanted to rest. She slowly collapsed into Guyla's arms and Guyla gently laid her on the kitchen floor. She died right there in Guyla's arms.

Guyla's fear had come true in the sense that she was alone at the time. But she witnessed such peace in Mother's final moments that she would not have wished it any differently.

A few days later, we held the funeral service for Mother in Fort Collins. In true Colorado fashion, there was a blizzard that day. I had the privilege of officiating her service in the same church in which we had held Dad's service.

I had tremendous peace and comfort preaching her service. I *knew* where she was — I know where she *is*! Sometime in her later years, Mother had finally surrendered her life and trusted in Jesus Christ as her Savior. Her life had changed instantly. She and Dad had read the Bible together after breakfast each day. She became much more kind to people. She regularly attended church, the First Baptist Church in Fort Collins. She still worked as hard as ever, but she had a new purpose. She was born again. And she finally understood my passion for souls.

At her funeral service, I shared her testimony. I preached the Gospel. I told of her love for us boys, her dedication in rearing us to be the best we could be. With tears, I told how she had died. "But the day she died, February 25, 1987, she entered Heaven's gates," I said. "She is now living with God in Heaven where she will be for all of eternity. Praise the Lord!"

Mother left such a legacy that five months later, when Dave and Robbi had their youngest daughter, they named her Anna Marie Kate in honor of my mother.

Chapter 31

Fundamental Opposition

It started in the mid-80s, but I should have known and seen through the issues long before. Jack Hyles was a contemporary of mine, born just three years after me.

When the Baptist Bible College of Denver* began in 1952, the school elected Sam Bradford, pastor of Beth Eden Baptist Church, as its president. A decade later, the school had a new president: Dr. Jack Hyles. He lived in Hammond, Indiana, and visited the college once a month. He realized that he needed someone local who could run the school in his absence. Apparently, he thought of me, even though we had never actually met.

I was at home flat on my back recovering from my first back surgery. Jack Hyles and Paul Seanor, a good friend of mine, came to visit me, completely unannounced. Jack Hyles was the president of the college and Paul Seanor was the chairman of the board. They walked into the house, and Guyla led them to my bedroom. That was the first time I met Jack Hyles.

"We'd like you to be the vice president of the school," Hyles told me. "I've heard that you are well known nationally and are an energetic, soul-winning preacher. I cannot run a school from over a thousand miles away. I need someone here locally to manage the place. I will

---
* Now a branch of Faith Baptist Bible College and Theological Seminary in Ankeny, Iowa

come once a month for three days and speak in chapel and review the management of the school."

"Well, thank you," I replied. "I'll pray about it and let you know."

"Oh, you don't need to pray," he immediately said. "I already told you what to do."

I should have immediately realized the danger and sin of what he had said — he was making himself to have more authority than God — but I did not. He had the dangerous philosophy of "I told you what to do, so do it. You don't need to pray and ask God. He is telling you what to do through what I've said."

No preacher should *ever* have that mentality. God speaks through His Spirit to an individual. Sometimes He will use what the preacher has said to provide direction, but it is *always* confirmed in the heart of the individual through the voice of the Holy Spirit and God's Word.

After praying about it over the weekend, I agreed to become vice president of the school, but after six short months, significant changes took place. Many on the board were so opposed to Jack Hyles that they demanded his resignation. Primarily, they disliked his strong evangelism. When he resigned on a Friday afternoon, Hyles looked over at me and asked what I was going to do. I did not know exactly what I should do. I prayed about it and realized that the board would soon dislike me for the same reason they disliked Jack Hyles. On Monday morning, I also resigned.

Jack Hyles and I became friends and I had him speak at South Sheridan a number of times. However, in the mid-80s, that all changed.

Carl Herbster was a good friend of mine and a pastor in Kansas City, Missouri. Every year, he hosted a Christian education conference. Part of the conference included a question and answer time specifically for pastors. Jack Hyles and I were both asked to speak and then answer questions from the audience.

Before it came time for the question and answer session, I suggested to Carl, "Jack is much better at answering questions than I am. Why

Fundamental Opposition

don't we just have him do it? I'll be in the audience and he can be the one to answer."

Both men agreed to the recommendation, so we began our question and answer time with me in the audience and Jack Hyles on the platform.

After a few questions, someone asked, "If there was a preacher who got mixed up with another woman and had an affair, what should happen to him and his ministry?"

"You know," Hyles said, looking around, "Ed Nelson is supposed to be up here with me answering some questions. Why don't we give that one to him? Ed, where are you?"

I stood up and said emphatically, "The man should be removed from the church immediately. He has disqualified himself from the ministry and should never be a pastor again." I sat down.

Just a few questions later, another person asked a similar question regarding a pastor and some inappropriate relations with a female staff member. Again, Jack Hyles looked at me and said, "Ed, why don't you take that one?"

I stood up and said the same thing, "The man should resign immediately and the staff member should be fired. They have both sinned and the pastor is no longer blameless. He is disqualified from the office of the pastor."

That happened *five* times in the course of *one* hour. Each time Hyles was presented with a question regarding sexual immorality and the office of the pastorate, he turned to me and told me to answer the question.

Following that service, I went to Carl. "Did you see what happened in that last session?" I asked. "Five times Jack was asked the same type of question. Each time, he asked me to answer the question. And those were the *only* questions Jack handed off to me the entire time."

Carl was just as surprised and disappointed as I was. "I have made a decision today," I told him. "I will never again share the same platform or preach anywhere that Jack Hyles is preaching."

Two weeks later, I received an invitation from a Colorado church asking me to preach. "We're having Jack Hyles and would love to have you too," the pastor said.

"I'm sorry, but two weeks ago, I made a conscious decision that I will never again be on the same platform as Jack Hyles," I told him, explaining what had just transpired in Kansas City.

That decision cost me broken fellowship and friendships for many years with many people, but I knew that I had made the right decision and I would not turn back.

In 1988, the world's perception of Jack Hyles changed. Rumors started flying that he was having an affair with another woman. I heard these rumors and wondered, but I did not talk about it. I had no facts, just rumors.

The rumors kept flying. I kept out of it, but I wanted to know the truth. In years past, I had preached many times with Jack Hyles. I considered him a friend, and I was concerned for him. So I wrote him a handwritten letter dated May 20, 1988, telling him that I had heard the rumors and wanted to give him the opportunity to address them directly. I specifically wrote it by hand because I did not want anyone on my staff to know about the rumors I had heard.

When I had not received a reply from him four months later, I sent another handwritten letter. One of the missionaries we supported had written Jack Hyles a letter and received a response. Still, no letter came for me. On March 22, 1989, I wrote a third letter. This one, I let my secretary type.

> Dear Brother Hyles:
>
> In May of 1988 I wrote you a handwritten letter asking you whether accusations I heard were true. I have never had an answer to that letter. . . .
>
> Believe me, I wish the very best for you and long for the gifts you have to be used to the glory of God. I weep over the stories that I

have heard. I am not verifying that they are true, but I do have difficulty understanding why you could not write me.

Finally, four months later — 13 months after my first letter — I received a reply.

> Ed:
>
> I doubt very seriously if this letter will interest you, because it is the truth, but I feel I must write it at least once, and I assure you I will not write you again.
>
> In case you are interested, the truth is as follows:
>
> - In my entire life I have had one woman and one woman only, and that is the mother of my children. . . .
>
> - I have never in 42 years of pastoring kept anybody on my staff whom I knew was guilty of immorality. When such could be proved, they have been asked immediately to resign. It is fair to say, however, that to me an accusation does not mean guilt, and a person is innocent until he is PROVED guilty. . . .
>
> Whether you believe it or not, the above is truth. To whatever degree you have spoken otherwise, you have spoken without proof, and you have lied.
>
> Sincerely,
>
> Jack Hyles
>
> P.S. There is no need to answer; I will not read it.

I was sorely disappointed when I read his letter. He never answered my questions. In my mind, it confirmed that the rumors were true, and indeed it was discovered shortly thereafter that my friend, Jack Hyles, *was* involved in an immoral relationship. His son, son-in-law, and others in churches across the country followed his example. Sexual scandals came to light for months and years after the affair of Jack Hyles came to light. It broke my heart.

I wish I had seen through the carnality and sin of Jack Hyles long before I did. I truly did receive many blessings from him, as did *many* people. He preached at South Sheridan many times. But all throughout the years I had known him, there were some things on which I vehemently disagreed with him — especially his view of women and his own pride. After that conference with Carl Herbster, I had never invited Jack Hyles to preach for our church again, and I had refused to speak on any platform or participate in any conference where he was also speaking.

It turned out that the rumors were true. Once his sin and immorality were exposed, the results were heart wrenching to watch unfold. His sin not only ruined his church, but it also ruined hundreds of other churches. *Many* Hyles-model churches discovered their pastors were having immoral affairs as well. Many churches were torn apart. Even more families were devastated. And worst of all, Jack Hyles had convinced thousands in his congregation into thinking that he and these other pastors had done absolutely nothing wrong.

It was incredibly sad for me to watch someone who had been an icon of Independent Fundamental Baptist churches be destroyed by his own sin. Satan had won and succeeded in tearing down a great leader and damaging the reputation of all Independent Fundamental Baptist churches in the minds of many.

I lost many friends over my stance against Jack Hyles. Yet, I was determined to live by the Word of God, not denomination or religion. I did not care who the person was or claimed to be. If *anyone*, liberal or conservative, committed sin that was clearly contrary to the Word of God, I would stand against them. I had a Biblical basis for my stance too. 2 John 9-11 tells believers to not have anything to do with a person who rejects the doctrine of Christ, yet proclaims to believe it.

I had stood against Billy Graham and the ecumenical evangelism movement in the 60s and again in the 80s. His liberal theology promoted and was supported by churches that did not believe in Jesus as the *only* way to salvation and had crusade leaders who refused to even pray in the name of Jesus. I now stood against Jack Hyles in 1989. He falsely believed that his conservative, "fundamental" theology licensed him to engage in whatever sin he desired — in this case, years of an immoral relationship with another woman. That was *not* what true Independent Fundamentalism was, is, or ever should be. That was not true Christianity.

Chapter 32

Politics

Before I received my calling to leave the farm and become a preacher, the only other career I desired to have was a career in politics. I aspired to a position of power and influence and followed local and state politics closely. At the age of 19, I was asked to speak at Republican county conventions. I could speak well, even though most of the time I did not know what I was speaking about. The Weld County politicians were waiting for the day I turned 21 so I could start my career as a county commissioner.

When I was called to preach, however, I abandoned all political ambition and threw myself wholeheartedly into ministry preparation and work. I left politics to the politicians and did not get involved other than voting. I registered as an Independent, even though I usually voted for the Republican candidate. Yet, even in that, there were some elections that I just did not see as important, primarily the school board elections and other county official positions. I followed the politics of the day, but I just did not want to get involved. I was under the impression that politics and Christianity were opposites. Voting was enough for me. Until, one day, my mind was changed.

In the early 1970s, a good friend and fellow preacher, Al Janney, called me. He wanted to start an association of Christian schools across the country, and he wondered if I would be willing to help him. He called a few other pastors, one of them being Wayne Van Gelderen, who also agreed to help.

Al had already started the Florida Association of Christian Schools, but he wanted to take it to a national level. I was asked to be on the executive board and immediately began working on gathering the support of Christian schools in Colorado. On November 30, 1972, we gathered in Dallas, Texas, for what would be known as the first recorded board meeting of the American Association of Christian Schools (AACS). In that meeting, Al set forth the question: "Where is the separatist organization, on a national level, that will champion our cause?" We established that the AACS would provide its members leadership, legislative protection, and high-quality educational programs.

Within a few months of establishing the AACS, we had enough Christian schools in Colorado that agreed to band together and form the Colorado Association of Christian Schools (CACS) — the state level of the national organization. Within the decade, this organization proved to be key in keeping the freedom of Christian schools in the state of Colorado — something that politicians tried to take away.

As part of the executive committee of the AACS, I attended the annual meetings in Washington, D.C., each February. In 1975, U.S. Representative John Conlan of Arizona — a Christian man — hosted a meeting in Washington, D.C., for Christian leaders. About 40 men attended including Jerry Falwell, Sr., pastor of Thomas Road Baptist Church and president of Liberty University; Bob Jones, Jr., president of Bob Jones University; W. A. Criswell, pastor of First Baptist Church in Dallas; Myron Cedarholm, president of Maranatha Baptist Bible College; and Theodore Epp, director of Back to the Bible Broadcast. The executive board of the AACS also attended.

When Congressman Conlan spoke, he stated, "We need to try and save America. Christians need to get involved in politics."

This was a tremendous shock to me. I had not been involved in politics at all, thinking it was unwise to mix Christianity and politics. And this man, who was a successful politician as well as a committed Christian, was telling all of us that we *should* be involved. And not only that we should be involved, but that we could *really* make a difference in our country. I was very convicted.

When I returned home to Colorado, I read in the paper that while I was in Washington, D.C., there had been a school board election in my county, Jefferson County. Only two percent of the county's registered voters had voted. I had not voted, and for the first time, I saw the importance of it. *Two percent decide who the school board members will be?* I thought. I decided I should have been there. I should have voted.

So a few days later, Guyla and I went to the Republican headquarters in Jefferson County. To the lady who greeted us, I said, "We haven't been involved in politics, and my wife and I have just been convinced that we should be more involved. We would like to register as Republicans so that we can be involved in the primaries and everything else. What do we do?"

"Well," said the lady, "we would be happy to register you!"

As we filled out the forms, the lady spoke up again. "I just looked up your precinct and they don't have a committeeman — the chairman of the precinct. Would you be willing to do that?"

I knew nothing about it, but I said, "Sure, I'll do it. Tell me what to do."

"You will be the man in your precinct that we contact regarding elections," she explained. "You will act as the link between our party and the voters."

It sounded simple enough to me, and from my early days of political ambition, I had seen that starting at the grass roots was the way to go.

They asked if I knew of a woman who might like to be the committeewoman, so I recommended Frances Shallenberger, the mother-in-law of my son John. Frances agreed, and we now had two from our church who were involved in politics.

The next Sunday, I told the church what I had learned from the Washington meetings, as well as my decision to become a committeeman. "I wonder if you would go to see if you could become a committee chairman or chairwoman too."

Many in the congregation took my advice, and registered at the Republican headquarters in several counties including Denver, Jefferson, Arapahoe, and Douglas. Within a few weeks, 60 members became precinct committeemen or committeewomen in Colorado counties.

Other members of our church began attending the precinct caucus meetings. Together, we elected delegates to the county, district, and state conventions. We began making an impact in the politics of Colorado. Our church became known as a powerful political machine in Jefferson County and Colorado politics.

At one point or another, almost all the conservative politicians who were running for office visited one of our church services. They came to me and asked if I would help them get the votes. So I formed a committee which interviewed each politician who came to us. The committee included me and four or five other men including Ed Byrd, John Mitchell, Chuck Schindel, and several others.

That is how I met Bill Armstrong. He had already served one term in the Colorado House of Representatives, becoming the youngest member of the State House, and two terms in the Colorado Senate, serving as President of the Senate both terms. Like most politicians in Colorado, he had come to our church asking for our support. Because his political values aligned with the Bible, we supported his campaigns.

In 1972, Bill Armstrong was elected to the U.S. House of Representatives. Sometime during the next year, Armstrong came to me

Ed with Bill and Ellen Armstrong

and told me that he had accepted the Lord as his personal Savior. He told me that a dentist from Alabama had gotten involved in politics and had come to Washington, D.C., to witness. The man had come to Armstrong's office and said he wanted to talk to him about Christ.

Armstrong did not really want to hear it, but agreed to have dinner with the man. At the end of the dinner, Bill Armstrong accepted Christ, and his life changed forever.

Along with Bill Armstrong, I met with *many* other congressmen and congresswomen, senators, county officials, state officials, and other politicians who were running for office.

One day, a man who was running for governor came to see me. Our committee met with him, asked him questions, and after a while discovered he was pro-choice. He supported abortion. Immediately, we told him, "No, we cannot support you. Your policies aren't right, so we will not support you. We believe aborting babies is wrong and sinful."

A week later, he resigned from the race. In the newspaper article that covered the story, he said that there was a pastor in Jefferson County who told him the church would not support him. The paper said something to the effect of, "If you can't have that pastor support you, you can't win the election."

Even though I became very involved in politics, I was extremely careful not to bring the state into the church. I knew many preachers who got involved in politics and then preached about it non-stop. I did not let it become an obsession for me. Nor did I tell my people which candidates to vote for or which party to support. Instead, I informed my congregation with pamphlets, and I kept preaching the Word of God.

We put out fliers saying who the candidates were and what their policies were. We told our congregation what to look for in a candidate. "We are not going to tell you how to vote," I would tell the people, "but vote! It's your privilege and responsibility as a Christian and as an American citizen. Vote! Look at the policies and vote your convictions."

And our church did! One Colorado news reporter stated that our church's conservative influence was "a force Colorado Republican moderates will have to cope with for some time." The convictions and votes of the South Sheridan Baptist Church members changed the politics in Denver for many years.

* * * * *

In 1984, when President Reagan was running for his second term, I was elected as a delegate to the Republican National Convention in Dallas, Texas. After that experience, it was enough to make me decide never to do that again.

Tim was in his second year at Duke Law School. He flew to Dallas and met me for the Republican National Convention. It was an honor to be there, and we learned a lot. However, the biggest impression I came away with was what Dr. Bob Jones, Jr., had told me 40 years earlier. Politics is just putting props under something that is going to fall anyway. Republicans, Democrats, Independents, none of them are going to solve the nation's problems. The place to solve problems is with the Lord.

I felt terribly out of place at the convention. There was much drinking and drunkenness among the other delegates. There were off-color jokes and comments that left me very uncomfortable. I was honored to be there and represent Colorado Republicans, but I was very grateful to come home.

One good thing that came out of the convention, though, was that I met a Jefferson County Sheriff by the name of Harold Bray. He was a Christian, and a few weeks after I met him, he and his wife showed up at South Sheridan for the services. "We like what you're preaching and what is going on here," they told me after several Sundays. "We are here for you."

A little while later, he asked me to dedicate the new Jefferson County Jail and County Building in Golden, Colorado. I spoke and dedicated

Politics

the building. Then together, Sheriff Bray and I cut the red ribbon to officially open the building.

* * * * *

A Note to Future Generations…

I encourage Christians to become involved in politics, at least to vote and to know what is going on. I try to learn the names of all those running for office and try to follow them. If God has called you to a career in politics, be the best politician you possibly can be, but realize that you will have some serious battles to face — battles between your country and your God. Start in the grassroots system, the caucuses and precinct meetings.

Above all, keep the Lord in first place. Recognize that political parties are not going to solve the world's problems. Only Jesus can. We live in a sin-cursed world and according to the Bible, evil will get worse and worse (2 Timothy 3:13). The nations of the world will go progressively farther and farther from God.

Take a stand for what is right. Take a stand against homosexuality. Take a stand against abortion. Take a stand against the crime and violence. Take a stand against the world's mindset that there is no absolute truth. There is! It is the Word of God. You can trust it and depend on it never to fail you.

The end of the world is coming. God tells us that evil will get worse and worse, and we see signs of that all around us — mass shootings and suicides, natural disasters, pandemics, men and women flippantly using God's name in vain and cursing, the glorification and explicit portrayal of sexual relations outside of marriage, and the LGBTQ movement. These signs are a manifestation of mankind's hatred of God and love for immorality. Eventually, God is just going to say, "Enough."

Be faithful until that day comes. And whatever you do, stand for the truth of the Gospel of Jesus Christ and the righteousness that can only be found in Him. We do not know when Christ is coming, but "*even so, come, Lord Jesus*" *(Revelation 22:20).*

Chapter 33

She Kept Her Word

By the mid-1970s, there were between 20 and 30 Christian schools that belonged to the Colorado Association of Christian Schools (CACS). Each year, we held an annual convention somewhere in the state. It was a great time of fellowship, and our schools really banded together to form a substantial group of private school influence in our state.

In 1977, we were notified of some new rules that the Colorado State Board of Education was trying to pass concerning all non-public schools. The rules would have made it necessary for us to close our schools because these new rules violated what we stood for. And the state was going to make us abide by its new rules. The state expected us to quit, and this was their motive. Only they did not account for the political influence the schools and churches in the CACS had.

I got the churches and schools together and said, "We're going to fight this."

The state had set a date for the school board to vote on these new policies. There were five members on the Board of Education at the time: Robin Johnston, Jacquie Haughton, Bill Graham, Allen Lamb, and Mary Feilbert.

Allen Lamb was from Greeley and went to the same church I had attended as a boy — one that did not preach the Gospel. As a boy, Allen and I had been good friends, but after I was called to preach, I rarely saw him. Now, nearly four decades later, he was one of the five on the Board of Education — the same board that was trying to pass the rules that would threaten our schools.

I began organizing churches and schools to petition their school board district representatives to vote "No" in the meeting, but I also decided to take some personal action.

I contacted Mr. Lamb, and he asked me to come see him. I explained the reasoning behind my opposition and just what these new rules would mean to our schools.

"Could I go to some of your schools?" he asked.

"Sure! Come anytime."

He visited Silver State and a few other Christian schools in our area. "You know," he said after his visits, "I can understand why you're fighting us. I don't agree with these rules either. I can see you ought to stand against us."

So he agreed to stand with us when it came to the vote. After the visits, he publicly announced that if he had grandchildren in Denver, he would put them in Silver State Baptist School because they would get a better education. He also talked to one of the other board members who also agreed to stand with us.

Two of the other three were opposed to us and had no desire to meet with us. They only wanted to pass this ruling that would end up shutting down all Christian schools in the state.

The last one, then, was Jacquie Haughton. She was a Republican who had just recently been elected to the board.

In those days, I was active enough in the political realm that candidates would come by and ask to visit with me and ask for my support. She had come to the church asking for our support to be elected to the Board of Education in the 1976 election. I had asked her, "What we want to know is where will you stand regarding the Christian schools?"

She had replied, "I will always stand with the Christian schools."

"Well," I had said, "if that be the case, we will put our support behind you." And we did. We publicly promoted her, and she was elected to the office — a six-year term.

Now, we were in the midst of this battle between our schools and the Board of Education. The board had invited the public to come and express themselves before the board members voted. Representatives from churches and Christian schools across the state came to be part of the meeting and hear the verdict.

In reading my Bible that morning, I had read Proverbs 21:1, *"The king's heart is in the hand of the Lord, as the rivers of water: he turneth it whithersoever he will."*

Our group met before going into the meeting room, and I quoted that verse. "Let's take that verse as our verse today," I said. "The king's heart is in the hand of the Lord and He is able to turn it."

We concluded with a time of prayer and then filed into the hearing room. We had so many people in the room that we overcrowded the entire space — we could not get everyone into the room that had come. Our people had really shown up!

"We have to adjourn and go to another room," they said, and they moved the meeting to a much bigger room at the old Supreme Court building. We overflowed that room as well. People were standing along the walls, and others who could not fit were standing outside the room and down the hallways. There was not a seat left in the entire room, so I sat on the floor, right in front of the board members' chairs. I was going to speak, along with other CACS members. There were also some out-of-state speakers who had come, one of whom was the head of a national Christian organization.

After we had all spoken to the board and presented our case, it was time for the vote. Allen Lamb and the other man voted "no." "We are opposed to these regulations."

Two members voted "yes," in favor of the regulations. Now it came down to Jacquie Haughton.

I was sitting right in the middle of the floor, and she was sitting in the middle seat on the platform. I fixed my eye right on her; she could see me very well.

She began to moan and shake her head back and forth. "Oh, oh, oh, oh, this is difficult!" We waited for three or four minutes while she made up her mind. Finally, she looked at me again and said, "No."

The place went wild. When she voted no, that stopped the regulations from taking effect. The Christian schools in Colorado were safe.

Several people came up to me afterwards and said, "We know how you won. It was that you brought in the man who is the head of a national Christian organization. He spoke and that helped her make up her mind."

"No," I said. "I'll tell you what helped us. One day, Jacquie Haughton came to our church seeking our support for her candidacy. We asked her, 'If there is any problem with the state, will you stand with us?' She said, 'I will.' The Lord turned her heart like I read in Proverbs 21:1 this morning, and she kept her word."

Chapter 34

SHOWERS OF BLESSING

G OD OFTEN WORKS through people, bringing about His will through the actions of others. He is sovereignly working behind the scenes, but He uses the brains, the talents, the thoughts, and the actions of people to do what He had planned all along. How it is that people have a free will and yet are directed by God at the same time, I do not understand. But I know it happens every day.

There are times, however, when God works the extraordinary, the miraculous. Many people discredit God by saying, "That was a freak thing." Or, "Wow. What a coincidence!" But there are just some things that cannot be explained other than, "It was God."

During my first semester at Bob Jones College, I had come across the book written by E.M. Bounds, *Power Through Prayer*. After reading this book, I had determined, as a freshman Preacher Boy, that I was going to pray and believe that God would work the miraculous. And He has — multiple times. He has moved rain storms, demolished well-established towns which were not receptive to the Gospel, and healed individuals — He healed me! I have seen Him provide funds when there were none to be found. All throughout my life, I have seen God work the miraculous. And sometimes, the miracles were accompanied by showers.

* * * * *

IN JUNE of 1981, John Mitchell invited Tim and me to go with him, his three sons, and his two sons-in-law on a fishing trip to Alaska. It was prime king salmon season, and Tim and I were thrilled to be on this trip with our friends. After flying into Anchorage, we boarded a float plane and flew inland about an hour up the Yentna River where we found our reserved fishing lodge.

The fishing lodge was located in a remote spot on the bank of the river and was accessed only by float plane or boat. It was beautiful! We stayed in some log cabins which surrounded a main lodge where we ate our meals. The property also included a shower-house, a generator building, and several other outbuildings. Small metal barrels, which contained the year's supply of aviation fuel, were set on their sides and stacked in a pyramid along the walls of the generator building. The entire property was surrounded by trees which ranged in height from 6 to over 60 feet tall. And, of course, the river surrounded it all, bringing in a variety of wildlife and activity — especially salmon.

We had a great time fishing and spending time in the Alaskan sunshine. Summers in Alaska were much different than any of us were accustomed to. It was "dark" — more like dusk — for only three hours each night. As a result, time had no meaning for us. We fished when we felt like it, slept when we were tired, and ate when we were hungry. There was no set schedule. "Just relax!" John had told us.

I went out early one morning with Tim, just the two of us. He caught one fish, then another, then another. "I haven't caught anything yet!" I said. "Not even a bite on the line."

"Here, try my pole," Tim said. We switched poles, and immediately, he caught another fish — on my pole.

We switched sides of the boat. He caught another one. I was getting more frustrated by the minute. Finally, we called it quits. Tim had caught 6 or 7 fish. I had caught zero.

A few days later, I was taking a shower after lunch. (Like I said, time did not matter to us on this trip.) Tim and Max were out on the river

Showers of Blessing

Left to right: Me, Jeff Musgrave, Tim, John Mitchell, Sam Mitchell, Randy Jaeggli, Tom Mitchell, and Max Mitchell

fishing. Jeff had just showered and was blow-drying his hair. The others were on the shore, loading up to go fishing. All of a sudden, from inside the shower house, I heard a KA-BOOM, and the lights went out. *Well, that's strange,* I thought.

Since I was almost finished with my shower, I turned off the water, dried off, and got dressed. I went outside to see what had happened, and oh, what a sight met my eyes!

The boom I had heard in the shower was an explosion. One of the diesel-run generators had caught fire. As I walked outside, I heard shouting and saw everyone clambering into boats. "We have to get out of here!" the lodge owner was yelling.

I turned and saw a column of fire billowing from the generator house. The flames themselves were up 15–20 feet in the air. The fire was growing larger and more ferocious by the second. We all had seen the aviation fuel right next to the generator house and knew how flammable it was. Any moment now, the flames would reach the aviation fuel and blow the entire property to pieces.

I ran from the shower house toward the shore. The lodge owner and one of his staff members were the only ones left. They were in the last boat waiting for me. The boats were relatively small — only three or four people could fit in each one. Three boats had pushed off into the river and were mid-stream. The lodge owner and one other person were standing on the beach watching the fire (and anxiously waiting for me to just get in the last boat).

"Where are we going?" I yelled as I approached the lodge owner.

"Down the river to get a phone. Our phones are out, and we've got to call the fire department."

"How long will it take to get there?" I asked.

"45 minutes."

"You can't!" I cried. "This is your livelihood. We can't just leave."

They stopped and just stared at me standing stubbornly on shore.

"We can't wait 45 minutes," I insisted. "The fire will get to those tanks. It will blow up and everything will be gone."

"We're going to pray," I said. I did not wait for a response from the others. I simply knelt right there on the shore and prayed.

"Lord," I began, "We don't want to have this camp destroyed and all the buildings ruined. Lord, would you stop that fire? Intervene right now and put a stop to that fire. Thank you, Lord."

The others were too surprised and terrified to close their eyes while I prayed. They told me afterwards that while I was praying, they literally watched the flames go down. A few minutes later, the 20-foot flames were completely extinguished — all of us watching in awe and amazement. After waiting a couple of hours for the area to cool off, we surveyed the damage. Aside from the burned generator, nothing else had caught fire. Every single barrel of aviation fuel had mushroomed out on each end. We could see that at any second, that aviation fuel would have exploded. God had miraculously saved us and the lodge and had answered my prayer.

* * * * *

Showers of Blessing

W<small>EDDING CEREMONIES</small> are a normal part of pastoral duties, and I conducted many weddings throughout the years. I performed the wedding ceremonies for many couples from the church — for each of my children to their spouses, for many Silver State graduates, and for many young people from the church. So it was no surprise to me when Becky Hunt, a long time member of South Sheridan, and David Mullennex, a man who had recently been saved, baptized, and joined the church, asked me to perform their wedding ceremony.

For the previous year or so, Dave had been attending our church, and I had seen the relationship between Becky and Dave grow. I had met with them both and given advice and premarital counsel.

The wedding date was set for August 22, 1981, at 2:00 in the afternoon. It was to be held outside in the Pastoral Gardens on the church grounds, a gorgeous place designed and landscaped for beautiful outdoor weddings. But *many* people, including Becky's mother, Guyla, and I, expressed our concerns about an outdoor wedding in August — and with good reason.

In Colorado, especially in late August, it is almost guaranteed that there will be a thunderstorm around 1 or 2 o'clock in the afternoon. Several of us recommended that they move the wedding inside the church, but Becky insisted it be outside in the Pastoral Gardens. Plans went forward, and we agreed to keep the wedding outside, all of us praying for clear skies and warm weather.

Saturday, August 22, we woke up to cloudy skies and an unusual steady drizzle of rain. This was no quick storm that would dump rain and then pass on. This storm was here to stay for the day.

The bridal party continued getting ready, hoping and praying for a break in the storm, and finally we got one. Although it remained overcast, the drizzle stopped. We dried off the chairs we had set up on the lawn and brought out the church organ, covering it with a canvas to protect it in case it started raining again.

I had a daily radio broadcast at 11:45 A.M. each day, including Saturdays. I was in my office that morning preparing to go on air when I heard a loud clap of thunder. I finished the 15-minute radio program and rushed outside. Large black clouds were coming in from the west. Our unusual rainy day was now a full-fledged thunderstorm. We were in for a downpour — a real gully washer.

I was not dressed for the wedding yet, so I drove the mile and a half home, dressed quickly, and was just putting on the last shoe when I saw a flash of lightning immediately followed by a clap of thunder. I dropped the shoe, ran to the window, and saw lightning flashing every few seconds. *Oh my!* I thought to myself. I immediately prayed, *Oh Lord, we can't have this. We are all set up and rain like this will ruin the ceremony and the organ. We must not have it.*

I quickly put on my shoe and headed over to the church. The family, the groom, and the groomsmen were meeting together in one room. The bride and bridesmaids were in our office building, a former house that was at the edge of the Pastoral Gardens.

I went and prayed with the groom and groomsmen and prayed that God would stop the rain. For some reason, at the end of my prayer, I said, "Thanks, God, for stopping the rain." Then while they took their places, I went to the bride and bridesmaids to pray with them.

Becky was close to tears when I arrived. "Pastor, how can I go out with it raining like this?" she cried.

"We're going to pray," I said firmly. We all bowed our heads and I prayed, "Lord, we don't need the rain. We must not have it. We are all set up for this wedding and it's too late to move back indoors. Please don't let it rain."

Then, for some reason, I said again, "Thanks, Lord, for stopping the rain. Amen." I did not intend to say that either time, but I did.

I looked up at Becky and said, "You can go out now."

"But Pastor, it's still raining. Hard!"

The Mullennex wedding
Photo courtesy of Dave Mullennex

"Open the door and it will stop," I said. Why I said that, I do not know. But someone opened the door, Becky stepped out, and instantly, the rain stopped.

All the guests had been gathering under a canopy we had set up for the reception. Others waited in their cars. When the rain stopped, we gathered a few men together, quickly dried off the seats again, uncovered the organ, and began the ceremony. We had not one drop of rain during the entire service. We could see it raining south of us, north of us, west of us, and east of us. But it was not raining where we were. In fact, when Becky came down the aisle, the sun broke through the clouds and a sunbeam shone right on the aisle as she walked down.

I performed the ceremony as planned, just a little quicker than I had planned or prepared. But I did everything that was necessary, and we remained dry for the entire service.

I announced, "Mr. and Mrs. David Mullennex," and the newly married couple proceeded to the designated spot outside for the receiving line. We were just about to finish the receiving line when I saw the rain marching across the field. By my judgment, we had about three minutes before the wall of rain was upon us. I yelled for everyone to rush under cover. We grabbed the gifts and cards and anything else that would be ruined by the rain, and brought it inside. Some men quickly moved the organ indoors. The bride and groom and bridal party rushed into the office, and everyone else gathered under the canopy or in their vehicles. No sooner did everyone reach cover than the skies released the rain — it was a total downpour.

The photographer, a member of the church, came up to me and said, "I'm sick about what you did."

"What do you mean?" I asked.

"You prayed for the wedding. You prayed for the receiving line. But you didn't pray for the pictures. Now, I have to take them inside. And we were going to have such nice outdoor pictures!"

* * * * *

IN ADDITION to hundreds of weddings, we were also engaged in *many* building and advancement projects for South Sheridan Baptist Church. Starting with the Miracle in '61 campaign, our church growth never stopped. We had built the new educational building and then purchased adjoining pieces of property. We renovated the existing buildings, but within a short amount of time, we were once again bursting at the seams. We needed the current auditorium space to be turned into classrooms. Thus, we needed a new auditorium — one that could seat our congregation of over 1,000 people.

As part of our financial budget, we set aside a certain amount of money in a building and advancement fund. We had about $10,000 in the fund, but we desperately needed more money in order to start the auditorium project.

This was the same year that I had determined I would take cold showers every morning simply as a matter of self-discipline. So one Friday morning, I was taking a cold shower and was praying while I showered quickly — after all, the water was only 60 degrees! "Lord, what are we going to do? How are we going to get that building?" All of a sudden, it seemed to be impressed upon me, *why don't you go ahead and start the building?* We had a little in the building fund, but it would not do much. It seemed that the Holy Spirit impressed on me, *why don't you go ahead and start and watch what God does?*

I called the deacons together and told them that God had impressed upon me that we needed to get started on the auditorium. Two days later, during the Sunday morning service, I told the congregation my experience and what I believed the Holy Spirit was impressing upon me. "I did not hear any voices or anything," I told them, "but I just seemed to be impressed. I'd like to go ahead and start the building project, but I want the church to vote to approve it."

I said, "If we raise $10,000 in the next month, we will have enough money to start the excavation for our new auditorium."

Now, we had *never* received $10,000 for the building fund in *any* month — not even close to it.

You know what? The church voted to do it. At the end of the month, we tallied up the offering for the building fund — we had received a little over $11,000. We announced it to the congregation on Sunday that God had provided, and so we were moving forward with the project. On Monday morning, the excavators were there and began digging the hole. It was quite a hole! It took all the money out of the building fund. Everything we had, including the $11,000, went into that hole.

I could see the hole from my study. As it got bigger and bigger and the money went down with each payment, I thought, *what have I done?* I prayed and pleaded, "O God, you've got to do something." The hole was finished, and now we had *no* money!

We raised money a few different ways for this project. We had our weekly offerings, and also hosted a few school and church fundraisers. We also had a bond program.

When we first started thinking about this building project, we started a bond program with A.B. Culbertson and Co. in Texas. Chuck Schindel was our bond sales chairman. We had sold about $200,000 worth of bonds, but all of a sudden, the bonds quit selling. We were left with close to $80,000 worth of bonds still to sell, and no one would buy them. Even worse was that the bond company would not release *any* of the $200,000 until *all* of the sales were completed. And, we had a hole in the ground and no money to continue.

I did not know what to do. We prayed and asked God for wisdom. We did not want to be a poor testimony to the community — starting a project but not being able to complete it. Some of the deacons suggested that we borrow money. Our church was in very good shape financially, so it made logical sense, but I had an aversion to borrowing money from a bank — especially since we were in the middle of this bond program. I simply did not want to borrow any more money, and a few of the deacons agreed with me. I believed that if the Lord was in it, He would take care of our needs. He had done so for all of the previous building and advancement projects thus far, so I believed He would do it again.

In deacons' meetings, we brainstormed for hours trying to come up with some ideas and ways we could continue the project without borrowing money. Some of them strongly encouraged me to take another cold shower. "And make it *very* cold this time!" they said laughing.

The shower did not work. I had no other ideas. Against my better judgment, we decided to go ahead and apply for a bank loan. Chuck Schindel prepared a financial presentation for the bank loan committee. I picked him up the morning of the meeting, and together we drove down to United Bank in downtown Denver. We sat down around a long oval table, the loan committee on one side, Chuck on the other, and me on the end, next to Chuck.

He gave his financial presentation, and I must admit, he did a very fine job. He explained how our church was in great shape. We really did not have any debt. We had a large campus, great attendance, everything was growing. We had a surplus in our budget. It really was a great picture he painted.

But I was uncomfortable with the whole thing. I let him finish and when he sat down, I immediately pounded my fist on the table. "I've got something to say," I said firmly. I stood up straight to my full six feet, four inches.

"Now, this young man—" I pointed at Chuck, "what he said is true. The Lord has really blessed our church. But I want you to know something. We don't have any rich people in our church, and if you give us this loan, I don't have any idea how we are going to pay it back. Lord-willing, we'll be able to. But I just felt like you should know that I have no idea how we're going to pay it back."

Having said what was on my heart, I sat down.

Everyone sat there in silence, eyes wide open, looking back and forth between Chuck Schindel and me. They hemmed and hawed and eventually told us they would have their decision on whether to loan us money within a week.

When we walked out of the bank, I could tell Chuck was extremely upset with me. He did not say a word. "I think you're upset," I told him as we walked by the busy downtown streets. He did not respond. I figured the best way to cheer him up was to be kind and take him out for lunch. "The Brown Palace is only a block away," I said. "I'm going to take you there for lunch."

"I don't want to go to the Brown Palace," he said coldly.

"We're going there anyway. I'm driving, and if you want to get back without walking, then you're going to have to go to lunch with me."

He sulkily followed me into the Brown Palace, a top-class hotel with a high-scale restaurant inside. I ordered my meal, then Chuck ordered his. The cheapest item on the menu was a hamburger. It was $5 — significantly more than the 15-cent hamburger we could get at McDonald's at that time. Chuck continued to be in a sour mood, and when our food came, it only made his attitude worse. His $5 hamburger was two pieces of bread, one thin beef patty, and a pickle. No ketchup, lettuce, tomato, onion — nothing extra. He asked the waiter for a piece of lettuce and a slice of tomato. They charged us 50 cents for each extra item, which made him even more upset.

We ate a silent lunch, and then I drove him home. The entire time, I tried talking to him but was met with nothing but grumpiness.

Twenty-four hours later, we received a call from the loan committee at United Bank. They had denied our request.

That news only made Chuck Schindel *more* upset with me. I knew that the cause of his attitude was because of what I had said in that meeting with the bank. But I had felt so impressed that I needed the bank to understand that we had no money to pay them back. I just *knew* I had done the right thing.

Chuck did not speak to me for two weeks. I did not know what to do to make amends. And then, one Saturday morning before the sun was up, a farmer from Fort Morgan, Colorado, called me.

Because I got up at 4:00 A.M. every morning and knew farmers did the same, I thought nothing of the early hour. He said, "I hear you've got bonds for sale."

"We sure do," I said.

"What's the interest rate?" he asked.

"Seven percent," I told him.

"Oh," he said, "that sounds good. I'd like to buy $30,000 worth of your bonds."

We had *never* had a sale like that before!

Showers of Blessing

"Well, we'll come out to see you yet this morning," I told the man.

Since Chuck Schindel was the chairman of the bond campaign, I immediately called him and said, "Chuck, are you out of bed?" It was 5:00 in the morning.

"What do you want?" he groggily said.

"Get your glad rags on," I told him. "You and I are going for a ride."

"Where are we going? Do you know what time it is?"

"Yes, I do. I'll be there in about 45 minutes. Get your glad rags on."

"Where are we going?" he asked again.

"Fort Morgan."

"Why?"

"A rancher called me and wants to buy some bonds. We're going. I'll be over in 45 minutes."

I immediately drove to the church and counted out the bonds. They were all one-thousand dollar denominations, and I counted out 30 of them and signed them all over to the farmer — something I should have waited to do until we had met with him.

When I picked up Chuck, he got into the car without a word. I explained to him the whole phone conversation with the farmer. Chuck still seemed off, like he had his nose out of joint.

We arrived at the farm in Fort Morgan and met the man wanting to buy the bonds. We discovered that he went to the Nazarene church. He handed Chuck the check for $30,000 as I began counting out the bonds. "1, 2, 3," and I came to "28, 29, 30, 31." I said, "Well, I must have miscounted." So I counted them again and it came out to 31.

"Oh, I'm so sorry," I said to the man. "We have 31, and they're already signed over to you. I can't do anything about it."

He said, "That's just like you Baptists. You're going to take advantage of every cent! You believe you can't lose your salvation, and so you just cheat on me now because you're not worried about hurting God and your salvation." Then he laughed and wrote a check for another $1,000.

Within two weeks of that large sale, every single bond we had was sold. A.B. Culbertson released the funds and we continued with the auditorium and finished it without borrowing another penny.

At the end of the two weeks of sales, Chuck came into my office. With tears streaming down his cheeks, he asked me to forgive him for his anger and bad attitude which I readily forgave.

In the 30 years as pastor at South Sheridan, we had over 25 building and advancement projects and grew the campus size to nearly 20 acres — 4 city blocks in length. When I turned over the church to Les Heinze, our church was debt free. God had truly showered His blessings upon our church.

Chapter 35

BEHIND THE IRON CURTAIN

IN THE EARLY 1980s, the United States was in the heart of the Cold War with the Union of Soviet Socialist Republics (USSR), also known as the Soviet Union. After World War II had ended, the Soviet Union remained closed to other countries and tightened their grip on socialist and communist rules — especially with regard to religion. In 1959, the Soviet Union had imposed new regulations on churches, Baptist churches in particular, that made it increasingly difficult for congregations to worship together. Suddenly, the churches split into two sides: those who would follow the Russian State and those who would follow God. One particular man rose to leadership over the latter group. His name was Georgi Vins.

Georgi Vins was no stranger to persecution. Though he discovered it only a few years before his own death, his father had been killed in prison for his faith. Georgi himself had been arrested several times and had spent the latter part of the 1960s in prison. Although he, his wife, and their four children went into hiding after his release from prison, he continued to preach the Gospel of Jesus Christ.

Only five years after his release from prison, he was caught again. After a trial in Kiev in January of 1975, Georgi Vins was sentenced to five years in a labor camp to be followed by five years of internal exile. He would become the Soviet Union's most famous religious prisoner.

After four years of imprisonment in the labor camp, Georgi was awakened, told to change into his own clothes, and then flown on a plane to Moscow. The next day, he was given new clothes and informed that because of his anti-Soviet activity, his Soviet citizenship was being revoked. He was being expelled. The officer bearing the news commanded him to write down the names of his closest relatives so they could leave the country with him.

After completing that task, he and four other prisoners were blindfolded and then ushered onto a plane. When the plane landed, they were in New York City, and the prisoners learned why they were suddenly released. They had been part of a trade agreement between the White House and the Soviet embassy in Washington: they were being exchanged for two convicted spies.

Six weeks later, Georgi's wife, children, mother, and niece arrived in America. After four long years, the family was back together again, experiencing a kind of freedom they had never imagined.

The Vins family settled in Elkhart, Indiana, where they all learned English. Georgi began preaching and speaking wherever he could on the suffering of the churches and Christians in the USSR. Trying to drum up help for his persecuted people, he spoke to missions agencies, colleges, and many other organizations. He even spoke at the White House and to a joint session of the United States Congress.

After several years, Georgi founded Russian Gospel Ministries — a ministry that supported his native, persecuted believers in the Soviet Union. He was passionate about it and begged Christians around the world to write letters to the Kremlin asking for humane treatment for these brothers and sisters in Christ.

It was through these letters that I heard about him.

* * * * *

As pastor of South Sheridan Baptist Church, I brought in many different special guests and speakers to help edify and educate our congregation. Some were Christian athletes who had a clear testimony for the Lord. Others were well-known evangelists and preachers of like faith and doctrine. Many were missionaries who were either home on furlough or were raising support to go to the field. Missions had always been a huge heartbeat of mine, so when I first heard of Georgi Vins in 1985, I decided to contact him and ask if he would speak at our church.

He agreed. Over the next three years, Georgi spoke multiple times at South Sheridan. He and I developed a close relationship as he expressed to me and to the church the importance and urgency of sharing the Gospel in Ukraine, Russia, Belorussia (Belarus), and even Siberia.

In 1987, he again expressed to me his desire to return to his people, but he did not yet dare to go. He would risk his life, not just his citizenship, the next time he entered the USSR. So Georgi asked Guyla and me to go in his place and represent the Fundamental Baptists of America.

We agreed and immediately began preparation. The trip would take place in May of 1988, and we would stay for two weeks. Natasha, Georgi's daughter, would travel with us, but no one could know that we knew her and vice versa until she initiated contact. The risk of imprisonment or being kicked out of the country was too great for all of us.

"You must go as tourists," Georgi told us. So we booked our trip with a tour group he recommended. The plan was for us to travel wherever they went, but in the evenings, we would break away from the tour group to contact the Underground Church. Natasha would fill us in on all the details and the ins and outs of going to the villages at the appropriate times.

We carefully planned out all the details we could. Then the day came for us to leave. We packed our bags, put a few Russian Bibles in our suitcases, and boarded the plane for Moscow. Guyla and I sat near the front of the plane, and when we saw Natasha board, we gave no indication that we even recognized her.

After several connecting flights and a long, two-day journey, we finally arrived in Moscow. After picking up our precious bags, we made our way toward a man who was holding a sign that read, "Mr. & Mrs. Ed Nelson."

With hardly a word — we spoke no Russian and he spoke very little English — the man led us to a waiting vehicle and drove us straight to the hotel. The man knew Natasha, but again, for everyone's safety, no one acknowledged that we knew each other.

Guyla and I had been instructed by Georgi to look like tourists, and we certainly embraced the tourist life. We did much sight-seeing every day, visiting the iconic places in the city and taking many pictures. We toured some of the government-approved Baptist churches. They were beautiful buildings inside and out. But they were very obviously restrained and controlled by the government.

The people were poor — much poorer than we had expected. It shocked both of us. Though many nationals put on smiles as our touring group went by, the smiles did not reach the eyes. The eyes showed us the hopelessness and oppression of the country which we were visiting. On several occasions, we saw a line of people several blocks long. When we asked what they were waiting for, our tour guide simply responded, "Toothbrushes," or "Shoestrings," or "Soap," or "Eggs." There was a very long line for nearly everything that anyone would need to buy.

The poverty of these dear people gripped our hearts with pity and compassion. We wanted to help and to reach out to the suffering people

"Tourists" in Soviet Russia

we saw. Yet we knew we could not and dared not risk the wrath and attention of the government — that was the last thing we wanted.

* * * * *

Early one morning, a few days after we had arrived in Moscow, Natasha came to us at the hotel and said, "I have a taxi waiting. You need to come with me right away."

In the taxi, Natasha did not say a word, but told the driver the address. When we stopped, we were parked in front of a big, old apartment building in the middle of the countryside. Natasha led us up the stairs and to an apartment door. At her knock, the door opened barely a crack. Through the crack, we saw what looked like a man. For a long, full minute, the man's eyeball moved up and down and thoroughly looked over all of us. Finally, the man carefully opened the door, whisked us inside, and immediately closed and locked the door behind us.

Guyla and I had no idea what was happening. We trusted Natasha, but what was going on? The man was the only person in the apartment. He motioned for us to sit down at a crude table with a lamp on it. Natasha seated herself beside us, and the man began asking us questions through Natasha.

"What do you think of Billy Graham? Have you cooperated with him?"

Right in that moment, I recalled reading and watching on the news how Billy Graham had visited Moscow and held a crusade. When he came back to America, one of the questions a reporter asked him was, "Did you see religious persecution while in the Soviet Union?"

His reply had been something to the effect of, "No, I did not see any signs of the persecution of Christians. There was a measure of religious freedom in Russia."

As I explained to the man how I had not participated in the Billy Graham crusades and had opposed them, his face changed drastically.

"We thought everyone in America supported Billy Graham," he said in wonder. "And his words about the freedom of religion here are completely untrue!"

His face grew troubled as he continued to speak. "Billy Graham came here to Moscow and went to the Baptist Church* — the one that is controlled by the government. The pastor there preaches only what the government tells him to preach. They are scared and have let this government control their faith instead of standing up for Jesus Christ!

"Meanwhile, there are hundreds of men and women who are in prison camps or have been executed because they stand for the Bible and won't give in. The rest of us have to stay in hiding. Every time we meet for church, we risk being jailed or killed. And here this Billy Graham says there is no persecution. Bah!"

Our hearts ached for the man as we listened to his story. We had heard enough from Georgi to know a good deal of the kinds of persecution that occurred daily in the Soviet Union. At that time, over 200 Christians were in prison because they preached the Gospel.

Yet, here we were in the country, seeing the people and their faces stricken with hopelessness. Hearing this man's story and the pain of countless friends and family members who had paid the price for the Gospel was overwhelming.

After satisfactorily answering his questions on our Billy Graham position, the man continued to ask us doctrinal questions for several hours. What did we believe about baptism? About the second coming of Christ? About the tribulation? We were drilled with question after question.

As the questions kept coming, I began to pick up on why we were there in that out-of-the-way apartment. This man belonged to the Underground Church. He was probably a pastor, and we were being questioned to determine where we stood on all of these issues before he would let us preach to his church.

Right about the time I came to that conclusion, another man en-

---

* Moscow Church of Evangelical Christian Baptists

tered the apartment and began questioning us. A few hours later, we were joined by yet another man. Every one of them had the same first question: what did we think about Billy Graham and had we joined his crusades in the States? To each, my answer remained the same: "No, we did not join with him. We are opposed to any ecumenical evangelistic crusades and have had nothing to do with him or his ministry or anything similar."

The entire day passed. We did not break for lunch. We were not allowed to leave or do anything besides answer the hundreds of questions. Finally, long after dark had come, the first man stood up and said (through Natasha), "It's all right. You are all right. You can come to preach at our churches now."

The other men in the room looked on, each nodding his agreement. Natasha led us outside to a waiting car, and we returned to the hotel. Once in the safety and privacy of our own room, Guyla and I talked about the outcome of the day: we were now accepted in the Underground Church of the Soviet Union.

* * * * *

From that day on, our schedule was different. We remained tourists throughout the entire day, going everywhere with our touring group. We visited Moscow, Leningrad (now St. Petersburg), and various other towns and cities along the way. Natasha had her own way of getting around the country. Somehow, wherever we went, she was there too. While we were very much part of the tourist group, each evening, Guyla and I would excuse ourselves from the nightly activities and slip off to meet Natasha. On Sundays, we simply said, "We won't be joining you this morning," and went to preach at a Sunday service instead.

We took extra precautions and maneuvers to ensure that no one followed us. From the hotel, we would take a taxi to a bus station; then we would take a bus to the train station, where we would take a train to a location near where we would meet the Russian believers. Once off the train, we would walk. Sometimes we walked until we were no longer in town, but in a forest. Sometimes we met in a small apartment or an abandoned building. Sometimes we gathered in someone's secluded backyard. Wherever it was, Natasha met us each evening at a pre-determined location and led us to the site where I was to preach. It was almost always under the cover of darkness with only the moon to light the way.

In the heart of a forest on the outskirts of Moscow, we began our first service in Soviet Russia. There were about 50 people there including Guyla, Natasha, and me. We sang a few hymns (Guyla and I sang in English), and then I began to preach.

A normal sermon length for me when preaching in America was about 40 minutes. When it became obvious that I was wrapping up, Natasha told me that the people wanted me to continue preaching. The first sermon I preached in the forest at the edge of Moscow lasted over two hours, but the people stood the entire two hours listening to me preach with Natasha translating. It was truly thrilling to be able to preach to people who were so hungry for the Word of God!

In Leningrad, we met in an upstairs apartment building close to the center of town. It was the end of May, so the weather outside was relatively warm, and a slight breeze through an open window would have been welcomed for our crowd of 50 in that small apartment. But government spies could be anywhere listening to conversations, even through open windows; so for the safety of our secret meeting, we kept all the windows closed. Within a short while, it became almost unbearably hot. The air was so stuffy that we all struggled to breathe. There was no air conditioning. No fans. Nothing to move the air. But the believers gathered together there did not seem to care. They were hearing the Word of God preached.

For the remainder of the two weeks in the Soviet Union, we settled on a normal schedule: tour with the group for the day; carefully maneuver the public transportation to meet Natasha; and then preach for hours

Behind the Iron Curtain

Services for the Underground Church were held in forests, closed apartments, or secluded yards. Natasha translated almost every service. (June 1988)

each evening. It was both exhausting and exhilarating

At the end of the two weeks, Guyla and I returned home. Our lives had been changed forever. All we wanted to do was to go back and be with those dear people and share the Word of God with them! We began to prepare to do just that. Part of that preparation included enrolling in a six-week Russian course during the summer of 1989 at the University of Denver.

The man who taught our class was a unique individual. He was a Russian man who had been raised in a Roman Catholic home. While most Catholics do not agree with us on the doctrine of salvation through faith alone, this man did. He was a believing Roman Catholic who had placed his entire hope of eternity in Heaven in the saving blood of Jesus Christ alone, not his good works.

Over the duration of the class, he told me how he had attended a university in Russia. Because he was a Catholic, and not of Russian Orthodox faith, he was arrested and sent to a prison camp.

One day not long into his time in prison, the guards began taking ten men each day and shooting them. Ten were killed by a firing squad every morning. Eventually, it was his turn. He and nine other men were forced to kneel in front of 10 guards with shotguns pointed at them. At the command, "Fire!" the guards pulled their triggers. Not a single gun went off. Each guard checked his gun, then the order was given again: "Fire!" Again, the guards pulled the triggers and nothing happened. The guns would not go off.

Not knowing what else to do, the guards put all the men back in prison. After brief deliberations between the prison officials and the guards, my teacher was exiled to America instead of being executed.

We learned much in that class, but we were still a long way from being able to speak Russian. Guyla and I figured that the best way for us to continue learning Russian was to be immersed in the language. So the following summer, we enrolled in a class at Indiana University in Bloomington, Indiana. Though they said it would be an immersion class with no English spoken, the teacher did speak English enough to tell us what was going on. We made much progress with the help of that class, although we were still far from fluent. Russian is a very difficult language to learn!

On June 2, 1989, our 40th wedding anniversary, Guyla and I celebrated by taking a month-long trip to the Soviet Union. We met with the Underground Church in Moscow, Kiev, Kharkov, Rostov-on-Don and Leningrad, and saw souls accept Christ at every service. Although the trip seemed very similar to our first trip, there were a few monumental differences. All of the religious prisoners had been released and were back home with their families. People on the streets readily accepted our gospel literature. The unregistered churches had begun erecting shelters in yards for their services. These were tremendous steps toward a measure of religious freedom for our Russian brothers and sisters in Christ.

Yet, we all knew that this was simply a brief respite from the persecution. We took the same precautions in order to avoid being followed or arrested. If arrests were made, we were more than willing to accept that as a consequence for preaching the Gospel. However, we would rather not be caught — and we were not.

While we were there, Guyla and I did have the privilege of getting a closer look at the communist oppression. An American friend, Jonathan, his wife Donna, and their three-year-old daughter lived in Moscow. Jonathan was studying Russian law in conjunction with a law degree he was working on at Columbia University in New York. He also worked as a lawyer for the World Bank and had many projects in Russia and surrounding countries.

Before we left on this trip, they had written to us asking us to visit and share a meal with them. I told him that I could read Russian well enough to ride the train and get off at his particular station. He met us there and we walked for over three quarters of a mile to get to his house.

On the way, Jonathan said, "We will go past one of the five best supermarkets in all of Russia." He wondered if we would like to stop in and see it, to which we responded that we would love to see it.

We went in and were utterly shocked at the sight before us. There were no modern cash registers. Instead, there were some old adding machines that tallied up the bill. "My wife and I came here two weeks ago and counted every item in the store that could be purchased," he said. "It came to 55 items."

"We wanted to have chicken," he continued, "and there was none to be found in this store, so we went out and found one and bought it. Then we had to dress it, but didn't know how to do that. So we asked some people to help us. We put the chicken in hot water, pulled the feathers out, and then cooked the rest for the soup. The chicken was so skinny that there was hardly any meat in the soup at all."

Jonathan pointed to the back of the store. "There are three quarts of milk over there," he said, "but if you buy them, they are sour already."

"Look at the vegetables," Guyla marveled. "They are all rotten except this one head of lettuce."

As we continued on toward Jonathan's house, he mentioned that the government officials had their own supermarkets that looked very much like an American supermarket. The food was fresh and plentiful, but the average Russian citizen had incredibly little from which to choose.

When we returned to Denver from that trip, Guyla and I went to our local supermarket. We walked down the cereal aisle and counted the different varieties of cereal available to purchase. There were 220 different kinds of breakfast cereals. We went to the soap aisle and counted those. They numbered over 200 as well. There was more of one variety of food and soap than had been in the entire store in Russia.

I asked the store manager, "How many items do you have in this store?"

"Over 100,000," was his reply. We realized then just how blessed and spoiled we really are in America.

* * * * *

In late October, 1989, I returned to the Soviet Union, without Guyla this time. Only a few days into my two-week trip, I learned that the Berlin Wall had fallen. I heard the news and became very concerned as to how the Soviet government might react. Amazingly enough, it almost seemed as if they did not care. At that point in history, they had the attitude that all the European issues centered in Germany were Germany's problems. They no longer had to deal with it. It was Germany that had built the wall and torn the wall down. According to Pavel Palazhchenko — the man who translated conversations between Soviet president Mikhail Gorbachev and U.S. president Ronald Reagan — "Gorbachev was happy. Happy with the fact that finally the problem of the wall was eliminated. It didn't exist anymore. And it was eliminated by Germans themselves. We were not involved in this liquidation and not responsible for the consequences."

Despite the freedom people now experienced in East Germany, the religious persecution and oppression was still a very real threat in the Soviet Union. I had to be extra careful preaching.

Two years later, the Iron Curtain finally collapsed. After almost 70 years of oppression, socialism, and severe religious persecution, the Russian and Ukrainian believers finally experienced true freedom.

* * * * *

Shortly following the collapse of the Iron Curtain, Guyla and I were on a plane heading back to Russia. On this trip, we had several different people join us at various times: Dr. Bob Jones, III, and his wife Beneth; Wayne Van Gelderen, Sr.; Ernest Pickering; and several other preachers. Beneth and Guyla were the only ladies who traveled with us besides Natasha.

We flew into Moscow and took an overnight train to Kiev. Everywhere we went, we saw the extreme poverty. Guyla and I had seen it before, but it was a total shock to the others in our group.

We were often entertained for meals in a Russian believer's

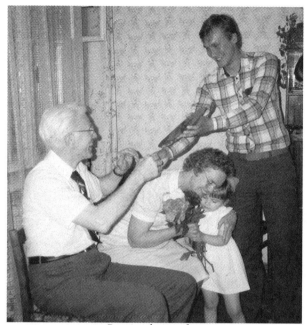
Russian hospitality

home. Very seldom was there any meat. What meat there was looked like a sausage that was full of little white bits of fat — hardly any meat within the sausage. We ate a lot of borscht, which is a type of red beet soup, as well as lots of potatoes and vegetables that had been raised in their gardens. They were giving us their very best, and it was costly to them. Yet they gave joyfully — we were blessed and taken care of well.

We had two goals for the trip. One, encourage the believers and share the Gospel with everyone we met. Two, encourage and minister to the pastors and believers who had just been released from the GULAG — the prison camps.

The religious freedom was incredible to witness. No longer did we sneak around the towns hoping that we were not being followed. Instead, we went to the subway stations, bus stops, housing developments, wherever we could find a crowd of people, and we openly and loudly proclaimed the Gospel of Jesus Christ.

One Saturday afternoon, we selected a particular station that was close to many houses and apartment buildings. Tall, gray nine-story buildings loomed above us. Because it was a train station, bus station, and taxi station all in one place, it was a prime location for us to hold services. It was raining hard, and water was pouring off the street into a large culvert — hardly an ideal situation. Yet here we were, gathered together, ready to preach on the streets.

We put boards over the top of the culvert so we could stand on something out of the water, sang a few hymns in English, and a crowd began gathering around us. The people going to and from the stations stopped, and several joined in the singing, only in their Russian language. By the time we were finished singing the few songs, we estimated a crowd of over 1,000 people had gathered.

I spoke first for about 20 minutes. When I gave an invitation, over 40 people came forward to accept the Lord. I took those to the back of the crowd and began praying with them individually. I dealt with each one personally. Natasha was with me doing the translating.

While I was there dealing with those, others came from the crowd and joined my small group saying, "I didn't come forward, but I would like to be saved too. Can you help me?" It was almost unbelievable.

Meanwhile, we had a Russian band with some trumpets, trombones, and other brass instruments playing hymns. They began playing and within a short while, another crowd of similar size had gathered.

Ernest Pickering spoke next, and when he gave an invitation, about 40 more people came forward to trust Christ. He followed my example and led the people to the back of the crowd and dealt with each one individually. He also had others from the crowd ask to join after the invitation had closed.

Again, the band played and another crowd gathered.

Dr. Bob spoke next and preached a message on the resurrection of Christ. When he gave a simple invitation for people to come forward and accept Christ, again, over 40 came forward. It was amazing!

Large crowds gathered for street meetings.

The Ukrainian pastors were also there to work with those who came forward. They took them and showed them from the Bible how they could be saved. It was still raining quite hard, but the people stayed where they were. They wanted to hear more, even though we all were soaked to the skin.

We began passing out gospel literature and tracts with the plan of salvation in them. People were knocking each other over trying to get their hands on the pamphlets.

At the end of our time at the stations, Dr. Bob came up to me with tears in his eyes. "Ed, I believe there were some *genuine* conversions here tonight," and I heartily agreed.

We Americans felt that we needed to go to our hotels, dry off, and get some sleep. The Ukrainian believers did not want to quit, so they continued holding meetings well into the night and saw many more souls saved.

The next day, we went to the subway station and held mini services there. We American pastors preached on a rotation of five minutes each with Natasha and a few others translating for each of us. When we were not preaching, we stood at the back of the crowd passing out tracts and gospel literature and talking to people as best we could.

At the end of the day, Dr. Bob told all of us that as he was passing out literature, two older ladies came up to receive theirs. When he handed them the pamphlet, they just looked at each other and stared. "Just look at this," they had said. (Natasha was standing close by and had translated for Dr. Bob.) "For 70 years, we've been denied the Bible. And now, we have the truth for the first time in 70 years."

Our days were filled with evangelism on the streets. We experienced a unique kind of openness that had not been present up until this point. It was glorious! Every evening, we held church services for the believers in the towns. The services lasted at *least* three hours. Children sat on wooden benches. Adults sat on the same. Whenever the benches were full, the people stood. It amazed me that the children sat still on those hard wooden benches for that long. Most children in America were not nearly so patient — and they were sitting on plush pews! The people did whatever it took to hear the Bible preached. They had been spiritually famished for 70 years, and now, they could freely hear the Word of God. It truly was amazing.

> *Sadly, the hunger and quest for truth was short-lived. By the time we came back to Russia and Ukraine a year later, it was much more challenging to reach the people. They did not have the same eagerness to hear the Gospel or to know what truth is. And although there was religious freedom, the government still did not like the Gospel being preached. They made things very difficult for the believers to share their faith.*

On the last day of that trip, we experienced a deep heartache. Natasha came and told us that we were required to go to the pastor's house. A group of men, believers and pastors from Odessa on the Black Sea, had come up to Kharkov to deliver a message to Georgi Vins through his daughter, Natasha.

The leader of the group of men spoke up. He saw himself as the new leader of all the free churches in the underground movement. "Tell your father to stay out of our country," he said while shaking his finger in Natasha's face. "He was a traitor. He left us. Betrayed us. He went to the comforts of America and left us here suffering. He is not welcome here anymore." The man was angrily spitting out the words. "You tell him to never show his face here again."

Natasha was weeping, as were all of us American pastors. It was horrible to watch. They did not care that Georgi Vins had been expelled by his own people and the government for the sake of the Gospel. He had been exiled. They did not seem to remember that while in America, he had published hundreds of thousands of bulletins with pictures, prison numbers, and profiles on each imprisoned pastor. He had begged thousands of Americans to write letters to the Kremlin asking for humane treatment for these men. It was heartbreaking to see that the very men whom Georgi had worked to free and relieve from pain, had turned against him.

When we were allowed to leave the pastor's house, I told my fellow companions, "That man was a Diotrephes."*

* * * * *

STARTING WITH my first trip to the Soviet Union in 1988, over the course of 15 years, I traveled to Russia and Ukraine 18 times. On at least six of those trips, Guyla accompanied me.

In 1993, a group of about 15 men traveled with me to Russia: Steve Pettit, Kevin Schaal, and Jeff Musgrave, to name a few.

In 1984, Jeff had started a church out of South Sheridan. It was a growing church that really supported missions. In the year before Jeff came to Russia with me, the congregation raised $20,000 to build a church in Russia. That was the main reason Jeff came with me on this trip — to give the money toward a new Russian church.

---

* 3 John 9-10 — *I wrote unto the church: but Diotrephes, who loveth to have the preeminence among them, receiveth us not. . . . his deeds which he doeth, prating against us with malicious words: and not content therewith, neither doth he himself receive the brethren, and forbiddeth them that would, and casteth them out of the church.*

At my recommendation, Paul Whitfield, a builder I knew, also came with us to provide insight into how to proceed with the construction. I took Jeff and Paul with me everywhere I went: Blagoveshchensk, Vyazemsky, Ussuriysk, Khabarovsk — we stayed in the towns on the east side of the country.

We traveled mostly by train to get from city to city. At every stop, there were people on the platform whom I knew. The minute I got off, I heard, "Pastor Nelson! There is Pastor Nelson!" Of course, I stood out like a sore thumb standing tall at my six feet, four inches with my shock of white hair.

In Blagoveshchensk, the Baptist church was hosting a revival meeting and had requested that we come and preach. Jeff, Paul, and I stayed long enough to speak once, meet people, and get to know some of the local pastors. Then we left the others to continue the meetings while we traveled back down the coast to Ussuriysk with Natasha.

We stopped in Khabarovsk on the way down the coast. It was there that I got hurt — so badly hurt that they wanted to take me to the hospital. I vehemently refused. I had made enough trips to visit believers in the Russian hospitals that I *knew* I did not want to be a patient. It was said that the same needle was used for 50 patients. I would manage just fine until I got back to America.

The accident had happened while we were at the train station in Khabarovsk. Each of the 15 men on the trip had brought a 50-pound box of books for us to pass out to the Russian pastors. I was carrying two boxes, one on either shoulder, walking down the stairs to get to the train. I do not know whether my foot slipped out from under me, or the stairway broke, or exactly what happened. But one minute, I was walking down the stairs with the books, and the next moment, the boxes were flying through the air and I was falling backwards. I landed *hard*, hitting the corner of a step with my tailbone.

We made it on the train, and when we got to Blagoveshchensk, the bruise on my tailbone was a deep, deep brown and as big as a cantaloupe. I could not carry any of the boxes of books for the remainder of the trip. My tailbone hurt so badly that I was doing well to walk.

From then on, Natasha would stay by the pile of books, I would stand near the train, and Jeff and Paul would carry the boxes from one spot to the other.

Eventually, we made it to Ussuriysk. Jeff had become violently ill on the way down. There were street vendors at each train stop and, as there was no food on the train itself, he was hungry enough to try anything and everything. He got food poisoning and was very sick to his stomach.

We traveled through the night to get to the house where we were to stay for a week. It was a simple Russian home with no indoor plumbing — just an outhouse located a short distance from the house. The house was heated by a wood-burning stove and water-piping system. It was very simple, but it worked. In fact, it worked so well that sick-to-his-stomach Jeff passed out from the heat. Twice. He woke up the first time to find me slapping his face asking, "Does this happen often?"

Since the house did not have an indoor bathroom or running water, the hosts told us they would take us to their son's apartment in the city. He got hot water once each week at his apartment, so we could shower there. Jeff overheard the couple talking and thought he heard them say we would get showers in the morning. We all got our shower kits and towels ready and were waiting the next morning. It turned out that what was actually said was that we were going to have *rain* showers in the morning.

Our hosts felt so bad about the misunderstanding that they figured out another way that we could take showers. "I know what we'll do," the man said. "One of our other sons works at the water treatment plant. They have a sauna and a shower there that you could use."

So off we went to the water treatment facility. The sauna was a homemade steam room; there were rocks that had been heated until they were extremely hot, and two benches on which we could sit. Then the son showed us how to pour water over the rocks to create the steam for the sauna.

We were given a branch with dried oak leaves on it, wool gloves, and a pointed ski cap. We were told to hit ourselves with the branch to exfoliate the skin. Then we were to sit in the sauna for 15 minutes, naked except for the cap and gloves, and then exit to take a shower. There was only one shower available, so we timed everything out so it would be one person at a time. Paul went first, then Jeff, then me.

When Paul was in the shower and Jeff was close to being done in the sauna, I entered for my time in the steam room. I still had a very messed up tailbone, so Jeff helped me in, beat me with the branch a few times, and helped me put on the wool gloves and cap. I could not handle it. I began fading very quickly. It was incredibly hot and humid. It felt close to 150º F. My 70-year-old body had difficulty adjusting to the heat and steam.

I sat down to begin my 15 minutes and immediately jumped up hollering. I had sat directly on the head of a hot nail and burned my already sore backside. Jeff kindly let me exit to the shower first to ease the pain of the burn and tailbone.

When I returned to the States, I discovered that I had actually broken my tailbone.

* * * * *

One of the cities I visited often was Khabarovsk, a city on the east side of Russia, very close to the sea coast. It was home to over one million people and was one of the larger cities in the region. Several years after the large group of men traveled with me, I returned to Khabarovsk, this time with only five others.

One Saturday afternoon, I said, "Let's go down to the market and have a service." When we arrived, we began singing "Jesus Saves" in English. It was not long until a crowd of about 100 people had gathered around us.

Once the song ended, I stood up on a bench and began preaching. I observed that all the men wore pants and shirts made of rough material. The clothes looked old and worn. The ladies, likewise, had very worn and rough material for their clothing, but they always wore either a skirt and blouse or a dress. As I preached, I noticed a lady standing at the very edge of the crowd, a lady whose clothing was made of fine material. Her dress stood out amidst the faded colors of the worn fabrics.

I watched her throughout my message, and she seemed to be hanging onto every word that I spoke. When I gave the invitation, she timidly came forward, along with several others.

Natasha saw her moving and whispered to me, "See if you can get others to deal with these people. I want to deal with her. Her dress means that she's a little better off than most of the women here."

Natasha ushered the lady aside and began talking with her.

"How did you like the service?" she asked.

"I liked it," the lady replied. "I would like to become a Christian, but I cannot."

"Why not?" Natasha questioned.

"Because I've sent so many people to prison. I have been a judge here in Khabarovsk for years and have had a lot of cases come before me — Jews, Baptists, Pentecostals — I sentenced all of them to prison. I don't think God would ever forgive me for that. I must have sent at least 200 people to the prison camps!" she moaned. "I am sorry that I did it, but it was what the law said, and I had to obey the law. I don't think anybody like me could ever get saved."

Natasha listened carefully, and then simply opened her Bible to Acts chapter nine. She showed this judge how Saul was a man who had been breathing out threats and killing many Christians. He was on his way to Damascus to arrest and slaughter many more Christians when he was blinded by a shining light from Heaven. He asked the Lord, "Who art Thou?" And the Lord's answer was, "*I am Jesus whom thou persecutest*"

(Acts 9:5). Jesus, the voice from Heaven, told Saul to go into Damascus and wait. A man named Ananias would speak to him in three days.

When the Lord told Ananias to speak to Saul, Ananias reminded God of how much evil Saul had done to Christians in Jerusalem and how Saul had come to Damascus to persecute the believers there too.

Though Ananias objected, the Lord told him, "*Go thy way: for he is a chosen vessel unto me, to bear my name before the Gentiles, and kings, and the children of Israel: For I will shew him how great things he must suffer for my name's sake*" *(Acts 9:15–16)*.

Ananias obeyed and as soon as he was done speaking to him, Saul received his sight again and immediately began preaching the Gospel. Saul was saved that day and became Paul, an ambassador of the Gospel and an author of many of the books of the New Testament.

When the judge heard that, she excitedly interjected, "He was like this? He was killing Christians too?"

"Yes."

"Well, maybe I *can* get saved then!" Immediately, the judge bowed her head and prayed to ask Christ's forgiveness for the sins she had done. When she finished praying, we could visibly see that she was a changed woman. Before, her face had shown much fear and guilt. Now, she was free and had total peace.

Natasha told her where we would be on Sunday morning for church. The next day, the judge came to church, was baptized, joined the church, and went on to live for the Lord.

* * * * *

ANOTHER TIME, we were in Vladivostok, a different town on the coast of eastern Russia. A group of believers invited me to come hold a revival meeting for them. They rented a school building for the occasion at $2.00 a night — shockingly inexpensive for us Americans.

On the night of the first meeting, the school auditorium was filled with over 400 people when we arrived. The principal met us at the door, took us around, and showed us the entire facility. She made sure the windows were opened to allow proper airflow and she helped the ushers seat people. She was just there, and she stayed for the entire service.

Afterwards, she came to me and asked, "Could you come tomorrow and speak to our school?"

"Well, yes," I said. It was the first time I had ever been invited into a Russian school.

"Wonderful. We start at 8:00. We will see you in the morning."

We were back the next morning at 8:00. I spoke for the school assembly. When it was over, a teacher came to me and asked, "Could you come to my class and speak in English? We are teaching our students English. You can talk about whatever you wish."

So I went and presented the Gospel. When I went to the door to leave, another teacher came up and asked, "Could you come and just tell us about Evolution and Creation?"

This was the science class, so I went to the class and showed them the difference between Evolution and Creation. I showed them from the Bible how God had created the world in six days and had rested on the seventh day.

When I went to leave that class, another teacher asked me to speak in her class. This happened all day long. I stayed the entire school day teaching in different classes. At the end of the day, the principal thanked me for all my help and gave me some food.

When we held the revival meeting at the school that evening, many of the students and teachers came to the service and trusted Christ as their personal Savior.

* * * * *

IN ANOTHER town where I was preaching evening services, I noticed that there were three women who attended — every night. One night, they came forward and said, "We want to thank you for coming, but we just don't see how we can live for the Lord. We have driven over 60 kilometers* just to get here. The only church we have in our town is a Russian Orthodox church. They do not preach what you have been telling us."

After more conversation, I discovered that they were faithfully attending the Russian Orthodox Church. "Now," they continued, "if what you are saying is true, then what they are saying at our church is not true. How do we know what to believe?"

I asked, "Which one uses the Bible?"

"You do."

"You have to go where the Bible is honored and preached," I replied. After that, all three ladies professed Christ as Savior. When I returned a year later, all three were attending the Baptist church in which I had preached previously. They traveled the 60 kilometers each Sunday just to hear the Word of God. All three ladies were living for the Lord.

* * * * *

Over the course of the 18 trips I made to Russia and Ukraine, I was amazed to notice that the poverty of the people did not change much, despite the relaxation of the Iron Curtain oppression.

On one occasion, I was out walking around Blagoveshchensk with the family with whom I was staying. The whole family was with me — an older man, his wife, his children, and his grandchildren. I saw an ice cream shop and pointed in that direction. I bought each of them a big ice cream cone. When the older gentleman received his, he began weeping. "This is the first time I have ever had ice cream," he said. "I couldn't afford it before."

* * * * *

Every time I returned from a trip to Russia or Ukraine, I gave a presentation to the church on what I had seen and what the travels had included.

---
* 40 miles

A good friend and member of South Sheridan, John Mitchell, grew increasingly burdened that the Russian pastors did not have the resources to study the Word of God like American pastors had. One important tool, a *Strong's Concordance*, was not available in Russian, so John commissioned three Russian/Ukrainian students at Bob Jones University — Alexander Kravchenko, Pavlo Parfenyuk, and Vycheslav Starikov — to translate the *Strong's Concordance* into the Russian language using the Russian Synodal Text (RST) from Wycliffe Bible Translators. It took several years, but they finally completed it. John came to me and said, "The book is translated. Now we just need the funds to print it and distribute it."

So I launched a fundraising effort through my evangelistic association and worked with several other pastors to raise over $100,000 to print the books in the Russian language through a printer in Germany. The next trip I took to Russia in 1998, I brought cases of books with me. We wanted the people to value the books, so we did not want to pass them out for free. But we did want the people to be able to afford them.

Following the fall of the Soviet Union, the Russian economy had taken a plunge. In the early 1990s, millions of Russian citizens were making $1.90 or less per day. Gradually, the average salary increased, but in 1998, when the Russian Concordance was completed, Russia's economy collapsed. Instead of having 1.1 million people living on $1.90 or less, there were 3.4 million in that economic bracket by 1999. Many pastors and church members were

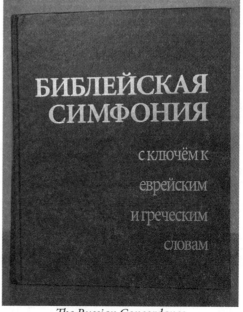

The Russian Concordance

among those impacted. As a result, we determined to sell the concordance for close to $10 — what it cost us to print the books.

The Russian Concordance changed the way the pastors preached. It taught them how to really study the Word of God and go deep into the Bible. There was a marked difference both in the pastors and their congregations the next time I went to Russia. God was growing His people on the other side of the world, and I was privileged to be a part of spreading the truth of the Gospel to those who desperately desired to hear it.

After 18 trips to Russia, I had a different perspective on life. I had seen extreme poverty and utter hopelessness. I had gotten a glimpse of the suffering of my Russian and Ukrainian brothers and sisters in Christ. I had seen religious oppression that churches in America cannot comprehend. Over a period of 15 years, God gave Guyla and me (and many others with us) the unique privilege of sharing Christ with people in Russia and Ukraine — people who, just like Americans, need to hear about the hope of Heaven and the freedom that only Jesus brings.

Chapter 36

TUCSON

I RETIRED FROM the pastorate of South Sheridan Baptist Church on May 20, 1990 — 30 years from when I had begun. We had started out with 20 families and a Quonset hut. We had survived a church split over ecumenical evangelism and the Billy Graham crusade in Denver, yet our church had grown faster than any other church in the city. On my last Sunday, we had about 1,400 members regularly attending.

Silver State Baptist School had begun with only 30 students. Now, 26 years later, we rejoiced at seeing fruit from the thousands of students that had passed through our doors. The academic and spiritual impact of the school was nationally recognized, and our students were spread across the globe — many in full-time Christian ministry.

During our years at South Sheridan, we had completed 25 building and advancement projects. With the exception of two houses, the church property now covered nearly 20 acres and extended four city blocks.

As for the political impact, over 60 church members were committeemen or committeewomen in their respective districts. Our church was incredibly active in screening and supporting candidates for various political offices.

In addition to all of that, we had begun with a missions budget of $1,000 per year. When I left, we were giving over $250,000 each year to missions.

The end of an era — 30 years at South Sheridan Baptist Church

We had faced battles, criticism, slander, and hardships; yet, through it all, we had stood for the Truth — the Word of God — and had not compromised the Gospel of Jesus Christ. God had built the church, and now, after 30 years, Guyla and I felt that God was leading us back into evangelism.

The church called our assistant pastor, Les Heinze, to be the senior pastor, so following our last service at South Sheridan, I turned the church over to Les, and Guyla and I hit the road. As a departing gift, the church gave us a brand new white Ford F250 and a fifth-wheel trailer. It was a diesel truck that had two gas tanks so we could drive farther between fuel stops. It was quite the leisurely ride — at least as leisurely as could be expected from a truck towing a trailer!

That year, we traveled all over the States holding revival meetings. We also took another trip to Russia.

After several years with the truck and trailer, we decided to sell our rig and upgrade to a motor home. We needed a washer and dryer and found a great deal on a wonderful "new house" for us.

We loved traveling. What better way to start our 70s than traveling and preaching the Gospel in churches across America? But once again,

I experienced the same thing that happened each time I got back into evangelism: I began to miss the pastorate.

* * * * *

At the same time God was building the work of South Sheridan Baptist Church in Lakewood, Colorado, He was also building another work in the Midwest: Bethel Baptist Church in Schaumburg, Illinois. This church began in 1959 with a group of three families. A year later, they voted to call a good friend of mine, Frank Bumpus, to be their pastor.

Guyla and I had been to this church many times to preach and visit their school. Though they started small, the church had grown tremendously! Their brand new auditorium could seat 2,400 people.

Some of their church members did not enjoy the Midwest winters, and I did not blame them! It was bitterly cold, especially with the lake-effect wind and snow from Lake Michigan. So the church had several members who were "snowbirds." Each November or December, they would leave Illinois and go to live in a warmer climate until the nice weather came back in spring.

Frank Bumpus was one of these snowbirds — but not because he did not like the cold weather. He had leukemia. Doctors told him to stay out of the cold climate during the winter. One of the families in Schaumburg also had a house in Tucson, Arizona, that they let Frank and his wife Ruth use during the winter.

In October of 1995, Guyla and I went to Troy, Michigan, for the annual Baptist World Mission board meeting. Frank Bumpus was there for the meeting as well. "Ed, it's good to see you!" he said warmly. "Would you come with me for a few minutes?"

I went with him as he led me to a private room. "Let me tell you what this is all about. You know, you are an evangelist, and as an evangelist, you should be starting churches."

"As you know, I have leukemia," he continued. "The doctors recommend that I go to a warmer climate, so I have been going to Tucson four times a year. There is a family from our church in Schaumburg that goes to Arizona for the winter. Since I need to be in the warmer weather during the colder months, they have offered to let us stay in one of the houses they own in Tucson.

"When we have been in Tucson, we've noticed there is a lack of Gospel-preaching, thriving churches throughout the city. I think they need a new church in Tucson!" he said emphatically.

"I told Guyla that we ought to start a church again sometime," I replied. "If the right opportunity came along, we should consider it."

"The next time I go to Tucson will be right after Christmas. Could you and Guyla come down then and look it over?" he asked.

"Well, I suppose I could," I said after thinking a minute. "I have scheduled a break from my meetings during the holidays." So Frank made arrangements for us to come down.

Guyla and I went to Tucson between Christmas and New Years. We were introduced to Arthur Coats, a pastor in Tucson, who graciously allowed me to preach at his church that Sunday morning. It was a small group of people meeting in a store front.

Following lunch with the Coats, Frank, Ruth, Guyla, and I met up with the family from Schaumburg. There was a vacant church building in southeast Tucson that was for sale. Frank and the family had scheduled a meeting with the former deacons of this church to gather more information — or so I thought. After discussing a few details and looking over the building, the family from Schaumburg made an offer to purchase the building, which the deacons immediately accepted. Guyla and I were shocked.

Then, the family turned to us and said, "We would like you to use this building to start a new church here in Tucson — as soon as you possibly can. Would you be willing to come?"

"I just don't see how I can do that," I replied. "I have speaking engagements and revival meetings scheduled for the next several months."

They did not argue or try to convince me, but over the remainder of our time in Tucson, it seemed that God was opening doors for us to start a church in Tucson. I talked with Arthur Coats and Frank Bumpus about it. They both were very much in favor of us starting a church in Tucson. Guyla and I prayed much for wisdom and decided that we would cancel our meetings and come to Tucson to start a church.

Frank, Ruth, and the family from Schaumburg were thrilled, and I was delighted to be getting back into the pastorate.

During the next few months, Frank and I worked out the logistics for the new church. It would be a mission church — Bethel Baptist Church in Schaumburg would support us as missionaries. Their deacons would be our deacons. Technically, Pastor Bumpus would be the pastor and I would work under him until the church was able to be self-supporting. And we would call the church, Bethel Baptist Church of Tucson.

Frank was not very familiar with this type of church planting, but I had done it a few times when I was pastoring South Sheridan and knew that it would be the best way to get the work off the ground.

From January to June, Guyla and I prepared for this new endeavor. We traded in our motor home for a new car. I preached many of the revival meetings I had already committed to for the spring. I spoke again with Arthur Coats who told me that his church decided to dissolve and several families from his congregation wanted to join in our work of planting the church.

Then, toward the end of April, I was preaching in South Carolina and ran into a young man who was a Silver State graduate and long-time family friend of ours, Adam Roland. He was taking graduate courses at Clemson University but did not have clear direction for his future. I suggested he come to Arizona and work at the church. He was very talented, particularly in music, and I thought he could be a great help to our church.

Guyla and I moved to Tucson early in the summer of 1996, and a few weeks later, Adam Roland arrived. Guyla and I had not had any time to shop for a house because we were busy getting everything else in order. Thankfully, because it was the "off-season" for the Bumpuses and the family from Schaumburg— they were back in Illinois — the family kindly let Guyla and me stay in one of the houses they owned until we could find a suitable apartment.

We set a date for our first service in the new building. However, a few weeks before the service, we discovered a large infestation of pack rats in the building. Pack rats are a type of rat that are extremely destructive. They chew through wires, insulation, drywall, and pipes. In a short amount of time, they can absolutely destroy buildings. They are also contaminated with many diseases that are harmful and sometimes deadly for humans.

These rats had ruined some of the electrical wiring in the church, and we did *not* want to have diseases spread throughout our congregation. We got some rat poison and bait and worked extremely hard to get rid of the rats. But it was not in time for our first service.

The first service of Bethel Baptist Church in Tucson was in the living room of our borrowed home. We had about 20 people attend that first service. The house worked well for the time we used it. Thankfully, within a few weeks, we had no more pack rats in the church and the destruction was completely repaired.

Guyla was incredible. She went with me on visitation every single day. Monday through Saturday, we knocked on doors, inviting people to attend our church. We knocked on most of the doors in East Tucson. It was not long before the few families we began with turned into 10, and then 20 families.

By the time we reached our first anniversary, we were no longer a mission of Bethel Baptist in Schaumburg, Illinois. We were our own church body, self-supporting and self-governing, with me as the pastor,

Bethel Baptist Church — Tucson, Arizona

Adam Roland as our assistant pastor and music director, and Arthur Coats and some other men as our own deacons. We were a very diverse group of believers. We had a number of African American families, several Hispanic families, a few white families, and a few other ethnicities in our church. It was thrilling to see how the Gospel is not limited to or defined by a particular ethnic group. We are all created in God's image, and we all need Jesus as our Savior.

By 1999, the church had grown so much that we needed a larger facility to accomodate our growing congregation of over 200 members. The generous family from Schaumburg learned of our need and found a beautiful 20-acre property that would be perfect for building a bigger church building. They pledged a substantial amount to our church to help fund the purchase of the land. At the end of 1999, we launched a building campaign, "A Miracle in the New Millennium."

Unfortunately, some issues arose during the next year about the future pastoral leadership of the church. As a result, the family from Schaumburg rescinded their monetary pledge. At the same time, Adam Roland and his family left with a few other families from Bethel and started a new church 11 miles down the road.

Because of all that transpired, we were unable to purchase land for a new building, and with the multiple families that left, we no longer needed a bigger facility. Instead, with the building campaign funds we had already raised, we scaled back our plans and built two new classroom buildings on our existing property, paying for them in cash.

Before the issues arose involving our building campaign, I was approached by a man in the church, Greg Dawson, about church planting. We had held a men's prayer meeting one Saturday morning, and in the prayer meeting, I had said, "Lord, we ought to be starting a new church again. So help us to get another church started."

After the meeting, a man came up to me. Greg and his wife Carmen were one of the African American couples in the church and were very godly people. They had recently moved to Tucson because Greg was assigned to Davis-Monthan Air Force Base. He had a long history of working with youth and children, so shortly after they became members, I asked him to take over the youth in our church.

"Pastor," he said to me after the prayer meeting, "would you trust me to work under you to start a new church to reach the black community here in Tucson?"

I said, "Greg, I'd trust you anywhere."

After many meetings and much prayer and discussion together, our church voted to send out Greg and Carmen to start another church about eight miles away. We started it as a mission church, exactly as our church had begun. I would be the pastor with Greg working under me as the missionary pastor. Our church would support them. Our deacons would be their deacons. All of this would be in place until their church was able to support itself.

After a year and a half of prayer, planning, and preparation, on September 30, 2001, Bethel Baptist Church Mission met for the first time. Less than two years later, the church was on its own: Shining Light Baptist Church.

The Dawson family was not the only family to leave Bethel Baptist Church, though. We had eight families join with the Dawsons in this new church plant. I was sad to see them go, but I was also excited for the work they were joining. Shining Light Baptist Church had a great pastor and some wonderful families assisting him.

* * * * *

OVER THE next few years, our church continued to grow as God blessed the ministry of Bethel Baptist Church. We hired a new assistant pastor, Joel Mosier, and together with his family, they were a tremendous help to the church, especially with our youth. Guyla and I both turned 80 years old, though age did not deter us much. We were slower physically than we had been in our 70s, but I had far too much energy to even think about retiring. When someone asked me if I was going to retire, I replied jokingly, "Go home and wash your mouth out with soap. I don't use that word."

We had been at the church for just over eight years when yet another battle arose — a battle over the King James Version (KJV) of the Bible.

I have always preached out of the KJV. It was the first version of the Bible I ever owned. It was the translation from which I was taught at Bob Jones University. It was the version from which I memorized verses. It is simply the translation I have used my entire life.

However, I am not one who believes that the KJV is the *only* inspired Word of God. I do not believe in what is known as "double inspiration" — the belief that both the original manuscript and the translation are separately inspired by God. I believe that the original manuscripts for the Bible were inspired by God — literally, God-breathed. But the translations that have come from the original manuscripts are not directly inspired by God. God wrote His Word through the men who wrote the original manuscripts as described in 2 Peter 1:21 — *"For the prophecy came not in old time by the will of man: but holy men of God spake as they were moved by the Holy Ghost."*

Other men and women have taken the original, inspired manuscripts and translated them to give us the Bibles we have today in many languages around the world. God tells us in 2 Timothy 3:16 that *"All scripture is given by inspiration of God, and is profitable for doctrine, for reproof, for correction, for instruction in righteousness."*

There are different methods of translating — one that translates word for word, and one that translates the overarching thought. I completely agree with those that translate the Bible word for word. It takes the original manuscript and translates it exactly as the writer and God intended it to be. Those that simply translate the thought as opposed to the actual words can get very far off from what the original manuscript said.

I had learned all of this in college and studied it throughout my 50 years of ministry. I firmly believe that God has preserved His Word throughout the many different languages that are in the world today. Jesus reassures us of this truth when He promises, *"Heaven and earth shall pass away, but my words shall not pass away"* (Matthew 24:35; Mark 13:31). We can trust God to keep His promise — we have the very words of God in our hands when we read our Bibles.

I had faced battles before, but I had never had an issue regarding Bible versions within any of my churches. Now, I had church members wanting me to say that whoever does not use the KJV is not using the Word of God. They called any translation other than the KJV the "Devil's Translation."

I have already mentioned that I always used the KJV in my ministry. I preached from it. It was the official translation for each of my churches. Whenever anyone taught or preached at our church, I asked that he or she use the KJV. But there were people in our church in Tucson who believed I was not King James *enough*.

It became so divisive in our church that I decided to bring a message about the topic. At the end, I said, "You know, if any of you are convinced otherwise about this topic and are going to sow discord among us about this issue, there are a lot of King James only churches around. You can join them. We are going to continue using the King James Version, but we are not identified as a King James only church."

Tuscon

At the conclusion of my message, over a third of the congregation left and never came back. Once again, we were heartbroken to see people leave, but we believed that what we were preaching and teaching was what God desired. We were going to do right, no matter the cost. And God continued to bless us.

Within a year of the translation issue, I became burdened and convinced that my work in Tucson was done and it was time to hand the reins over to someone else. God called Joel Mosier and his family to move to Pennsylvania to become assistant pastor at a church there. Since there was no one else on staff at Bethel, I gave the pulpit committee the names of a few men whom I thought would make a good pastor for the church. In 2006 — ten years after we had started — the church called David Stertzbach to be the pastor, and Guyla and I moved away from Tucson to finally "retire."

Chapter 37

"Retired"

Guyla and I were both 82 when we "retired" — for the third time. By that time, our son Tim, who had purchased our house in Lakewood, had moved to Minnesota with his family.

Once we "retired" from the pastorate in Tucson, we thought about moving to be close to Tim; but after visiting Minnesota in the dead of winter, we decided it was far too cold and snowy for us. I am a Colorado boy through and through, and there was nowhere I would rather live than in my beautiful home state. We settled on a house in Castle Rock, Colorado, and began attending a church plant from South Sheridan — Highlands Baptist Church pastored by Jeff Musgrave.

In Arizona, we had owned two sedans. Once we moved back to Colorado, we found out very quickly that neither vehicle would work for the Colorado winters. Our first winter, we experienced unusually snowy weather. When I tried driving my car in the first snow storm, I got stuck in our cul-de-sac. Kind neighbors helped me shovel a path back to my garage where I waited out the storm.

When I informed Tim of what had happened, he immediately suggested that Guyla and I needed a new car — one with all-wheel drive — to which I agreed. So Guyla and I purchased the last car we would ever own, a 2007 Toyota Highlander.

The Holiday Blizzard 1

What a difference all-wheel drive makes! I felt as if I could go anywhere in any type of weather. It was a good thing, too, because only a few weeks later, "Holiday Blizzard 1" descended upon us and left drifts four feet deep in front of our garage.

I had just ordered a snowblower from Home Depot, but the drifts were so deep that I could not shovel my way out to go pick it up. I thought about trying out our new car, but decided against it — I did not want my neighbors to have to "rescue" me again. Fortunately, the snow melts quickly once the sun comes out, and within a few days, Guyla and I were able to be out and about again. We learned our way around Castle Rock, which proved to be a blessing before the winter was over.

Only a few months after joining Highlands Baptist Church as a member — something I had not experienced since college as I had always been the pastor — Pastor Gary Holloway from Harvest Baptist Church asked to speak with me.

Harvest Baptist Church was one of two Baptist churches in Castle Rock. Locals of what was then still a small-town community had no qualms about telling church leaders, "Castle Rock is the graveyard of churches." However, just like any other community in the world, the people needed to hear the Gospel of Jesus Christ. That is why Highlands Baptist, under the leadership of Pastor Jeff Musgrave, had sent a pastor and some of the members from his congregation to start this church.

From its beginning, the church struggled — just like most of the other churches that began in Castle Rock. The church began in 2000 under the leadership of Pastor and Mrs. Gary Holloway. They started with a handful of people both from the community and a few from Highlands as well. Within five years, they purchased a building on South Gilbert Street and were chartered as Harvest Baptist Church.

When I met with Pastor Holloway, he informed me that he and his wife Charis felt that the Lord was moving them on from Castle Rock. "Would you be willing to candidate for the pastorate here?" he asked.

I went home that evening and told Guyla about the conversation. We talked with Jeff Musgrave and asked for his opinion. We all prayed about it, and then Guyla and I decided that if the church would have us come, we would candidate for the pastorate.

The Holloways went away for a weekend, and I preached a candidating service. The following week, Guyla and I visited family while the church voted. It was unanimous. Less than a year after "retirement," I was back to work. At age 82, I was the pastor of Harvest Baptist Church.

*****

Pastoring a struggling church in a growing area is not easy for anyone. It is even more difficult when the pastor is 82 years old. Yet, Guyla and I both felt confident that this is what God would have us to do, so we embraced it! We went out knocking on doors. We visited all our church members and anyone new who visited. It was exciting! Our little church began to grow.

Within a year or two, we were able to bring on a man as assistant pastor. I thought he would be the man to whom I could hand over the church. He and his family seemed to love the people and love God's Word — and I genuinely believe that was the case!

However, one day, I received an anonymous letter that strongly advised me to look into this man's past. I read the letter, and then made some phone calls. I needed to verify facts and not simply rely on an anonymous accusation. What I discovered made me incredibly sad. I called the man into my office and told him what I had uncovered. "Is this true?" I asked him.

"Yes, it is. I was in counseling for a while, but I'm over the issue now. I've made things right, so I am fine continuing in the ministry."

"Maybe somewhere else," I said. "I don't believe you are blameless, and based upon your admission, I think you have been disqualified from the ministry."

The man insisted that he was fine and that reconciliation had been made. He begged me to let him stay.

"No," I said firmly. "Effective immediately, you are no longer on staff at this church, nor do I want you to come back."

Sunday morning, the man and his family were not there. I told the church that this man was not going to be working for the church anymore and that there were issues I did not want to discuss, but I had to let the man go.

I received much criticism over that decision. People did not understand, but I was not going to deliberately undermine or betray him or his family. If other people wanted to use him in the ministry, that was their decision. But I had made mine and would stick with it, no matter what people said about me.

A short while later, we called another man to the assistant pastorate. He had been the youth pastor at Highlands Baptist Church for a few years and felt God calling his family to move on from the church. The Lord led them to us, and in January of 2009, Josh and Priscilla Musgrave joined our team at Harvest Baptist Church.

He was an excellent man to have working with me. He was young; I was old. He had the energy and ability to do things that my body just simply could not do anymore.

* * * * *

ONE YEAR before Josh came, I had fallen on ice and broken my arm. That injury set me back for several months. Guyla and I were scheduled to travel to India at the beginning of October to speak at a pastor's conference, a Bible college graduation, and evangelistic services, as well as to visit and minister with Mathew Thomas — a long-time friend and former member of South Sheridan. Also living and working in the ministry with Mathew were his daughter and son-in-law Sophie and Santhosh George, and their two children, Joanna and Jonathan.

August came, and I still had limited mobility in my arm, specifically my fingers. We, however, were determined to go. I laugh now when

Inside Nelson Hall — a fellowship hall in a church in India dedicated to Guyla and me. Left to right: Santhosh and Sophie George, Emilee, Guyla, Me, Mathew Thomas

I think about it — two 84-year-olds traveling to the other side of the world, and one of them with a broken arm that was not yet healed.

Our children were hesitant about Guyla and I traveling to India alone, so it was a great relief to them when one of our granddaughters, Emilee, offered to travel with us in order "to take care of us." Ironically however, instead of Emilee taking care of us, we had to take care of her! She got food poisoning on the way from Denver to London. It continued throughout the layover in London, the flight to Mumbai, the flight to Cochin, and the drive to the Thomas/George house where we were to stay. Needless to say, it was quite the trip! Guyla and I both prayed much for her, and God answered our prayers. Within three days of landing in India, she was back to herself again, although she did get to experience the inside of an Indian hospital.

I preached almost daily with either Mathew or Santhosh translating. Guyla taught a few sessions to the pastors' wives, and Emilee played her violin for some of the services. God truly blessed our last trip out of the country.

After two weeks in India, we returned to America — still in one piece. Maybe traveling at 84 was not as dangerous as our kids thought!

* * * * *

Once Josh Musgrave came to Harvest, I slowly began handing over many of the church responsibilities to him. He was an excellent preacher and had a heart for the people — his whole family did. Over the next year, Guyla and I came to the conclusion that it was time for us to step aside. On March 28, 2010, Guyla and I left the church, and the congregation voted to call Josh Musgrave as the senior pastor of Harvest Baptist Church.

My time as pastor was finished. At 86 years of age, I had "retired" for the last time.

Chapter 38

"Gettin' Old Ain't for Sissies"

It was not until I was 87 that I really started feeling old. Up until that point, I had only experienced what I thought were minor health issues — several of them involving my throat. I had real trouble swallowing. The simple solution, the doctor told me, was an endoscopy to stretch out my throat so I could swallow better.

In July of 2011, I went in for a normal endoscopic throat-stretching. Within 24 hours of the procedure, I could not swallow anything — no water, no food, not even saliva. I called Tim and Dave, but I was having trouble breathing and talking to them on the phone. My throat had swelled shut. They convinced me to go to the emergency room, and I did not argue.

At the hospital, the doctors determined that I would require surgery to fix the problem and relieve the tension on the muscles. The emergency room transferred me to a hospital covered by my insurance, St. Anthony Hospital. I was very familiar with the name of the hospital because it had been in Denver since before I was born. However, they had just moved to a brand new campus in Lakewood a few weeks prior to my transfer. I was to be one of the first surgical patients in the new facility.

The surgery was scheduled for the next afternoon. About an hour before surgery, the nurse came in. I thought she was there to do pre-op preparation. Instead, she told me, "We are having to cancel your surgery. As you know, this is a brand new facility. Apparently when the drywall for the operating rooms was shipped from Asia, there were beetles that laid eggs in the drywall. They have now hatched, and there are beetles all over the operating rooms — we literally have bugs in our operating rooms. We have to move your surgery to tomorrow. By that time, we will have exterminated the beetles and sanitized the operating rooms."

There was nothing else for me to do but wait for the next morning when I could have the surgery.

About two hours later, I felt funny and started vomiting. About an hour later, the surgeon came into my room. "Mr. Nelson, did you feel all right this afternoon?" he asked.

I explained what had happened that afternoon including the funny feeling and vomiting. When I finished, he simply said, "You are a lucky man. If we had been in surgery as planned when this happened, you would not have come off that operating table alive. You had a heart attack."

God used those beetles in that drywall to prevent the scheduled surgery and spare my life!

Two stents, a throat surgery, and several weeks later, I was back up and ready to preach again. I must admit, though, I did feel a lot older.

A year later, Guyla had her own bout in the hospital. By this time, Tim and Monica had moved their family back to Colorado and lived about 10 minutes away from us. They figured we needed extra care — and I guess we did! Just a few months after they moved, Monica noticed that Guyla did not look well, so she took her to the doctor for bloodwork. The next day, we were sitting at breakfast when the doctor called. "Get her to the nearest hospital immediately!" he said. Her bloodwork had shown a hemoglobin level of 4. Normal is 14. The ER personnel saw her and said, "We have *never* seen anyone walk in with a 4. You're practically dead if you're at a 4."

Immediate testing showed that Guyla had colon cancer. Within two days, she was under the knife. The surgeon removed an eight inch section of her colon, the only section that had cancer in it. During her entire recovery at the hospital, nurses walked past the room, pointed, and said, "She was the 4."

At 88 years old, it took her quite some time to recuperate, but by the grace of God, she made a complete recovery.

Throughout the next few years, Guyla and I took turns with various illnesses, injuries, surgeries, and other difficulties. Our bodies definitely felt the age now! But we always were blessed to have the strength to regain health and the ability to minister through the opportunities God kept providing.

Early in 2013, I had a hip replacement surgery. Let me tell you, that is not for the faint of heart. The actual surgery went very smoothly, but the recovery and rehabilitation was excruciating. It was months before I was able to accomplish my goal of walking a mile.

Fortunately, by the time my 90th birthday came around, I was completely healed and rarin' to go. December 1, 2013, happened to land on a Sunday. Five churches in the Denver area — four of which I had helped start — gathered together and held a special evening service just for me at Red Rocks Baptist Church, the former South Sheridan Baptist Church. Friends shared fond memories, and we sang my favorite hymns. I was asked to preach and reminisce. It was a special day.

On the way to the service, I *doubly* realized my age when 40 minutes into the 45 minute drive, I realized I had left my Bible and my notes at home. I preached from Guyla's Bible which had much smaller print than mine. Fortunately, I had memorized most of the passages so I did not need to read too much of the smaller print.

I preached on Zechariah 4:6, *"Then he answered and spake unto me, saying, This is the word of the LORD unto Zerubbabel, saying, Not by might, nor by power, but by my spirit, saith the LORD of hosts."*

"In other words," I preached, "the Holy Spirit is the One who brings the power of God and gives the blessing of understanding the Word of God. It's so important for us preachers to realize that we need to rely on the Holy Spirit" — especially when we forget our notes!

To the shock of my children and grandchildren who were at the service, I even remembered a quote from Charles Spurgeon that I had studied and included in my forgotten notes. I am sure I did not quote him exactly word-for-word, but the idea was there nonetheless.

> *If your church does not have the Holy Spirit's blessing upon it, you'd better close it up. Board up the doors and put a cross over the doors, a black cross with a big sign saying, 'God, have mercy on us.' If you preachers have not the Holy Spirit, you'd better quit preaching and your people had better stay at home. I think I speak not too plainly when I say that any church in the land without the Holy Spirit's blessing is more of a curse than a blessing. If you have not the Holy Spirit, Christian worker, you're standing in someone else's place. You're standing as a tree that bears no fruit where a fruitful tree might grow.*

It was a great time of reminiscing on the goodness and faithfulness of God. Early in our married lives, Guyla and I had taken Zechariah 4:6 and determined that we were going to depend on the power of the Holy Spirit to bless our work for God — and He certainly has.

I concluded the service with advice from an old man to the next generations: "You know what? We're in the minority — Baptists who believe in the fundamental truths of the Bible. But I don't care if we're in the minority. If we've got the Holy Spirit, we have the power of God."

* * * * *

THE NEXT six years were full of ups and downs: preaching at various churches, many of which I had started years ago with church planting or tent meetings; in and out of the hospital for various reasons; preaching at Bob Jones University at age 92; a few broken bones; doctors' visits; memory loss for Guyla; funerals of peers and friends; performing the wedding ceremonies for two of my granddaughters; and taking advantage of each opportunity to minister as the Lord led and we were able. It was particularly special to be invited to preach at many of the churches in Colorado that I had helped start.

I had pastored many older folks throughout my years, but I was learning firsthand just how difficult it is to age well. Getting old is hard!

Living in our house by ourselves became increasingly difficult. Though Guyla was healthy physically, it grew more and more obvious to me, Tim's family, and Dave and Robbi, that Guyla was mentally slipping. Our doctor, Dr. Michael Schindel, did some basic testing and officially diagnosed her with dementia.

Tim, Monica, and their kids lived 10 minutes away, which was a tremendous blessing to us when the smoke detector batteries went out at 2 A.M.; when I fell and could not get up; when Guyla did not feel like cooking. We found ourselves over at their house more frequently for dinner, and they came over often just to help out us old folks.

After months of this, we decided that the best solution was for us to move in with Tim and Monica. They were renting at the time in order to be close to us. The landlords informed them that the house was going on the market. The timing was perfect. Tim and Monica moved out of their house and moved into ours to help us get ready to sell it. For two 91-year-olds, the process of selling a house was exhausting. Over the next 40 days, we showed our house over 50 times — and it usually happened during lunch or nap time. Finally, our house sold, and Tim and I purchased an amazing house that had a main floor master for Tim and Monica, enough bedrooms for their children, *and* a main floor apartment for us. It was the perfect solution.

As Guyla's dementia progressed, Monica was able to jump in and take care of her and me. We fixed our own breakfasts and lunches, but

Homeowners for the last time

each evening, we traveled the "long distance" to Monica's kitchen where we ate dinner as a family. It was a rare occasion when we had less than 10 people at the dinner table — Tim and Monica, Mollie and her husband Rob, Meghan and her husband Nick, Emilee, Sam, Zach, and Monica's parents Ernst and Renate Stoeckmann. It was such a joyous time together. Often, we would laugh when the boys, who were teasing their siblings, received a classic, one-liner joke or reprimand from Grandma.

Though there were many things that Guyla forgot, she remembered important things. Every day, she and I would have our devotions together in our little living room. As we concluded, we would pray for each of our family members, many of the pastors in the area, missionaries, and friends with needs. She remembered every single family member's name.

For me, I must admit, it was a very difficult thing watching my brilliant wife slowly slip away as she forgot places, people, faces, and amazingly, some of the grammar and schooling she had taught for so many years. She still could rattle off the "correct" order of teaching the alphabet, but she began to lose a desire to do much of anything. She did not remember how to cook or clean. She slept more than anything else.

Whenever I wrote something, she still felt it was her duty to proofread my work; but often, she missed many grammatical errors or typos.

In 2018, our lives changed a lot. Guyla got sick with a really bad cold. After weeks of no healing, *much* sleeping, and lots of medicine, we grew concerned that she had pneumonia. Dr. Schindel ordered an x-ray to see if her lungs were clear. He found something far more serious. It seemed that Guyla's cancer had returned and metastasized to her lungs.

The bloodwork confirmed the results of the x-ray. In order to preserve Guyla's normal quality of life, we chose not to treat the cancer. Over the next few weeks, Guyla recovered from the cold, and miraculously, she had zero symptoms from the cancer. She had no shortness of breath, no pain, no coughing, nothing. We were all amazed at the graciousness of God.

Another big change happened that year. I gave up my keys.

At 94½, I was still driving — not long distances, but Tim and Monica let me drive to the bank, the grocery store, the gas station, and other local places in town. When my parents got to the point when they could not drive, Dad fought me when I told him he needed to give up the keys. I told Tim that I would not fight him, but I *really* did not want to give up driving just yet. I thought I was just fine!

Until. . . I did not see the bear.

Our neighborhood has a bear that enjoyed a feast of watermelon from our trash cans shortly after we moved in. The bear had cubs, and they also ravaged any trash or food they could get their paws on.

Guyla was not up to walking much, but I walked almost daily. I used a walker instead of my cane so I had better balance. It had a built-in seat, so whenever I got tired, I could just sit down. I was at the end of our cul-de-sac resting before beginning the 200-foot walk back to the house. All of a sudden, Tim started yelling and walking rapidly toward me. I stood up and had started walking again when Tim reached me. "Do you not see the bear?" he asked.

"What bear?"

"Right there!" he said pointing. "It's about 50 feet away from you."

All I could see was a dark blob. I have macular degeneration, an eye condition that is typically caused by aging. As it grows worse over time, it can cause people to lose their central vision, either partially or completely. I knew my eyesight had been getting worse, but I did not know it was *that* bad!

It was not until Tim pointed out the bear that I got scared. He helped me home, and I told him, "I've decided. I'm handing over the keys right now." And I never drove again.

Well — almost never. In January 2020, Tim let me drive one more time when my Toyota Highlander reached 200,000 miles. It was the first vehicle I had ever owned that had reached that mileage. When Tim and Monica discovered that, they decided to make a big party out of it. Tim drove my car the 2.4 miles up the road to our church property. No one, including me, thought it was a good idea for me to be on an actual road. Our church, Castleview Baptist Church, owns 19 acres off of Crowfoot Valley Road in Castle Rock, so Tim figured the open land was the perfect place to drive into the 200,000th mile.

There was only one hiccup. I had not driven in over two years, and Tim and Dave forgot to refresh my memory on where the brake and gas pedals were.

The church property lies on the top of a ridge in Castle Rock, and it has a steep ravine in the middle of the land with a small road connecting the two peninsulas. I was on the first peninsula driving through mile 199,999. When I turned around and headed toward the main road (Crowfoot Valley Road), I did not remember where the brake pedal was. As I moved my foot around trying to find it, I accidently pushed the gas. Instead of slowing down, we sped up. Dave was sitting in the

Driving my car over 200,000 miles

front passenger seat next to me and tried to reach the brake pedal with his hand, but could not reach. He threw the car into park. It did nothing. But in order to get it *out* of park, the brake pedal needed to be pressed.

We were still heading straight toward the road. With only 20 feet to go before hitting the wire fence separating us from the oncoming cars, Dave grabbed the steering wheel and turned sharply to the left — directly into a downhill embankment of scrub oak.

We crashed through some large scrub oak branches and bushes and were heading straight toward the steep ravine. Once again, Dave grabbed the steering wheel and swerved onto the dirt road connecting the peninsulas. The car, still in park, finally stopped. And everyone breathed a sigh of relief.

At that point, Tim and Dave made sure I was well acquainted with the pedals and workings of the car. I took it out of park and drove right through a sign Tim's kids had made: 200,000 MILES.

Maybe there is a reason why most 96-year-olds do not drive.

* * * * *

THE YEAR 2019 brought much pain, both emotional and physical, but also much joy.

Within the first four months, I was in the emergency room four times. On the last visit, we discovered that I had stress fractures on my spine. Let me tell you, stress fractures are painful! Dr. Schindel said that he thought the cause of the fractures was simply because I was sitting down too hard. I changed how I seat myself in chairs, and I have not had stress fractures since.

One week into my recovery, Guyla woke up in pain. It was Good Friday, so Emilee had the day off of work. She came in and checked out where Guyla was complaining about the pain. It was her lung. Monica called Dr. Schindel who simply said, "I'm sorry. I've been waiting for this call for quite a while."

We called in hospice, and they helped us figure out a plan to keep Guyla's pain managed. That Friday, she only took two Advil the entire day. By Monday, she was on a narcotic pain medicine every four hours. We knew then that her body was finally showing symptoms of her cancer, and it had progressed substantially since her pain had gotten so bad. She did not have much time left, and somehow, we just knew it. We were praying that she would make it to our 70th wedding anniversary on June 2. On April 30, we shared this on our Facebook page:

> Almost 70 years ago, I said "in sickness and in health. . . 'til death do us part" as a covenant promise to my dear wife Guyla. Now, at 95 years of age, we believe she is in her last days.
>
> A few years ago, she was sick with colon cancer. The doctors removed all of it, but we believe it has come back in her lungs. By God's grace, for a year now, she has had no side effects — no pain, no shortness of breath, nothing. However, two weeks ago, she woke up with severe pain, the result of the cancer worsening. We are able to make her comfortable at home, and the hospice nurses and our family are taking great care of both her and me. The nurses and doctors have given her only a few weeks to live. . . .

> Thank you for your prayers and support through these days. We praise the Lord for all He has done and continue to praise Him.
>
> "Being confident of this very thing, that He which hath begun a good work in you will perform it until the day of Jesus Christ" (Philippians 1:6). This is Guyla's life verse.

Ruth decided to come out immediately. Kathy would have come, but she was recovering from her own health battle and was not strong enough to walk, let alone travel. Guyla had a *great* two days with Ruth. Guyla was mentally sharp and lucid — something we had not seen very often in recent days.

Two days after Ruth came, she took me to get my hair cut. Guyla tried to get ready and come with us, but she was just too tired. We came home, and Ruth fixed lunch. About the time she was going to the bedroom to get Guyla up from her nap, we heard a faint, "Help! Help!"

Guyla had fallen. We rushed in and found her on the floor, her head near the closet door. Monica and Ruth carefully picked her up and set her in the chair nearby. Monica was convinced she had broken her hip. We called Dr. Schindel and hospice. The hospice nurse arrived first. She took one look at Guyla sitting in the chair, and said, "She definitely does *not* have a broken hip. No one would be able to sit that peacefully and pain-free with a broken hip."

A few hours later, Dr. Schindel came and did his own examination — much more thorough than the hospice nurse. "She definitely *does* have a broken hip."

We deliberated on whether to take Guyla to the hospital or just let her stay home, and we finally decided that she would be most comfortable at home, especially with her dementia.

She fell around 1:30 p.m. By 9:00 p.m., we had moved her to a hospital bed set up in our living room. Almost all of us fully expected her to be awake in the morning, looking out the front window at the birds and the flowers. But she never woke up. During the evening, she had slipped into a coma.

Three agonizing days later, my dear, sweet Guyla passed from life here on Earth and began her eternity with her Lord and Savior Jesus Christ. On May 4, 2019, at approximately 9:25 P.M., Guyla was finally Home, just 28 days shy of our 70th anniversary. Oh, what a thrill it is to know the truth of 2 Corinthians 5:8, *"We are confident, I say, and willing rather to be absent from the body, and to be present with the Lord."*

The funeral service was held at Red Rocks Baptist Church on Thursday, May 16. Four of our children, 9 of our 14 grandchildren, and 2 of our great-grandchildren were able to attend. Our children and their spouses each shared one or two words that described Mom — smart, witty, unremarkably remarkable, kind, gracious, beautiful — and they were all true of her.

As the cards and memories came flooding in, I got a new sense of wonder at the woman God had given me as my wife. She was always special to me — I just did not fully realize how special a lady she was to so many others; how brilliant; how kind; how humble. Over our many years of ministry together, I received praise from others for my preaching of the Word, but she was right there beside me, giving a listening ear, wise advice, or a shoulder to cry on. She was just *there* for the people of our churches. She was a teacher to the teachers. I was amazed to hear of the many children and adults who learned to read or to teach simply through Guyla's curriculum or advice. After her death, I realized how rare women like Guyla are in this world. And I saw in a new way just how much of a gift God had bestowed upon me by giving me someone as faithful, loyal, and totally committed to the will of God as my dear Guyla.

She was the biggest instrument of grace that God ever brought into my life. She was the force behind my ministry. Her demeanor, her speech, her actions, her love — her being my life companion made me who I am. Without her, I could never have seen the blessing of all the years of miraculous ministry. I could have never faced the battles we had to face. Silver State Baptist School would never have succeeded. She

Frances Guyla Nelson, 1924 – 2019

helped me immeasurably to be a pastor whom God could use. I could not have done one fraction of what I have done in my lifetime without her standing beside me and helping me every day. Next to my Lord, she was my everything. And now she was gone.

Though in her later years Guyla did not and could not do much because of her dementia, she was still there. She kept me going. I took care of her. I fixed her breakfast. We had devotions and prayed together. I studied downstairs. I fixed her lunch. We took our afternoon naps, and then we watched the news. My entire life had centered around her as we had grown older. And now, she was just not there.

In the days that followed, I discovered old habits that revolved around her care. When I would get up during the night, I would get out of bed as quietly as possible so I would not wake her. Then I would remember, she was not there.

It was hard! After 69 years and 11 months of marriage, I did not know what to do without her. And the longer I continue to live without her, the more I miss her. Oh, how I look forward to the day when I, too, can be *"caught up together in the clouds to meet the Lord in the air; and so shall we ever be with the Lord" (1 Thessalonians 4:17).*

* * * * *

ON JULY 4, just two months after Guyla's passing, Monica, Emilee, and Zachary took me to Idaho Springs for some of their favorite pizza, Beau Jo's. There was a long wait, so I asked if we could go see the First Baptist Church building in town. On the way, I told them the brief version of how I had started the church back in 1947 with a tent meeting.

When we arrived at the church building, we found a lady there picking up some tables for a BBQ the church was having that evening. She let us see the inside and told us how the church was looking for a new pastor. We shared some of the history we had with the church, encouraged one another, and even sang some hymns together. Monica mentioned that maybe I could come and preach sometime for them.

What do you know? A month later, I was asked to preach on Labor Day weekend. It was thrilling for me to stand in the pulpit of one of the first churches I had helped to start 72 years earlier.

Exactly three months later was my 96th birthday, December 1, 2019. I had preached on my 90th birthday and never thought I would make it to 96 — but I did! I really wanted the opportunity to preach on my 96th birthday, too, but I did not want to push myself on any church. Outside of family, I had only told one other person of my desire, and that was Dr. Dean Miller, Sr., the man who had been one of my assistants at South Sheridan.

I should have known better. He told his son, Dean Miller, Jr., pastor of Front Range Baptist Church in Fort Collins. Within a week of my telling Dean, Sr., I had an invitation to preach — on my birthday.

It was such a special day. In addition to the Front Range Baptist Church congregation, many friends and family joined us for the service that day. Pastor Dean, Jr., went above and beyond to make me feel special. He organized a birthday greeting video from friends and pastors including Dr. Bob Jones, III; Pastor Tate Throndson; Pastor Jud Riley; and Dr. R.B. Oullette. Their kindness was unexpected and made my 96th birthday that much more memorable.

Preaching on my 96th birthday

My goal was the same at 96 years of age as it was at 21 — to win souls to Jesus; to encourage believers in their faith; and, more than anything, to bring glory to God.

* * * * *

Looking back on my life, I see so many areas where I wish I had done things differently. I have failed so many times. I have driven people away with words I have said or things I have (or have not) done. I have sinned and have not loved God or people enough.

Yet, my God is a faithful God. He is a forgiving God. He is merciful and does not give me what I deserve. He has answered my prayers far more abundantly than I could have imagined. He has stretched me greater than I thought possible. He has humbled me; transformed me; encouraged me. I have endeavored to live my life by the power of the Spirit of God and directed by the Word of God. One of the many poems about the Bible which I memorized during my pastorate at South Sheridan sums up the value and treasure I have found in my Bible.

> *This Holy Book I'd rather own*
>   *Than all the gold and gems*
> *That e'er in monarch's coffers shone,*
>   *Than all their diadems.*
>
> *Nay, were the seas one chrysolite,*
>   *The earth one golden ball,*
> *And diamonds all the stars of night,*
>   *This Book outweighs them all.*
>
> *Ah, no, the soul ne'er found relief*
>   *In glittering hoards of wealth;*
> *Gems dazzle not the eye of grief,*
>   *Gold cannot purchase health.*
>
> *But here a blessed balm appears*
>   *To heal the deepest woe;*
> *And they who read this Book in tears*
>   *Their tears shall cease to flow.*
>
> *Thou truest friend man ever knew*
>   *Thy constancy I've tried;*
> *When all were false I found Thee true,*
>   *My counselor and guide.*
>
> *The mines of earth no treasures give*
>   *That can this volume buy;*
> *In teaching me the way to live,*
>   *It taught me how to die.*
>
>   — *Author Unknown*

All throughout my life, I have heard people say that is important to live well. I agree — we ought to live our lives for the glory of God and run the race of the Christian faith every single day. But in my old age, I have learned that it is equally important to finish well. To keep on and not quit. To keep fighting. To keep running. Satan does not give up his fight on believers once they hit a certain age. Just because I have been in the ministry for over 70 years does not mean that I have somehow made it to the stage where I am no longer tempted to sin. I am tempted every single day. The fight for the faith is not over, nor will it be until I see my Savior face to face.

So this is my story. The story of a simple farm boy whom God miraculously saved and transformed by the Spirit of God to preach the Word and bring souls to Jesus. It truly is a miracle — the miracle of taking me, a sinner, and saving me by His grace.

> *Only a sinner saved by grace!*
> *Only a sinner saved by grace!*
> *This is my story, to God be the glory —*
> *I'm only a sinner saved by grace!*
>   — James M. Gray

Acknowledgements

Writing a book is no easy task. There are many people who have their hand in creating the finished product, and I want to bestow praise and thankfulness on those who deserve it.

Guyla — *thank you for being my faithful companion, my best proofreader, and my partner in ministry for nearly 70 years. I wish you could have proofread this book, but thankfully you taught our children well.*

Kathy, Ruth, Dave, Tim, and Monica — *thanks for the countless hours you spent editing, proofreading, and reviewing the book. Thanks, also, for the support you have given me as your dad.*

Ed and Lorene Byrd; Dr. Bob Jones, III; Sophie (Thomas) George and Sumi (Thomas) Sara; Poulose Kochakkan, Dave Mullennex; Jeff and Anna Musgrave; Dr. Steve Pettit; Chuck and Becky Schindel; and Dr. Wayne and Beverly Van Gelderen — *thank you for the time you spent answering questions and researching facts, and thank you for helping me remember and correcting me when I remembered incorrectly.*

Carolyn Perdue — *thank you for providing copies of the Mile-Hi Evangelist and other historical documents for our research.*

Emilee — *thank you for the hours you spent in getting this book written and published. You put your life and soul into the book, researched* more than I ever thought possible, and really helped me tell my story. I am grateful.

To my former assistant pastors and staff members — *thank you for serving faithfully alongside me in the futherance of His service.*

And to former church members in my congregations — *thank you for the privilege of being your pastor.*

— Ed Nelson

* * * * *

In addition, I would like to add my gratitude . . .

Grandpa — *thank you for trusting me to help you write this book, for your faithfulness throughout your life, for your unusual ability to stand for truth no matter the cost, and for teaching me that it is impossible to have a "horse-drawn tractor" like I had in Draft 1.*

Mom and Dad — *thank you for your constant support and for encouraging me to keep going, especially on the days when the words were not coming to me and the editing was overwhelming.*

Meghan Books, Lauren Wiggs, and Mollie Yoder — *thank you for proofreading the book and correcting my mistakes.*

Sam Nelson — *thank you for donating airline tickets to assist with the audiobook recording.*

Zach Nelson — *thank you for being the voice of the audiobook even while you were in the middle of a college semester.*

Bob Johansen, Matthew Steel, and Ashley Gwillim — *thank you for your service in recording and mastering the audiobook. Special thanks to Ashley for assisting Zach with the voicing of the book characters.*

And to the countless number of people who have prayed for this book, checked on the progress, and supported me through this process — thank you.

— Emilee Nelson

Notes

Chapter 1: The Accident

Page 5   **I remember one night**: Ken Nelson, in conversation with Ed Nelson, May 2019.

Page 5   **Northern Lights**: Floyd E. Merrill, 'Northern Lights in Fine Display Near Midnight,' *Greeley Daily Tribune*, 18 September, 1941.

Chapter 2: My Family

Page 7   **Arrived in Chicago on May 21, 1884**: Obituary of John Magni Nelson, 'J. M. Nelson Dies Tuesday After Illness of Many Months,' *Windsor Beacon*, 14 December, 1939.

Page 7   **In 1886**: 'Welcome to the Colorado State Capitol,' Colorado General Assembly, accessed 6 October, 2020, https://leg.colorado.gov/Visit-Learn.

Page 8   **In 1894, Magni moved**: Obituary, 'J.M. Nelson Dies.'

Page 8   **In 1904**: Obituary, 'J.M. Nelson Dies.'

Page 10   **December 29, 1920**: 'Ernest D. Nelson Weds Former Idaho Springs Girl,' *Windsor Beacon*, 30 December, 1920.

Page 7   **I won first place**: 'Labor Day Carnival Parade,' *Windsor Beacon*, 4 September, 1941.

Page 10   **December 29, 1920**: 'Ernest Nelson Wins Top Colorado Honor In Soil Conservation,' *Windsor Beacon*, 10 December, 1959.

Page 19   **Rotary Club Master Farmer**: 'Obituary of Ernest D. Nelson,' *Windsor Beacon*, 7 March, 1985.

Page 23   **Senior Class President**: 'Windsor High Class Presidents,' *Greeley Daily Tribune*, 16 May, 1941.

Page 24 — **Scholarship for $100**: '3 Weld Boys Awarded $100 Scholarships,' *Greeley Daily Tribune,* 20 August, 1942.

Chapter 3: Frozen to the Farm

Page 25 — **From the NBC Newsroom:** WeAreHistoryTeachers, 'The Pearl Harbor Attack Emergency Radio Broadcast Announcement (December 07, 1941),' YouTube video, 04:02, 14 June, 2018, https://youtu.be/tdtaRvWd3t4.

Page 26 — **Yesterday, December 7, 1941**: A&E Television, 'The United States Declares War on Japan,' HISTORY, accessed 6 October, 2020, https://www.history.com/this-day-in-history/the-united-states-declares-war-on-japan.

Page 26 — **4-F rating**: 'Classifications,' Selected Service System, 2020, https://www.sss.gov/about/return-to-draft/.

Page 33 — **War ended in September**: A&E Television Networks, 'World War II,' HISTORY, accessed 6 October, 2020, https://www.history.com/topics/world-war-ii/world-war-ii-history.

Chapter 4: The Call to Preach

Page 44 — **Souls for Jesus:** Words by Gillis Partin, 1918-, Music by BJU Ministerial Students, 1941, Arranged by Dwight Gustafson, 1930–2014; © Copyright 1979 by Bob Jones University. All rights reserved. Used with permission.

Page 44 — **Do Right**: Quote from Chapel Sayings by Dr. Bob Jones, Sr. Used with permission.

Page 45 — **The Greatest Ability**: Quote from Chapel Sayings by Dr. Bob Jones, Sr. Used with permission.

Page 45 — **The way to keep**: Quote from Chapel Sayings by Dr. Bob Jones, Sr. Used with permission.

Chapter 6: Ministry Lessons 101

Page 56 — **The Navigators**: 'History of The Navigators,' The Navigators, accessed 6 October, 2020, https://www.navigators.org/about/history/.

Page 56 — **Every preacher who**: E. M. Bounds, *The Power Through Prayer,* originally published 1910, © 2011 paperback edition, printed 2 July, 2019, 6.

Page 57 — **The way to learn**: Quote from Chapel Sayings by Dr. Bob Jones, Sr. Used with permission.

Page 58 — **Take the train**: 'Windsor: Besels on Vacation. In Religious Work. Goes to Puerto Rico,' *Fort Collins Coloradoan,* 21 June, 1946.

PAGE 62   **Old Fashioned Revival Hour**: 'About Us,' Old Fashioned Revival Hour, accessed 2 June, 2020, https://www.ofrh.com/about-us.

Chapter 9: Rocky Mountain Evangelist

PAGE 80   **Under 200 residents**: 'Number of Inhabitants — Colorado,' United States Census Bureau, https://www2.census.gov/library/publications/decennial/1950/population-volume-1/vol-01-09.pdf.

PAGE 81   **A grade school...**: Amanda Kesting and Caitlin Hendee, 'The Original Location of This Colorado Mountain Town is Now 250 Feet Underwater,' 9News, accessed 6 October, 2020, https://www.9news.com/article/life/style/colorado-guide/the-original-location-of-this-colorado-mountain-town-is-now-250-feet-underwater/73-508987368.

PAGE 85   **An article came out**: 'Dillon, Colorado Faces Extinction if Denver Builds Dam,' *Denver Post*, 9 March, 1953, 3.

Chapter 10: Guyla

PAGE 91   **Battle of Seven Pines**: The Editors of Encyclopedia Britannica, 'Battle of Seven Pines,' Encyclopedia Britannica, accessed 6 October, 2020, https://www.britannica.com/event/Battle-of-Seven-Pines.

PAGE 91   **Margaret Guyla**: Personal letter, no date, signed J. G. Lofton.

PAGE 94   **Valedictorian**: Tim Nelson, 'Guyla Nelson Eulogy,' 16 May, 2019.

PAGE 96   **99.3% average**: Nelson, 'Eulogy.'

PAGE 91   **Six academic schools**: 'History of BJU,' Bob Jones University, accessed 6 October, 2020, https://www.bju.edu/about/history.php.

Chapter 11: Preparing for the Mission Field

PAGE 99   **Achieved a new status**: Bob Jones University, "History of BJU."

PAGE 101 **Vice-president of the Ministerial Association**: BJU Vintage Staff, *1949 Vintage*, Bob Jones University, 53.

PAGE 102 **Student Body Chaplain**: 'Nelson Elected Chaplain University Student Body,' *Windsor Beacon*, 11 March, 1948.

PAGE 103 **Do right - even if the stars fall**: Quote from Chapel Sayings by Dr. Bob Jones, Sr. Used with permission.

PAGE 104 **General Douglas MacArthur's word to America saying**: Mikio Haruna, 'MacArthur Pondered Showa Conversion,' Japan Times, 2000, accessed 6 October, 2020, https://www.japantimes.co.jp/news/2000/05/04/national/history/macarthur-pondered-showa-conversion/#.XtfcmC-z10s.

Chapter 12: Six Months to Live

Page 107 — **Newspaper wrote an article**: 'Big Day For Ed Nelson. Wins Diploma and Bride Today,' *Windsor Beacon*, 2 June, 1949.

Page 107 — **Hotel Lake Louise**: 'History — A Look Back At Our Past,' Georgia Baptist Conference Center, accessed 6 October, 2020, https://mytoccoa.com/history/.

Page 107 — **Bright's Disease**: The Editors of Encyclopaedia Britannica, 'Bright Disease,' Encyclopædia Britannica, accessed 6 October, 2020, https://www.britannica.com/science/Bright-disease.

Page 112 — **Sulfathiazole**: John P. Swann, 'The 1941 Sulfathiazole Disaster and the Birth of Good Manufacturing Practices,' *Pharmacy in History* 41, no. 1 (1999): 16-25, accessed 6 October, 2020, www.jstor.org/stable/41111915.

Chapter 13: "If You Leave on Monday..."

Page 116 — **Penicillin... a newer drug**: 'Penicillin,' Wikipedia, accessed 6 October, 2020, https://en.wikipedia.org/wiki/Penicillin.

Chapter 15: God's Miraculous Provision

Page 132 — **Fathers were not allowed:** Deena Prichep, 'This Father's Day, Remembering a Time When Dads Weren't Welcome in Delivery Rooms,' National Public Radio, 2017, accessed 6 October, 2020, https://www.npr.org/sections/health-shots/2017/06/18/532921305/this-fathers-day-remembering-a-time-when-dads-werent-welcome-in-delivery-rooms.

Page 138 — **In August of 1950**: 'Our Story, His Glory,' Calvary Baptist Church, accessed 6 October, 2020, http://www.calvarycasper.com/our-story-his-glory.html.

Chapter 16: Hoffman Heights

Page 151 — **1,700 doors**: Kelly Jensen, 'Hoffman Heights in Aurora, a Neighborhood Born From WWII,' 9News, 2016, accessed 6 October, 2020, https://www.9news.com/article/life/style/colorado-guide/hoffman-heights-in-aurora-a-neighborhood-born-from-wwii/337546830.

Page 149 — **Conservative Baptist Association structure**: 'CB Northwest Identity Document,' CBNorthwest, accessed 6 October, 2020, https://www.cbnw.org/en/about/index.cfm.

Page 151 — **Robert's Rules of Order**: RROR, 11th ed., III, 17, accessed 6 October, 2020, http://www.rulesonline.com/rror-03.htm.

Page 156 — **Annexed into the city of Aurora**: Jensen, 'Hoffman Heights.'

Notes 399

Chapter 18: Spelling Matters

Page 178 **Thousand Oaks area:** Public Information Office, 'History,' City of Thousand Oaks, CA, accessed 5 June, 2020, https://www.toaks.org/departments/city-manager-s-offiice/public-information-office/history.

Page 179 **Begun… in the 1930s:** 'Our History,' Red Rocks Baptist Church, accessed 6 October, 2020, https://redrocksbaptistchurch.org/welcome/our-history/.

Page 179 **First church in Denver:** 'Church for Price of Small Home,' *Okmulgee County News,* 6 March, 1958, 3.

Chapter 19: Building a Church

Page 187 **May 29, 1960:** 'Our History,' Red Rocks Baptist Church.

Page 183 **Quonset hut:** David Green, 'Quonset Huts: A Practical Building Solution for the U.S. Navy During World War II,' *The Vintage News*, 2016, accessed 6 October, 2020, https://www.thevintagenews.com/2016/10/20/quonset-huts-a-practical-building-solution-for-the-u-s-navy-during-world-war-ii/.

Chapter 20: Controversy

Page 191 **First major organization of churches:** Winthrop S. Hudson, 'Baptist,' Encyclopædia Britannica, 2020, accessed 6 October, 2020, https://www.britannica.com/topic/Baptist.

Page 191 **Adoniram Judson and Luther Rice:** Hudson, 'Baptist.'

Page 191 **General Convention:** Hudson, 'Baptist.'

Page 192 **Southern Baptist Convention:** Hudson, 'Baptist.'

Page 192 **Northern Baptist Convention:** Hudson, 'Baptist.'

Page 192 **Modernism:** Hudson, 'Baptist.'

Page 193 **In 1943, after renewed:** Bruce Shelley, 'Those People Called Conservative Baptist,' CBNorthwest, accessed 6 October, 2020, https://www.cbnw.org/en/about/index.cfm.

Page 194 **Militant, scribal, fundamentalists…:** Shelley, "Those People."

Page 194 **Hard core and soft core:** 'History of Baptist World Mission,' Baptist World Mission, 2017, accessed 6 October, 2020, http://www.baptistworldmission.org/history-of-baptist-world-mission/.

Page 194 **They acknowledge that the Bible:** Richard Quebedeaux, *The Young Evangelicals: Revolution in Orthodoxy,* (Haper & Row, 1974), 37-38.

Page 194 **Seemingly more compatible:** Quebedeaux, *The Young Evangelicals.*

PAGE 196   **To be a consistent**: 'History of Baptist World Mission,' Baptist World Mission.

PAGE 197   **200 fundamental churches**: Shelley, 'Those People.'

Chapter 21: Church Split

PAGE 199   **John Glenn orbiting the earth**: Stephen J. Garber, 'The Friendship 7 Mission: A Major Achievement and a Sign of More to Come,' NASA, accessed 6 October, 2020, https://history.nasa.gov/friendship7/.

PAGE 200   **Begun in 1950 as the Conservative Baptist Seminary**: 'History,' Denver Seminary, accessed 6 October, 2020, https://denverseminary.edu/about/history/.

Chapter 22: Missions and Growth

PAGE 206   **Crusade came to Denver in July of 1965**: Patrick Traylor, 'Photos: Rev. Billy Graham in Colorado,' *Denver Post*, 21 February, 2018, https://www.denverpost.com/2018/02/21/billy-graham-colorado-photos/.

PAGE 207   **Jehovah's Witnesses do not even believe that Jesus is God**: 'Do Jehovah's Witnesses Believe in Jesus?' Jehovah's Witnesses, accessed 6 October, 2020, https://www.jw.org/en/jehovahs-witnesses/faq/believe-in-jesus/.

PAGE 210   **$146,000 for missions**: 'As I See Things', *Mile-Hi Evangelist*, 9, no. 34, 1974.

Chapter 23: A Trip Around the World

PAGE 212   **Neighborhood Bible Time**: 'Our History,' Neighborhood Bible Time, accessed 6 October, 2020, http://www.nbtime.org/new_link.html.

PAGE 213   **Balut is a developing bird embryo**: 'Balut (food),' Wikipedia, accessed 6 October, 2020, https://en.wikipedia.org/wiki/Balut_(food).

PAGE 219   **Israelites as slaves in 14th century B.C.**: Dewey Beegle, 'Moses,' Encyclopædia Britannica, accessed 6 October, 2020, https://www.britannica.com/biography/Moses-Hebrew-prophet.

Chapter 24: "Honey, We've Got a School"

PAGE 224   **It was March of 1964**: 'Silver State Baptist School: Its History and Philosophy,' Silver State Baptist School, 1.

PAGE 224   **One of thirty students**: 'Silver State,' 1.

PAGE 224   **Elmer Jantz**: 'Silver State,' 1.

PAGE 228   **120 students enrolled**: 'Silver State,' 2.

PAGE 228   **Sheridan Baptist Elementary School, 1967-68**: 'Silver State,' 2.

Page 228	**250 students enrolled**: 'Silver State,' 2.
Page 229	**In 1971, the board of Silver State**: 'Silver State,' 2.
Page 229	**On June 18, 1971**: 'Silver State,' 2.

Chapter 25: Building a School

Page 235	**We had enrolled about 875 students**: 'Silver State Baptist School,' *Mile-Hi Evangelist*, 9, no. 33, 1974.

Chapter 26: Revival

Page 239	**If the rats of sin**: Quote from Chapel Sayings by Dr. Bob Jones, Sr., Used with permission.

Chapter 27: Buses, Radio, & A Little Bit of Crazy

Page 244	**The largest crowd we had**: 'As I See Things,' *Mile-Hi Evangelist*, 10, no. 6, 1975.
Page 247	**President of Bob Jones University in 2014**: 'Office of the President — Steve Pettit,' Bob Jones University, accessed 6 October, 2020, https://www.bju.edu/about/university-leadership/president/.
Page 247	**Mathew Thomas information**: Personal interview with Sophie George, July 2020.
Page 252	**KLIR made station changes**: *Broadcasting Yearbook 1980*, pages C-34-35, https://worldradiohistory.com/Archive-BC-YB/1980/C-1%20Radio%20Broadcasting%20Yearbook%201980.pdf.

Chapter 28: The Shenanigans of the Nelson Kids

Page 257	**Footprints of Jesus that**: Text by Mary B.C. Slade, Public Domain.

Chapter 29: The Family Grows Up

Page 272	**Byron Jolivette & Denver Junior Police Band**: 'Denver Jr. Police Band,' *Greeley Daily Tribune*, 20 January, 1965, 1.

Chapter 31: Fundamental Opposition

Page 295	**Baptist Bible College of Denver**: 'History of Fatih,' Faith Baptist Bible College and Theological Seminary, accessed 6 October, 2020, https://faith.edu/about/history/.

Page 298   **Rumors started flying**: Michael Hirsley, 'Pastor Denies Adultury, 2 Other Charges,' *Chicago Tribune*, 25 May, 1989, https://www.chicagotribune.com/news/ct-xpm-1989-05-25-8902040083-story.html.

Page 300   **The rumors were true**: David Cloud, 'The Women Who Knew Jack Hyles,' Way Of Life Literature, 2012, accessed 6 October, 2020, https://www.wayoflife.org/reports/the_women_who_knew_jack_hyles.php.

Chapter 32: Politics

Page 304   **Florida Association of Christian Schools**: 'History of AACS,' American Association of Christian Schools, accessed 6 October, 2020, https://www.aacs.org/about-us/aacs-facts/.

Page 304   **On November 30, 1972**: 'History,' American Association.

Page 304   **Where is the separatist organization…**: "History," American Association.

Page 304   **U.S. Representative John Conlan of Arizona**: Gene Amole, 'Denver Delegate Preaches Politics,' *Rocky Mountain News*, 23 August, 1984, 54.

Page 306   **Bill Armstrong**: Associated Press, 'Ex-Colorado Sen. Bill Armstrong Remembered For Work, Faith,' *San Diego Union-Tribune*, 15 July, 2016, https://www.sandiegouniontribune.com/sdut-ex-colorado-sen-bill-armstrong-remembered-for-2016jul15-story.html.

Page 306   **Youngest member of the State House**: 'Bill Armstrong Obituary,' Colorado Christian University, accessed 6 October, 2020, https://www.ccu.edu/about/ccu-president/bill-armstrong/obituary/.

Page 306   **President of the Senate**: 'Bill Armstrong Obituary,' Colorado Christian University.

Page 306   **In 1972, Bill Armstrong**: 'William L. Armstrong,' Wikipedia, accessed 6 October, 2020, https://en.wikipedia.org/wiki/William_L._Armstrong.

Page 308   **A force Colorado Republican**: Gene Amole, 'Denver Delegate Preaches Politics,' *Rocky Mountain News*, 23 August, 1984, 54.

Chapter 33: She Kept Her Word

Page 311   **Board of Education members**: Mary Estill Buchanan, "1976 Colorado Abstract of Votes," page 2.

Page 312   **She was a Republican**: Buchanan, '1976.'

Notes 403

Chapter 35: Behind The Iron Curtain

Page 329   **In 1959, the Russian State...**: Library of Congress, 'Revelations from the Russian Archives: Anti-Religious Campaigns,' accessed 6 October, 2020, https://www.loc.gov/exhibits/archives/anti.html.

Page 329   **Georgi Vins information**: Felix Corley, 'Obituary: Pastor Georgi Vins,' *The Independent*, 17 January, 1998, https://www.independent.co.uk/news/obituaries/obituary-pastor-georgi-vins-1139170.html.

Page 330   **Soviet Union's most famous religious prisoner**: Corley, 'Obituary.'

Page 333   **Billy Graham had visited Moscow**: Rushworth Kidder, 'How Billy Graham Views His Controversial Moscow Trip,' *The Christian Science Monitor*, 3 June, 1982, https://www.csmonitor.com/1982/0603/060340.html.

Page 334   **Moscow Church of Evangelical Chiristian Baptists**: Serge Schmemann, 'Graham Preaches at Church in Moscow,' *New York Times*, 10 May, 1982, https://www.nytimes.com/1982/05/10/world/graham-preaches-at-church-in-moscow.html.

Page 341   **Berlin Wall had fallen**: History.com Editors, 'Berlin Wall,' HISTORY, 2009, accessed 6 October, 2020, https://www.history.com/topics/cold-war/berlin-wall.

Page 341   **Gorbachev was happy**: Andrei Belkevich, 'How the Fall of the Berlin Wall Was Seen in Russia,' Euronews, accessed 6 October, 2020, https://www.euronews.com/2014/11/03/how-the-fall-of-the-berlin-wall-was-seen-in-russia.

Page 342   **GULAG - the prison camps**: History.com Editors, 'Gulag,' HISTORY, 2018, accessed 6 October, 2020, https://www.history.com/topics/russia/gulag.

Page 354   **Russian economic information**: Ben Aris, 'Remembering Russia's 1998 Financial Crisis (Op-ed),' *Moscow Times*, 22 August, 2018, https://www.themoscowtimes.com/2018/08/22/remembering-russias-1998-financial-crash-op-ed-a62595.

Chapter 36: Tucson

Page 359   **Bethel Baptist Church in Schaumburg, Illinois**: 'Bethel Baptist Church History and Facts,' Bethel Baptist Church, accessed 6 October, 2020, https://www.bethelministries.org/wp-content/uploads/2018/06/Bethel-Baptist-Church-History-and-Quick-Facts.pdf.

Page 362   **Pack rats**: 'Pack Rats' DesertUSA, accessed 6 October, 2020, https://www.desertusa.com/animals/packrats.html.

PAGE 364   **Shining Light Baptist Church**: 'Our Pastor,' Shining Light Baptist Church, accessed 6 October, 2020, http://shininglight-baptistchurch.org/about-us/our-pastor/.

Chapter 37: "Retired"

PAGE 370   **Holiday Blizzard 1**: '2006 Holiday Blizzards,' Wikipedia, accessed 6 October, 2020, https://en.wikipedia.org/wiki/2006_Colorado_Holiday_Blizzards.

PAGE 371   **The church began in 2000**: 'About,' Calvary Crossway, accessed 6 October, 2020, http://calvarycrossway.org/about-2/.

PAGE 371   **Harvest Baptist Church**: 'About,' Calvary.

PAGE 374   **On March 28, 2010...Pastor Josh Musgrave**: 'Josh Musgrave,' Calvary Crossway, accessed 6 October, 2020, http://calvarycrossway.org/josh-musgrave/.

Chapter 38: "Gettin Old An't For Sissies"

PAGE 375   **St. Anthony Hospital**: 'St. Anthony Hospital — About Us,' Centura Health, accessed 6 October, 2020, https://www.centura.org/locations/st-anthony-hospital/about.

PAGE 376   **Beetles all over the operating room**: '"Teeny, Tiny" Beetle Shuts Down Operating Room at St. Anthony's,' CBS Denver Channel 4, 2011, accessed 6 October, 2020, https://denver.cbslocal.com/2011/07/27/teeny-tiny-beetle-shuts-down-operating-room-at-st-anthonys/.

PAGE 378   **If your church does not have the Holy Spirit's blessing**: transcription of 90th birthday celebration sermon from Red Rocks Baptist Church, used with permission.

PAGE 382   **Castleview Baptist Church, owns 19 acres**: Douglas County Assessor, Account #R0406799, Parcel #2349-180-00-019, 6 October, 2020, https://apps.douglas.co.us/assessor/web/#/details/2020/R0406799.

PAGE 391   **Only a sinner saved by grace!**: Text by James Martin Gray, Public domain.

Photo Credits

Cover	**Cover Mountain Image**: Longs Peak from Estes Park, 1880–1900, History Colorado, Accession # 86.200.1834.
Page 47	**Terminal Station**: Reproduced by permission from Will H. Stokes Family / ChattanoogaHistory.com.
Page 79	**Idaho Springs**: Reproduced by permission from The Denver Public Library, Western History Collection, X-63134.
Page 82	**Dillon, Colorado**: Main Street in Dillon, Colorado, 1950–1960, History Colorado, Accession # 2002.16.23.
Page 82	**Methodist Church, Dillon**: Reproduced by permission from The Denver Public Library, Western History Collection, X-7695.
Page 322	**The Mullennex Wedding**: Photo courtesy of Dave Mullennex

All other photos are taken from the Nelson Family Photo Library.

MORE BOOKS BY ED NELSON...

My Morning Manna, Volume 1 — Journey Through the Bible guides the reader straight through the Bible from Genesis 1 to Revelation 22. You will find that God's Word is relevant for today to meet every need in your life. Each daily devotional is written on a passage of Scripture from the assigned reading schedule and continues consecutively through the Bible.

My Morning Manna, Volume 2 — Journey Through the New Testament takes an in-depth look at the entire New Testament, covering approximately 25 verses per day. Your journey will include an examination of the life of Christ as revealed in the Gospels, the thrilling account of the early church and the missionary journeys of Paul, the practical teachings of the epistles, and the fascinating prophecies of Revelation.

My Morning Manna, Volume 3 — Journey Through the Psalms explores the book of Psalms in an exciting new way. Your journey inclues devotionals covering approximately 7 verses each day. Spend an entire year with David and the other psalmists as you take an in-depth look at one of the favorite books of the Bible.

Growing in Grace is designed to help a new believer become a mature Christian. It is the grace of God that saves us and that also sustains us after we are saved. Each of the 13 lessons guides the new believer to study important Bible principles. Helpful notes, practical assignments, memory verses, and a beginning prayer journal are included.